Faith and Oil

Faith and Oil

How the Alaska Pipeline
Shaped America's Religious Right

K. L. MARSHALL

RESOURCE *Publications* • Eugene, Oregon

FAITH AND OIL
How the Alaska Pipeline Shaped America's Religious Right

Copyright © 2020 K. L. Marshall. All rights reserved. Except for brief quotations in critical publications or reviews, no part of this book may be reproduced in any manner without prior written permission from the publisher. Write: Permissions, Wipf and Stock Publishers, 199 W. 8th Ave., Suite 3, Eugene, OR 97401.

Resource Publications
An Imprint of Wipf and Stock Publishers
199 W. 8th Ave., Suite 3
Eugene, OR 97401

www.wipfandstock.com

PAPERBACK ISBN: 978-1-7252-5666-8
HARDCOVER ISBN: 978-1-7252-5667-5
EBOOK ISBN: 978-1-7252-5668-2

Manufactured in the U.S.A. 04/17/20

Special thanks to all the wonderful people
Who shared their stories and experiences
Of their lives in Alaska;
Who opened up their spare bedrooms,
kitchen tables, and wood-burning stoves;
Who walked me through libraries and archives
Down Main Streets and across wooded trails;
And who helped shape my own Alaska experience.

This book would not have been possible without you.

For Granny,
Who gave me the courage to become who I always was
For Aunt Dianne,
Who never stopped being my biggest fan
For Grandma Marshall,
Who gave me the family I needed
And for Emir,
Who was and always will be my little buddy.

You are not lost, because I know where you are
And one day, I will see you again.

Contents

Preface		ix
Chapter 1	The Rockefeller Legacy: Big Oil, Fundamentalism, and the Republican Party	1
Chapter 2	The Oil Crisis of 1973 and the Alyeska Pipeline	19
Chapter 3	The Rise of the Religious Right	36
Chapter 4	Nationalism and Religion in the Moral Majority: Crafting the Identity Politics of the Religious Right	56
Chapter 5	Oil Politics and the Cold War: Alaska's Glocalized Economy Intersects With International Affairs	74
Chapter 6	The Price of America's Addiction to Oil	91
Chapter 7	The First Bush Years	109
Chapter 8	The Second Bush Years: Populism, Oil, and the Prosperity Gospel	124
Chapter 9	McCain-Palin 2008: Sarah Palin Becomes the New Face of the Religious Right	140
Chapter 10	The Birther Movement and the Tea Party	156
Chapter 11	Make America Great Again: The Religious Right's Support of Trump	171
Conclusion		188
Bibliography		191

Preface

When Katie Couric interviewed Sarah Palin during the 2008 presidential campaign, the Alaskan governor-turned-vice-presidential candidate said, "Alaska is a microcosm for the world." While Palin may not have been referring to the state's diversity, two years later, in 2010, the US Census named the Anchorage neighborhood of Mountain View as the most diverse neighborhood in the entire country. Three of the city's high schools are the three most diverse in the United States, and every other Anchorage public school ranks in the top one percent. In other words, by some measures, Alaska's largest city is more diverse than New York City, Chicago, Houston, and Los Angeles.

Travel about 35 miles north of Anchorage, to Sarah Palin's hometown of Wasilla and the broader Mat-Su Valley, and the sight is vastly different. Small fundamentalist churches dot the landscape, and upwards of 20% of children are homeschooled by their parents. Wasilla represents the ideal of "Middle America," the rural and suburban heartland where small-town politics uphold family values and a capitalist work ethic. Middle America stands for the family farm, the small business, and a Jeffersonian vision of democracy; to many, it also stands for homogeneity and the proverbial WASP—the White Anglo-Saxon Protestant. Though diversity in the Mat-Su Valley is increasing, Wasilla remains one of the least diverse cities in the country. In some ways, life in the Mat-Su Valley seems to be a reaction against the modern, diverse center of Anchorage.

Nothing in the state of Alaska is unaffected by its oil industry, which helps fuel the engine of modern America. Alaska's oil fields brought jobs and an influx of cash, and with it, Alaska Natives entered the cash economy and immigrants traveled to the state looking for work. Oil money flooded the state's coffers when an 800-mile pipeline was completed in 1977. Many people, resisting the modernization of Alaska, retreated into fundamentalist enclaves while themselves enjoying the benefits of the state's oil-based wealth. Within a 35-mile stretch of Alaska, one can find the epitome of modernity and a fundamentalist reaction against it, both created by an economy and culture built around the extraction of oil. Alaska truly is a microcosm for the world.

Nobody in the state has been more affected by its oil industry than the Alaska Natives, who have seen their lands polluted by oil and their millennia-old ways of life eroded. Many Alaska Natives have left their subsistence lifestyles and reshaped their cultures within the cash-based oil economy; efforts to increase drilling in the interior of Alaska promise to bring more money to the Native peoples, while Natives who resist drilling insist that they cannot eat oil or the money that it brings. The challenges that they have faced represent the challenges of indigenous peoples throughout the world who are struggling to hold onto their ways of life in the face of globalization and the continued growth of oil.

While working on this book, I was confronted with another way that Alaska is a microcosm of the world. During the 2008 election season, an arsonist set Wasilla Bible Church, where Sarah Palin attended with her family, on fire with worshippers gathered inside. This hate crime committed against conservative Christians in Wasilla is just one in a growing number of hate crimes being committed against Muslims, Jews, LGBTQ+ communities, immigrants, minorities, and other groups all across the world.

In light of the problems posed by modernity, globalization, and oil, the very real challenge today is of how to talk about these difficult issues in a way that invites civil discourse rather than increased division. As such, this book is not primarily about Sarah Palin or her church in Wasilla, though there is quite a bit of content about her. This book is about oil and how the resource has transformed the Religious Right—from fundamentalists to Pentecostals to the broader world of evangelicals and other conservative Christians—in such a way that a "theology of oil" is now a constant undercurrent in American public discourse.

Each chapter of this book is divided into five sections: an ideology (such as fundamentalism, nationalism, American exceptionalism, and Christian dominionism), a national event, a global event, a local event, and a glocal event. The glocal event describes how the preceding ideology and events coalesced in Alaska, particularly around the pipeline. As such, this book covers a very wide range of topics and does not have the space to give them the careful attention that they deserve. Each section could be turned into an entire book on its own. *Faith and Oil* is best read as a survey that gives a bird's-eye view of the breadth of entanglements between America's Religious Right and oil politics.

The first six chapters are broadly about the events that led to the construction of the Alaska pipeline and how it shaped the local culture in which Sarah Palin grew up. They will show how state, national, and international oil politics, coupled with the emergence of the Religious Right during the 1970s, shaped her faith, values, and views of politics. The rest of the book deals more specifically with how Palin herself emerged as a leader, first in the oil-based politics of Alaska and later in the faith-based politics of the United States. They will show how, on a national stage, she brought oil to the forefront of the Religious Right and helped shape how the bloc's constituents view themselves in relation to their country and in relation to eternity.

My hope is that in reading this, you find something that resonates with your own theological and/or political views and that you take up the challenge of reshaping how you think about oil. I also hope that in challenging your own beliefs about oil, you feel compassion for those that oil has left behind, including Alaska Natives and other indigenous peoples, and compelled to civil discourse regarding what a post-oil world, and post-oil Christianity, should look like.

Chapter 1

The Rockefeller Legacy

Big Oil, Fundamentalism, and the Republican Party

"WHAT CAN GOVERNMENT DO FOR YOU?"

You would be hard-pressed today to find a Republican politician asking that question, especially on the campaign trail, and genuinely expecting a positive response. The Republican Party, as we know it today, is characterized by its opposition to "Big Government," especially the government intruding into the lives of its citizens and imposing regulations on private businesses. However, in the first century of the party's existence, it looked a lot different than it does today.

"What can government do for you?" was a favorite catchphrase of Nelson Rockefeller, the grandson of the legendary oil tycoon, JD Rockefeller. "Rockie" used this phrase while campaigning for governor of New York, a position that he held from 1959 until 1973, as well as in his numerous bids to become the Republican candidate for president. Rockie was a liberal Republican, what was then known as a "Rockefeller Republican." As a Republican, he championed private businesses and believed that they promoted the public good. As a liberal, he promoted social values that favored minority groups and believed that government intervention could be a positive force.

JD Rockefeller, the first billionaire in history, became the man that ran the world through his massive oil industry. While the Rockefeller connection to Big Oil and Big Money has long been appreciated, what is less understood is JD's and other oilmen's relationships with the burgeoning fundamentalist movement of the late-nineteenth and early-twentieth centuries. The endowments that JD made to religious institutions and revival preachers were part of a broader movement of oil tycoons using their money to spearhead the fundamentalist movement. In turn, the fundamentalist movement developed a symbiotic relationship with Big Oil such that fundamentalists supported the Republican Party and conservative, business-minded politics.

IDEOLOGY: FUNDAMENTALISM

Evangelicalism refers to a stream of Protestant thought that emphasizes the need for individuals to experience a spiritual rebirth. Evangelicalism in the United States can be traced to the Great Awakening of the 1730s and 1740s, when the Anglican priest George Whitefield traveled throughout the American colonies to preach of the need for people to have personal encounters with God. Today, evangelicalism can be understood in terms of three primary tenets: that the Bible is inerrant, meaning that it is without flaw; that salvation only comes through a personal encounter with God through His Son, Jesus Christ; and that salvation is between an individual and God rather than being conferred on one by a priest. Evangelicals have been behind many reform movements in America, including the abolition of slavery, prison reform, women's suffrage, and the Civil Rights Movement.

Evangelicalism and Christian fundamentalism describe two different religious phenomena that are often confused with each other. Fundamentalists hold to all of the tenets of evangelicalism, as well as additional beliefs and practices that set them apart from evangelicals. Yet fundamentalism is more than adherence to a set of beliefs; it is a mode of being that sets "true believers" (the fundamentalists) in contradistinction to modern, secular society.

The term "fundamentalism" derives from a series of tracts published in 1910 called *The Fundamentals*. The tracts outlined the "fundamentals" of the Christian faith, which conservative Christian leaders feared were being lost with the growth of modern and liberal forms of Christianity. The five most essential fundamentals are: a literal understanding and interpretation of the Bible; complete inerrancy of the Bible; the virgin birth of Jesus Christ; His death as a substitutionary atonement; and His physical resurrection and impending return. Fundamentalists believe that these fundamentals represent the "pure" version of Christianity, as God originally intended it; the fundamentals became lost due to the hierarchical structures of the church during the Middle Ages and, in more recent times, processes of modernization. Fundamentalists see themselves as preserving the true form of the religion, after it was corrupted by liberalism and secularity. As such, Christian fundamentalists generally believe that they are practicing Christianity in the same way that it was practiced in the first century by the earliest followers of Jesus.

The fundamentalist movement in the United States began in the nineteenth century, a period that saw immense changes regarding the role that religion would play, both in people's personal lives and in society as a whole. Particularly, three crises ensured that the conservative followers of "traditional" Protestant Christianity would have to draw a line in the sand and say that they would not compromise on their faith. Those three crises were the rise of Darwinism, the development of higher criticism of the Bible, and the spread of the social gospel.

Darwinism is more than the theory of evolution for which Charles Darwin earned his fame. Rather, Darwinism refers to the entire system of belief that emerged from evolutionary thought, a system that seems to stand at odds with many long-standing Christian traditions; perhaps the most prominent struggle is that evolution teaches a different origin story than the creation account in the Bible's first book, Genesis. Some Christians feared that if the creation account could not be seen as fully authoritative in a literal sense, then perhaps the entire text of the Bible could be called into question. During the nineteenth century, Darwinism infiltrated universities, both in Europe and the United States, and caused a complete paradigm shift regarding not only what people believed but the basis of knowledge itself. Was knowledge to be found in science or in the scriptures? The ensuing struggle between evolutionism and creationism remains a battleground for many fundamentalists today.

Darwinism was not the only nineteenth-century movement that challenged the authority of the Bible. Another force came from within Christendom itself in the form of higher criticism. Instead of viewing the Bible as God's revealed scriptures to humankind, higher criticism subjected the Bible to the same scrutiny as other ancient texts. Tradition has long held that Moses wrote the first five books of the Bible, but higher criticism questioned this belief and asserted that someone else, or a group of people, had to have written them. Higher criticism also challenged the notion that King David had authored the psalms and that Jonah was literally eaten by a large fish (and lived to tell the tale!). Many higher critics saw evolution and Darwinism as compatible with this approach to the Bible, and what ensued was the liberalization and modernization of Protestant Christianity. Liberal Protestants saw higher criticism as something that freed the Bible from traditionalism and allowed them to practice their faith in a way that was compatible with the modern world. Conservative Protestants, who did not think that anyone had the right to challenge the authority of the Bible as the inspired Word of God, parted ways.

The third and final crisis, the social gospel, was the foil of the fundamentalist movement. It was marked by the theology of liberal Protestant Christianity, which embraced Darwinism and the growth of science as marks of progress. As society rapidly urbanized during the 1800s, urban poverty became a pressing concern for a liberal theologian named Walter Rauschenbusch, whose church in New York City overlooked the aptly named neighborhood of Hell's Kitchen. He believed that Christians had a theological mandate to respond to the urban crises of the day, and his theology formed the basis of what came to be known as the social gospel. Social gospellers were, for the most part, liberal Christians who believed that the practice of the true gospel required them to work to ameliorate society's ills.

Granted, many fundamentalists also believed that the gospel had to be lived out through acts of charity and service to the poor. What set the social gospel movement apart from the fundamentalist movement was that the social gospel embraced liberalism, while the fundamentalists remained conservative. Social gospellers used the emerging field of sociology to generate statistics regarding poverty and what effects their efforts had on ameliorating it. As Darwinists, they believed that society was in a state of progress and that this progress was biblical. For the liberal Christians of the social gospel movement, higher criticism did not negate the belief that the Bible was scripture or that they should apply it to their lives. Rather, higher criticism meant that they could approach the Bible with an open mind because it did not contradict the science of Darwinism. The social gospellers tied their faith and how they practiced it to science rather than to tradition and biblical literalism.

In many ways, the fundamentalist movement, when it emerged in the late-nineteenth century, was a reaction against the three crises of Darwinism, higher criticism, and the social gospel. The five fundamentals of the faith rebuff these ideologies completely, as a literal interpretation of the creation account in Genesis means that Darwinism has no place in the Bible or in the life of a Christian. Literalism also nullifies any conclusions drawn by higher criticism. Therefore, for fundamentalists, the call to social action came not from love of humankind but rather from submission to the will of God, as revealed in the Bible.

For fundamentalists, the fundamentals represent more than what a true Christian must believe; they are the diagnosis and the cure for modern society. American society (and the Western world in general) is sick because the people have strayed from faith in God. The symptoms of this sickness include social ills such as poverty and criminal behavior, and the cure is a return to the fundamentals of the Christian faith. Hence, fundamentalists tend to spend a great deal of time on charitable programs that combine care for the poor with distributing copies of the Bible, inviting people to attend church, and "soul-winning" (encouraging people to convert to Christianity). At its heart, Christian fundamentalism is less about adherence to the five fundamentals than it is about the question of how Christianity should respond to modernity and the social changes that came with it.

One critique of fundamentalism is that it takes highly complex systems, such as Christianity, and reduces them to simple formulas. Approximately two billion people in the world today profess that they are Christians, yet only a fraction believe in the five fundamentals (the most contentious one being a literal interpretation of the Bible, which many Christians reject). For many—though not all—fundamentalists, those who do not believe in the five fundamentals are not true Christians. Institutions long associated with Christianity, such as the Vatican, can be disregarded, as can any form of Christian thought that is not entirely compatible with the fundamentals. Thus, critics argue, fundamentalism reduces the diverse, complex, and dynamic religion of Christianity into something that is homogenous, simplistic, and static.

Adhering to the fundamentals gave the fundamentalists a means of preserving what they saw as the true form of Christianity in the face of theological liberalism in churches and the secularization of modern society. They were the ones who, in the words of fundamentalist Curtis Lee Laws, were ready to do battle royal for the fundamentals. Their allies in that battle would come from an unlikely place: men who made their fortune in oil.

NATIONAL: OIL BARONS ENDOWING BIBLE INSTITUTES

At the turn of the twentieth century, the fundamentalist movement had a high level of public visibility, even while its adherents practiced some level of separatism from secular, liberal society. They rarely associated with liberal Christians except to debate with them, as the fundamentalist politician William Jennings Bryan often did. Yet despite this separatism, the fundamentalist movement developed with a symbiotic relationship to the burgeoning oil industry.

A catalog of people who financed the fundamentalist movement reads almost like a Who's Who of businessmen who made their fortunes in oil. The mightiest of them all was JD Rockefeller, but equally important were those who risked their livelihoods to find oil at Texas' oil geyser, Spindletop, and those whose names are now associated with fundamentalist schools. Not that all oil businessmen gave money to the fundamentalist movement, or that all who gave to the fundamentalist movement were oil businessmen. Yet there was a high degree of overlap between men who made their fortunes in oil and men who helped finance the fundamentalist movement. According to Notre Dame historian Darren Dochuk,

> Countless Bible believers in North America's oil patches saw petroleum as their special providence to be used industriously for the advancement of kingdoms of their making. Viewing their place in the oil sector as divinely appointed, never doubting the virtues of their quest, they brought their theology to bear on temporal issues of energy governance, used monies accrued through secular business to build sacred empires (churches, missionary agencies), and relied on religion to facilitate and legitimate the construction of modern petroleum's most elaborate apparatuses of extraction.[1]

Oil barons supplied the money, and fundamentalists supplied the ideology of free enterprise and the Protestant work ethic.

Lyman Stewart was a fundamentalist who hoped to capitalize on the early oil boom of the 1860s so as to fund himself as a foreign missionary. He and other oil barons of his time believed that God favors those who work hard, but for Stewart, the Civil War (1861–1865) interrupted his business ambitions. He served in Union forces during the war and, having seen the depths of human depravity and the horrors people proved themselves capable of inflicting upon each other, wanted to use his means to create a more Christian society. For Stewart, this Christian society would embody a capitalist spirit and the so-called Protestant work ethic via industrialization, the engines of which would be fueled by oil. He became determined to strike enough oil to help create that Christian society and provide himself with the money to work overseas as a missionary.

---

1. Darren Dochuk, "Extracted Truths: The Politics of God and Black Gold on a Global Stage" in *Outside In: The Transnational Circuitry of US History*, ed. Andrew Preston and Doug Rossinow (Oxford: Oxford University Press, 2017), 155.

Stewart experienced several bankruptcies in his quest for oil; he believed that they happened because he stopped giving generously to the church. He would make sure not to repeat that mistake after he and his brother, Milton, made their fortune in California's booming oil business and founded Union Oil. Union Oil would never become a superstar in the world of Big Oil, but it would give the brothers a way of making sure that the time-honored truths of Christianity were not lost amidst the cacophony of modernity and liberalism. In 1910, Lyman and Milton Stewart were the ones who endowed the publication of *The Fundamentals*, the set of tracts from which the entire movement derived its name.

Shortly before endowing *The Fundamentals*, Lyman Stewart made another investment that would ensure that the Bible would remain the focus of Christianity. In 1908, he partnered with the Reverend TC Horton to endow a school that they named the Bible Institute of Los Angeles, today known by the acronym Biola. Reuben Torrey, one of the primary writers of *The Fundamentals*, became the school's dean in 1912.

Torrey's career in the fundamentalist movement began long before he became dean of Biola. A graduate of Yale Divinity School in 1878, Torrey had a longstanding relationship with the American revivalist Dwight Moody. In 1883, Moody founded the Chicago Evangelization Society, which later became Moody Bible Institute. Moody was less directly connected to the oil industry than other fundamentalist leaders, as the businessmen who funded his ministry operated in industries such as dry goods, manufacturing, and agriculture. What is telling about his ministry and the relationship that bound oil and fundamentalism together is his opposition to the social gospel. He believed that the movement detracted from the preaching of the Word of God, and that without a spiritual conversion, people who benefited from the charity of social gospellers were still destined for an eternity in hell.

After Moody's death, the pastor of his church, Paul Radar, converted Charles Fuller to Christianity. Fuller and Oral Roberts both became oilmen and used their profits to finance the fundamentalist schools that they founded—Fuller Seminary and Oral Roberts University (though Fuller Seminary today teaches from a more evangelical rather than fundamentalist approach).

Pattillo Higgins, the "prophet of Spindletop," believed that God had given him success in the oil industry when he and his partner, George Carroll, struck oil at Spindletop—near Beaumont, Texas—in January 1901. Their company—Gladys City Oil, Gas, and Manufacturing—funded local Baptist causes and institutions, and Carroll himself made an exorbitant gift of $75,000 to Baylor College (now Baylor University). Another significant donor to Baylor College, as well as other local Baptist institutions, was Kate

McKie, the widow of William Junius McKie. W.J. McKie was a lawyer and judge who specialized in Texas' burgeoning oil industry; after his death in 1927, his widow donated tens of thousands of dollars to Baylor. Regarding the relationship between oil dollars and Bible institutions in the South, Dochuk says,

> Since its beginnings, the Southern oil business has been dominated by petro-patriarchs who have used their company profits to fund evangelical institutions that legitimate their business pursuits. The marriage has always been a natural one: in the freewheeling culture of Southwestern oil—where high-risk, high-reward wildcatting has romanticized the rags-to-riches man who demands to be left alone—evangelicalism has celebrated its own fierce, masculine individualism. It is no wonder that this marriage has spawned a formidable ideology of up-by-the-bootstraps conservativism.[2]

In the early 1900s, the foil of the Bible Institute of Los Angeles and Baylor College was the Chicago Divinity School, also endowed by an oil baron, JD Rockefeller. The Chicago Divinity School became the flagship of the University of Chicago, and it was and remains much more liberal than Biola and Baylor. The first president of the Chicago Divinity School was William Rainey Harper, a Semiticist who embraced higher criticism. Harper's colleague, Shailer Mathews, rejected the teachings of the fundamentalist movement and wrote pieces such as *The Contributions of Science to Religion* and *Fundamentalism versus Modernism*. Centers for higher education in religion seemed to become the new battleground in which the oil barons would fight for supremacy. Their dollars would finance the ideology that they wanted the next generation of religious leaders to preach.

But the case was less simple than the conservative fundamentalists, like those of Biola, becoming pitted against the liberal modernists, like those of Chicago Divinity School. In addition to funding the liberal Chicago Divinity School, Rockefeller had partners in the fundamentalist movement, including the fire-and-brimstone revivalist preacher, Billy Sunday. Furthermore, in 1918, Rockefeller and his son, John Junior, made a philanthropic donation of $1 million to help begin a stock brokerage firm named GuideStone Financial Resources. Since its inception, GuideStone has specialized in providing financial services, such as retirement plans and health insurance, for churches and clergy, especially among fundamentalists and evangelicals. The partnership that the oil magnate had with GuideStone was so

---

2. Darren Dochuk, "Tea Party America and the Born-Again Politics of the Populist Right," in *New Labor Forum* vol. 21 No. 1 (Winter 2012), pp 14–21. Cited from page 19.

significant that, to commemorate the centennial of the financial services company, in 2018, the Southern Baptist Convention issued a resolution honoring JD Rockefeller, GuideStone, and its commitment to Christian ministers. Rockefeller seemed to be less concerned with the theological views promoted at an institute that he financed and more concerned about how his endowments would help him retain dominance in the oil business.

Here is where the motive for the engagement of Rockefeller—as well as other oil barons—in the fundamentalist movement begins to emerge: In addition to affirming the fundamentals of the Christian faith, the fundamentalist movement taught that laborers should submit to their managers. Billy Sunday, who Rockefeller supported, railed against the conflict between labor and capital and insisted that a day's honest work led to honest wages. He also preached about the virtues of free enterprise, the capitalist system, and American patriotism. For Sunday and like-minded fundamentalists, the interests of business and capitalism were not merely political issues; they were theological issues. They saw the Bible as affirming private property and other capitalist values, and to promote labor and workers' rights over management was to defy biblical teachings.

While Rockefeller paid higher-than-average wages to Standard Oil's employees, he opposed them joining labor unions, which were an outgrowth of the social gospel movement. In the early 1900s, workers at one of Rockefeller's companies, Colorado Fuel and Iron Company, secretly formed a union to challenge unfair wage practices and the unsafe conditions in the mines where they worked, as hundreds of miners had already died in workplace accidents. In 1913, the unionized workers began a strike that lasted for over a year. Rockefeller's son, John Junior, was managing the Colorado mines from his office on Broadway in New York City and tried unsuccessfully to break up the strike. The strike took a bloody turn on April 20, 1914, when the Colorado National Guard opened fire on the workers' tent city and then set it on fire; nearly two dozen men, women, and children died in the Ludlow Massacre. Though John Junior later improved the working conditions of the miners, the massacre demonstrated just how opposed oil barons and their ilk were to the demands of the social gospel.

To powerful people like JD Rockefeller, the social gospel was dangerous. The movement sought to do more than provide immediate aid to the poor; it sought to reform society so that people were no longer poor. Doing so meant establishing public schools, which would be paid for by the tax dollars of the wealthy. It meant allowing for the creation of labor unions, which would require people like Rockefeller to provide better working conditions. And it might mean the end of the Protestant work ethic, as the masses might come to feel entitled as wealth became more shared.

GLOBAL: JD ROCKEFELLER AND THE GLOBAL RISE OF BIG OIL

> I believe the power to make money is a gift from God.
> —JD Rockefeller

Though Lyman Stewart never succeeded in funding himself as a foreign missionary, oil dollars went far in supporting Christian missions. JD Rockefeller funded several foreign missionaries, including the parents of publishing magnate Henry Luce. Luce grew up in China, where his parents served, before founding a publishing empire that included the magazines *Time*, *Life*, and *Fortune*. He repaid his parents' benefactor by using his national platform to promote oil as God's blessing on America. Luce saw oil money as enabling foreign missions as well as making America powerful on the international scene. In 1903, long before Luce acquired *Life*, an article in the magazine praised Rockefeller for promoting the oil industry and commented on the need to remember the role of religion in his life. Rockefeller himself saw oil money as evidence that God favored him, and he saw the oil industry as his way of furthering God's kingdom on earth.

John Davison Rockefeller was born in 1839 into a family of modest means and religious piety. His father, a con artist, taught him shrewdness and thrift by cheating him every chance he could, while his mother, a housewife and devoted Baptist, taught him hard work and discipline. As a young adult, he began investing in the oil industry and, in 1870, created the company Standard Oil. Within a decade, Standard Oil controlled 90% of the oil refining in the United States, and John D. Rockefeller went on to became the first billionaire in history.

The defining Protestant movements of the late nineteenth century, during Rockefeller's most active business years, were those of the social gospel and fundamentalism. Instead of engaging in the theological debates of the day, Rockefeller rose above the fray by developing his own version of the social gospel. He said,

> I believe the power to make money is a gift from God. Having been endowed with the gifts I possess, I believe it is my duty to make money and still more money, and to use the money I make for the good of my fellow man according to the dictates of my conscience.[3]

---

3. Darren Dochuk, *Anointed with Oil: How Christianity and Crude Made Modern America* (Basic Books, 2019), 42.

This view of the ultra-rich having an obligation to engage in philanthropy is also known as the "Gospel of Wealth," after an article that Andrew Carnegie—second only to Rockefeller as the wealthiest man in the United States—wrote in 1889. In particular, Rockefeller's social gospel professed that he could enact the truest form of the Protestant work ethic by cleaning up the inefficiencies and wastefulness that plagued the country's nascent oil industry.

Before the ascendancy of Standard Oil, the oil industry had no regulation and was in danger of collapsing altogether. The "rule of capture" meant that whoever staked a claim and struck oil owned that resource. As a result, during the oil boom of the 1860s, men would set up dozens of derricks on the same hillside and develop their own companies to move the oil that they found from the ground into the market. Speculators haphazardly drilled down wherever their intuition told them to go, and many even used divining rods and other spiritualist tools to try to locate oil. The complete lack of coordination among the drillers caused financial and environmental catastrophes to become commonplace. Rivers and lakes became inundated with runoff oil, and wildlife suffered immensely from haphazard practices. People working on rigs had to sign death waivers because the work was so dangerous, and hundreds of people died as oil fires broke out. When a surplus of oil would hit the market, prices would drop so precipitously that companies would go bankrupt. With all these systemic problems, Rockefeller realized that he could not maintain wealth in the oil industry unless he controlled the entire market.

Rockefeller's vision required that he move upstream in the production process and coordinate all of the affairs involved in producing and refining oil. While the likes of Stewart and Fuller—fundamentalists who used their oil money to set up their own schools—embraced capitalist competition as a means of creating a more Christian society, Rockefeller's gospel of wealth, his version of the social gospel—of making money so that he could spend it "according to the dictates of my conscience"—meant cleaning out the wastefulness of the industry by buying out all of the competition.

And buy out all the competition he did. By 1872, two years after founding Standard Oil, he owned nearly every refinery in his adopted city of Cleveland, Ohio. His growing monopoly of oil led him to create a deal with the railroad companies that gave him more favorable rates than other oil companies. Since he paid less than other companies to transport his oil, he was able to price out his remaining competition until Standard Oil controlled 90% of the country's oil industry. By 1890, state and federal legislatures were enacting laws to try to break up Standard Oil's monopoly. Rockefeller evaded many legal challenges by reorganizing his company, sometimes moving properties and ownerships to different states, sometimes creating subsidiary companies that Standard Oil retained control of. With his version of the social gospel, Rockefeller did not see himself as accountable to laws passed to try to break up Standard Oil. He was doing God's work, and he believed that God had blessed his entrepreneurial ventures by making him rich.

Having taken control of the oil industry in the United States, Rockefeller set his sights on the rest of the world. With his oil industry booming, by the 1890s, the supply from the oil fields in the United States began to outpace the demand from consumers. Rockefeller took his surplus oil to China, where he called Standard Oil "Mei Foo;" Standard Oil began producing kerosene lamps called Mei Foo, which the company passed out to Chinese peasants for free or at steeply discounted rates. In turn, the population rapidly switched from using local vegetable oil to Standard Oil's kerosene. For Rockefeller, this expansion into overseas markets was a missionary enterprise, as he saw himself as improving people's quality of life and society at large, thereby bringing the Kingdom of God to earth.

By the mid-1890s, Rockefeller had all but retired, retaining the title of president of Standard Oil but devoting himself to leisure activities and philanthropy. Yet the Standard Oil juggernaut continued to advance, perhaps most notably into the untapped oil fields of the Middle East. In 1908, oil was discovered in the mountains of northwest Iran, setting off a frenzy of European oil companies obtaining mineral and drilling rights in the Middle East and Central Asia. The Turkish Petroleum Company—owned by European companies, including Deutsche Bank and the Anglo-Saxon Oil Company—struck oil in Iraq in 1927.

Standard Oil saw the opportunity and obtained exploration and drilling rights in Saudi Arabia, Iraq, Bahrain, and other countries in the region. In Bahrain, Standard Oil—operating as SOCAL (Standard Oil of California)—created the subsidiary Bahrain Petroleum Company (BAPCO), which struck oil in 1932. The company then negotiated exclusive rights to explore for 60 years in 930,000 square kilometers of land, which included the Arabian peninsula. In 1938, another subsidiary of Standard Oil, the California-Arabian Standard Oil Company, struck oil in Saudi Arabia. The oil fields of the Middle East, particularly the ones that Standard Oil developed in the Arabian peninsula, would prove to be the largest in the entire world.

In 1944, the California-Arabian Standard Oil Company became Arabian American Oil Company, or ARAMCO. Today, ARAMCO and Standard Oil remain major players in the global oil industry, though under different names. Standard Oil of New Jersey became Exxon, and SOCAL became Chevron. ARAMCO is now Saudi Aramco, the state-owned oil company that plays a prominent role in OPEC (Organization of Petroleum Exporting Companies). In China, Standard Oil created Mobil under the aegis Standard Oil Company of New York (SOCONY); Mobil remains a major oil company today. As this book will later show, the geopolitics that emerged from Standard Oil's global monopoly would go on to become embedded into fundamentalist thought.

Rockefeller's son, John Junior, eventually took over the company, but he devoted his life to giving away the fortune that his father had made. While fundamentalist charities actively sought religious converts, John Junior set up the Rockefeller Foundation, which promoted scientific modernization. Amongst other things, John Junior funded New York's Riverside Church, whose artwork commemorates Jesus and his 12 disciples, as well as scientists the likes of Albert Einstein, Charles Darwin, and Pythagoras. He hired Henry Emerson Fosdick, a noted figure in the fundamentalist-modernist controversy, as the church's minister. In keeping with the artistic representation of Darwin in the church's architecture, Fosdick was a liberal Christian who saw the Bible as a record of God's dealings with humanity, not a text that should be read literally. Ironically, John Junior took a stance against the fundamentalist movement that his father had helped empower.

JD Rockefeller helped shape not only America but the entire world in the image of oil. While he was neither a fundamentalist nor a social gospeller, his unique theology was still consistent with that of the fundamentalist oilmen's, in the sense that they all believed oil was a divine resource. They could use it to further the kingdom of God on earth by promoting social progress and funding Christian mission while creating their own utopias of wealth and prosperity.

LOCAL: NELSON ROCKEFELLER AS GOVERNOR OF NEW YORK

Under the influence of billionaires such as JD Rockefeller, by the end of the 1800s, the Republican Party had become the party that represented Big Business and capitalism (its foil, the Populist Party, represented workers, especially rural farmers; see Chapter 2). It promoted low taxes for the ultra-rich and the businesses that they ran and disparaged the idea that the government could reform society by providing aid to the poor. Then came the Great Depression of the 1930s, which saw the failure of hundreds of banks and the highest unemployment rate in the country's history. When the Democratic candidate Franklin Delano Roosevelt was elected president in 1932, he enacted dozens of socialist programs that provided relief to the poor, paid for by taxes on the wealthy. Big Business leaders, whose income was being redistributed among people who had not worked for it, feared that America's socialist government was on track to becoming communist.

Their fears were well-founded. A communist revolution in Russia in 1917 had created a state, the Soviet Union, in which citizens could not own private property or run private businesses. The state ran all the means of production—it owned all property and all businesses—and distributed income to citizens, many of whom suffered brutal oppression and persecution by their government. In the United States during the Great Depression, membership in the communist party exploded among unemployed people who believed that the capitalist system had failed, and business owners feared a communist uprising might take down the government. Following World War II, the capitalist United States and communist Soviet Union entered a decades-long stalemate known as the Cold War; the Republican support of private businesses and low taxes on the wealthy expanded as a means of countering the communist threat. JD Rockefeller's grandson, Nelson Rockefeller—known to many as "Rockie"—was a liberal Republican who, during the years of the Cold War, promoted a business-friendly agenda against the threat of communism while also advancing social policies that aimed to help the poor, minorities, and the environment.

"Liberalism" is not one thing in particular but rather a set of attitudes and beliefs regarding the relationship of an individual to society and to the state. People who consider themselves to be liberals generally emphasize the role of the state in ensuring social justice, particularly for the poor and for minority groups. They also advocate for policies that favor minority groups—including religious minorities, ethnic minorities, and the queer community—and allow them full participation in a democratic system. While liberals generally advocate for an economic system built on free enterprise, they allow for socialist policies, including the redistribution of wealth through taxes on the wealthy that fund welfare services for the poor.

"Conservativism" is not so much the opposite of liberalism as a critique of it, particularly when the liberal state fails to deliver on its promises; this reaction usually emerges when the central features of society—such as churches and the family—begin to feel challenged by liberal institutions. Conservatives tend to distrust welfare programs and see the redistribution of wealth as harming the capitalist system, which is based on private businesses rather than the government. During the fundamentalist movement, the fundamentalists generally promoted conservativism, both in their approach to the Bible and in their approach to politics. In the United States, liberalism is usually associated with the Democratic Party, while conservativism is mostly associated with the Republican Party. But during the

Cold War years of roughly the 1950s through the 1970s, Rockie occupied a middle ground between conservativism and liberalism.

As a liberal, Rockie believed that the government could have a positive impact on people's lives. His catchphrase, "What can government do for you?," reflected his view that the government had an obligation to enact public works projects that would benefit people. As governor of New York, he oversaw large-scale programs that included cleaning up the heavily polluted waterways of New York and expanding the State University of New York (SUNY) system. To help fund these projects, he instituted a statewide sales tax in 1965. As a Republican, he believed that the government needed to provide opportunities for private businesses by giving them a role in public projects. Therefore, his administration contracted private businesses to complete many of the building, environmental, and civil rights programs that he enacted.

Rockie's is perhaps most remembered for his liberal Republicanism that championed a positive role of the government in people's lives while advocating for private business. His influence during his four-term tenure as governor of New York improved the state's infrastructure—it had better public schools, tighter environmental regulations, cleaner air and water, and an increase in public parks and wilderness areas—while also increasing the role of private business. His politics reflected his Cold War ethos, that the government had to support private businesses while it worked to improve the lives of ordinary citizens. This ethos stood against the communist goals of state-controlled production and the elimination of private business.

In 1964, Rockie lost the Republican presidential nomination to Barry Goldwater, an ultra-conservative senator from the state of Arizona. As a senator, Goldwater had voted against the 1964 Civil Rights Act on the grounds that the government was overstepping its bounds by guaranteeing equal rights to African Americans and other racial minorities. Goldwater's nomination over Rockie's by the Republican Party marked the beginning of the end of liberal Republicanism, and the end was sealed by the 1968 election of the conservative Republican Richard Nixon.

The end of Rockie's presidential aspirations in 1968 (though some claim he never did give up on his desire to assume the White House) marked the beginning of the end of the liberal Republicans. The Republican Party became irrevocably conservative, so that today's Republicans continue to support private business but believe the government has no role in how those businesses are run; they also tend to support tax breaks for the wealthy rather than imposing taxes to fund services for the poor. Today's Republican Party advocates a small government, particularly in terms of welfare and environmental policies; deregulation of private businesses so that they can operate without cumbersome restrictions; lower business taxes so that companies can afford to hire more people; and lower personal taxes so that people have more control over their own money.

The last of the Rockefeller Republicans may have been John McCain, the moderate conservative who brought Sarah Palin onto the national scene in 2008 when he nominated her to be his vice-presidential candidate.

GLOCAL: THE REPUBLICAN PARTY IN ALASKA

> We support a simplified tax system that does not produce the effect of government-directed redistribution of wealth.
> —From the 2018 Alaska Republican Party Platform

The frontier has always occupied a special place in the American imagination. It is where people go to find their own way far from the bustling cities of the East Coast, live off the land, and if they're lucky, earn their fortunes. As pioneers on the frontier, they can live as libertarians, without the government intruding in their lives. Alaska, more than any other state, has long epitomized this frontier spirit. From fur traders to gold seekers to oil drillers, men—and sometimes women—with ambitions have gone to Alaska to find a simpler life in the rugged terrain while attempting to stake their claim in the land's immense wealth. Alaskans generally see themselves as fiercely independent and not in need of services that the government provides. People who move to the northernmost state are prepared to fend for themselves, as they must survive brutal winters that can dump upwards of 20 feet of snow and last for eight months out of the year. They do not want the government telling them what they can or cannot do, especially when they must rely on their own hard work and ingenuity in order to survive. Unsurprisingly, Alaska may be the most solidly Republican state in the country, and the Alaska Republican Party's platform is more conservative than the national one.

Yet at the time of Goldwater's nomination in 1964 and then Nixon's election in 1968, Alaska was not the bastion of conservative Republicanism that it is today, and in 1964, the state voted for the Democratic candidate, Lyndon B. Johnson, over Goldwater. Perhaps the disastrous Good Friday Earthquake that occurred earlier that year, when a 9.2-magnitude quake devastated parts of Alaska's southern coastline and killed 131 people, caused Alaskans to look more favorably towards government support, particularly in repairing roads, bridges, and other infrastructure that had been destroyed. Yet the 1964 election marked the last time that Alaska's electoral votes went to a Democrat. In the 1968 election, Nixon won a plurality of Alaska's vote, just enough to win an edge over the Democratic candidate, Hubert Humphrey. Following the 1968 election of Nixon, well over 50% of Alaska's electorate has consistently voted for the Republican presidential candidate.

The years between the 1968 and 1972 presidential elections saw some subtle shifts in Alaska's culture that, years later, would have a marked effect on how the state responded to the challenges of the twentieth century. In 1968, the largest oil field in North America was discovered at Prudhoe Bay, on the edge of the Arctic Ocean. That same year, Ted Stevens, a Republican, began his 40-year tenure representing Alaska in the United States Senate; he pushed for congress to approve development of the oil field and construction of an 800-mile pipeline that would bring the oil to market. In 1971, the fundamentalist pastor Jerry Prevo moved from the American South to Alaska's largest city, Anchorage, to begin working at Anchorage Baptist Temple. At a time when debates over oil dominated public life in Alaska, he began preaching a brand of fundamentalism that merged with American nationalism and Republican politics. He and his associates spearheaded church-planting efforts that saw the formation of fundamentalist churches throughout the state, beginning with the Mat-Su Valley, the borough that Sarah Palin called home. Prevo's influence over the next four decades would be so immense that he would later be named one of the 40 most influential men in Alaska.

The relationship between oil politics, Republicanism, Protestant fundamentalism and the broader category of evangelicalism, and American nationalism that emerged during this era of Alaskan history can be seen in the Alaska Republican Party's platform today. While the national 2016 Republican Party platform opposes abortion, the 2018 Alaska Republican Party's platform opposes abortion on the grounds that people are created in the image of God. The text of the platform reads,

> Man is made in the image of God; therefore, we embrace the sanctity of life from the moment of conception until natural death and will defend the sanctity of life.

The national Republican platform advocates for allowing the 10 Commandments to be posted in public places and for voluntary prayer to be brought back to public schools. The Alaska Republican platform goes further by promoting the teaching of American patriotism in public schools as part of the country's Judeo-Christian heritage. The platform reads,

> We support active promotion of patriotism in our schools, the teaching of the Judeo-Christian foundation of our country with the emphasis on the Constitution of the United States.

Regarding the operation of private businesses, the platform says,

> Free enterprise is the best system to deliver economic opportunity and prosperity. It should not be burdened by excessive regulation and taxation. Government must practice fiscal responsibility, so citizens can keep more of the money they earn.

In some ways, the state's Republican platform looks like a fundamentalist statement of faith. That faith is an amalgamation of the conservative business practices that the earliest fundamentalists came to support, as they found their financial support in oil companies at the turn of the twentieth century.

The faith expressed by Alaska's Republican platform resembles the same faith expressed by the state's most famous resident, Sarah Palin. Palin is not fundamentalist in the strictest sense; she has long attended a Pentecostal church, and while Pentecostalism has many similarities with fundamentalism (especially biblical literalism), there are some differences. Yet her faith was shaped by oil politics as much as by the ruggedness of Alaska's terrain and the brutality of its winters, by American nationalism as much as by the Bible and historical Christian thought. The rest of this book will look more closely at the ideologies and social changes that shaped the faith-based politics of America's Religious Right, especially on the frontier of Alaska, and how multiple international and national crises coalesced in the state's pipeline.

Chapter 2

The Oil Crisis of 1973 and the Alyeska Pipeline

Evangelicalism in the United States has its origins in the First Great Awakening, which occurred in the first half of the eighteenth century, prior to the Revolutionary War; the impact of the Great Awakening was so strong that it may have actually contributed to the Revolutionary War. Prior to the Revolution, the American colonies operated state-run churches that worked alongside the government in creating and enforcing legislation. In a move that departed from the state-run churches, the Great Awakening emphasized a personal, transformative encounter with God as the basis for individual salvation. As such, one effect of the Great Awakening was to undermine the authority of the state-run churches and create a zeal for religious freedom. That zeal became embedded in the First Amendment of the United States Constitution, which says that Congress will not make any laws respecting any religion.

    Protestant fundamentalism has somewhat different origins. It began with movements protesting against the state-run churches, namely the Anglican church but also the Catholic church and other denominations, in the United Kingdom in the early 1800s. These "millenarian" movements placed a heavy emphasis on the Second Coming of Jesus, which millenarians believe will herald the establishment of the "Millennial Reign" of his 1000-year rule on earth. Some leaders of the millenarian movement in Britain, such as John

Nelson Darby, taught that the "true church" of Christ was distinct from the state-run Anglican church and that "true Christians" had to separate from it. The movements spread across the Atlantic Ocean when British separatist theologians came to the United States to spread their teachings regarding the church and their apocalyptic views of the impending End Times. Protestant fundamentalism became a viable movement in the United States over a century after evangelicalism emerged in the First Great Awakening, and while a number of converts to fundamentalism may have been evangelicals, fundamentalism is a category distinct from evangelicalism.

Populism, which characterizes much of Alaskan politics, became a national force when Sarah Palin, the conservative governor of Alaska, ran alongside John McCain for the White House in 2008 and then emerged as a leader of the Tea Party. Palin's populism had been preceded by William Jennings Bryan, a fundamentalist politician who lived at the turn of the twentieth century, as well as Ted Stevens, a Republican who filled one of Alaska's spots in the United States Senate for four decades. Stevens' populism relied heavily on the discovery of oil on Alaska's North Slope, and he had to fight the early environmentalist movement to ensure that Alaska's oil could be accessed. And without a conflict in the Middle East in 1973, congress may have never approved construction of Alaska's pipeline. During the 1970s, the "theology of oil" that had begun in the fundamentalist movement of the late 1800s found its being in the oil fields of Alaska.

IDEOLOGY: POPULISM AND CIVIL RELIGION

William Jennings Bryan (born 1860, died 1925) was a fundamentalist politician who led the Populist Party of the late nineteenth century and argued for creationism in the 1925 Scopes "Monkey" Trial (see chapter 4). Bryan firmly believed not only that the American people were devout Christians but also that they were uncompromisingly good. For Bryan, the good American people were fundamentally opposed by an elite that was not only corrupt but that was, in a religious sense, evil. Furthermore, God was on the side of the people in their ongoing struggle against the elite. This belief led him to support the Populist Party that emerged in the Midwest in 1890 and become the democratic presidential candidate in 1896, though he lost to William McKinley. His nickname, "The Great Commoner," tied him to the masses of everyday, hard-working people that he championed.

Bryan exemplified two ideologies that often work under the surface of political and religious life in the United States: populism and civil religion. Populism today looks so different from Bryan's Populist Party (which merged with the Democratic Party) that many scholars do not even consider Bryan's movement to be truly populist. However, he set important precedents that would resurface when Sarah Palin burst onto the national scene in 2008.

Populism is a mode of political expression that occurs when "the people" feel ignored by "the establishment" of corrupt elite. While populism can take various forms, it is a mode of political thought in which society becomes divided into the opposing categories of "the people" and "the establishment" or "the elite" and in which "the people" attempt to reassert themselves. Western democracies, particularly in the United States, assert that sovereignty belongs to the people rather than a ruling class of elites, yet power and wealth still tend to become concentrated among a few. When the "pure people" revolt against what they see as the "corrupt elite," a populist movement may emerge that attempts to put sovereignty back into the hands of the people. Populism gives a voice to people's anger and frustration, especially when they feel as if those in power have ignored them.

Populist movements present themselves as moral causes because of how populists understand "the people" and "the elite." Neither group is defined by social status or financial wealth but rather by how moral the groups are: "the elite" are corrupt, while "the people" are pure. "The elite" are usually caricatured as being part of "the establishment," while "the people" are those that "the establishment" has long ignored. Billionaires, such as Donald Trump, can position themselves as one of "the people," as he did when he presented himself during his 2016 campaign as being a Washington outsider who would "clean the swamp." By presenting himself as one of "the people," he implied that his wealth does not matter, nor did his womanizing or xenophobic remarks. He was "pure," as opposed to the "corrupt" Washington elite. Populism is not limited to conservative movements, however; it can happen anywhere along the political spectrum whenever the candidate positions himself or herself as the champion of the people and the only candidate who is morally qualified for office.

These opposing groups, "the people" and "the elite," are homogenous, meaning that there are no differences among those who are "the people" nor any differences among those who are "the elite." Any who express a difference of opinion are not one of "the people;" therefore, they are either of "the elite" or, at worst, may be considered "enemies of the people." As such, populism denies pluralism, because pluralism requires that there be multiple groups representing diverse peoples. The two groups of "the people" and "the elite" are also entirely opposed to each other, so compromise between the two is not possible. According to a populist mindset, if one of the pure people is willing to compromise with one of the corrupt elite, then he or she is not only making a political error, but more importantly, a moral one.

Pundits tend to characterize populism as being opposed to democracy, but if one defines democracy exclusively as majority rule, then this claim is false. Populism is not opposed to democracy, as its aim is to return power to the people. But populism is against liberal democracy. Liberal democracy is not merely majority rule; it includes the protection of minority rights. Liberal democracy also provides for an independent judicial branch so that the legislative or executive branches cannot control the courts. Populists view their movements as a corrective to what they see as the failures of democracy because populism answers the central question of democracy: If "We, the people" form the basis of sovereignty in the government, who are "the people"?

Civil religion is not one religion in particular but rather a broad, national appeal to Providence over the fate of the country. The American civil religion has its roots in the Protestantism that dominated the country in its early years, but it is not the same as Protestantism, nor is it limited to Protestants. The American national motto, "In God We Trust," suggests that there is a higher sovereignty than that of the people, that is, God. The sovereign people endeavor to carry out the will of God on earth through their civic engagement and national life. The scriptures of the civil religion include the Declaration of Independence, the constitution, and the Gettysburg Address, and the civil sites of pilgrimage include locations such as the Lincoln Memorial, the Washington Monument, and the Liberty Bell. While populist movements attempt to put sovereignty back into the hands of the people, civil religion promotes the idea that true sovereignty over the nation belongs to God.

For William Jennings Bryan, an ardent proponent of both American civil religion and populism, the American nation was a community of faithful believers. The Christian faith and ethos made the nation's democratic system sacred, so much so that the voice of the people reflected the voice of God and His will for the nation. Bryan believed that the Christian religion was expressed politically through fair and equal participation in a democratic system. God works through the expression of majority rule which, though fallible, has the greatest potential of expressing truth and the divine will. This use of civil religion merged with populism, as together, they explicitly championed the Christian faith as the religion of America and made the consensus of the majority the test of God's plan for the nation.

The relationship between populism, civil religion, and oil exists in the idea that God put oil into the ground so that "the people" can benefit from it. This idea was promoted by early fundamentalists, such as Lyman Stewart, who saw oil as the means for creating a more Christian society. Likewise, Patillo Higgins, the "prophet of Spindletop," believed that God had directed him to the massive oil reserves near Beaumont, Texas and used the money from it to fund Christian charities and ministries. This ideology also became embedded in the Alaska pipeline, as "the people" of Alaska also came to see oil as God's blessing on their state.

If William Jennings Bryan was The Great Commoner, Sarah Palin was The Greater Commoner. She was a hockey mom (Alaska's version of a "soccer mom") from a small town, and faith and family came first in her life. She worked for the PTA at her kids' schools and had family members serving in the military. Alaskans spoke favorably of their governor, whom they proudly touted as populist, because she refused to be bought by the elites of oil companies that ran Alaska's oil fields. She wanted to make sure that everyday people had jobs instead of using her government position to satiate the oil companies, which many Alaskans saw as corrupt. She did not merely represent common, everyday people; she was one of them.

Like Bryan before her, Palin merged Christianity with the American civil religion, as she believed that the country's founding documents were Christian in origin. From the national platform she received in 2008 as vice-presidential candidate, she frequently evoked the American civil religion by referring to the people's God-given rights and God's blessing on America. As governor of Alaska, however, she much more strongly expressed the idea of America being a Christian nation. Her Christian beliefs influenced her politics, and her belief that America is a Christian nation shaped many of the policies that she enacted as governor (see Chapter 3, Chapter 4, and Chapter 7).

As a populist, she claimed to represent "the people"—hockey moms and those with family members serving in the military—against "the elites"—the supposedly corrupt oil executives and establishment politicians. But "the people" are not one homogenous whole; they are a diverse array of individuals whose interests do not always intersect with those of a populist leader. "The people" that she represented were not all of America but rather those who had similar political goals.

Palin's version of "the people" was very much shaped by the Alaska pipeline. "The people" were the everyday, hard-working folks who weathered Alaska's harsh climate and often subsisted by hunting and growing their own food. They relied on the pipeline to provide jobs and revenue for the state's budget. And they needed a champion who would fight for them against oil companies that attempted to halt production in order to cause oil prices to rise or who would acquire land on the oil fields but not drill. But those people are not representative of all of America, and as things turn out, they were not representative of all of Alaska.

NATIONAL: RISE OF ENVIRONMENTALISM IN AMERICA

Following the discovery of the massive oil fields in the Middle East, the United States began importing much of its oil from the region. Even with the financial cost of transporting it from the other side of the world, oil from the Middle East proved to be substantially cheaper than oil procured from fields in the United States. Access to cheap oil, especially in the decades after World War II, fueled a post-war boom in the United States that led to rapid economic development and higher standards of living. Yet the prosperity came at a cost, as obtaining oil from countries such as Saudi Arabia, Iraq, and Iran was causing the United States to become entangled in complicated political webs that did not serve its best interests. It was supporting dictators—such as the shah of Iran—who were guilty of massive human rights abuses, as well as having to commit its military resources to upholding those regimes. In the case of Iran, the outcome would be disastrous (see chapter 5).

There was another price to this oil-based prosperity, an ecological one. Throughout the 1960s, people became increasingly aware of the ecological damage that humans had caused. Burning fossil fuels, such as the oil that became the gas for cars, was polluting the air. The country's rivers and lakes were filling with toxic runoff from industrial plants, causing marine ecosystems to collapse. And the use of pesticides such as DDT, highlighted in the 1962 landmark book *Silent Spring*, was poisoning humans, plants, and animals. On April 22, 1970, environmentalists commemorated the first Earth Day to celebrate the planet and raise awareness of the need to care for it.

With the growing environmentalist movement and awareness of how human activity had damaged fragile ecosystems, many became hopeful that the United States would begin to transition away from oil and to clean, renewable sources of energy, such as wind, hydro, and solar. Reducing the country's dependence on oil would help clean up the air pollution in cities like New York, Chicago, and LA while providing jobs for people in developing renewable energy. In the late 1960s and early 1970s, though, environmental concerns would clash against oil companies in national debates about whether to construct the Alaska pipeline.

Native peoples of Alaska had long used oil that seeped out of the ground as fuel for fires, and by the end of the nineteenth century, oil companies were projecting that Alaska had immense oil reserves underground. When oil was discovered at the Kenai Peninsula in southern Alaska in 1957, oil companies clamored to undertake exploratory projects to find more oil fields in the state. Yet the harsh Arctic conditions stymied their efforts, as their instruments could not cope with temperatures that reached 60 degrees below zero and ice that was thousands of feet deep. In 1968, though, ARCO and Humble Oil discovered the largest oil field in North America at Prudhoe Bay, on Alaska's North Slope. The oil field was the eighteenth largest in the world, making it a rival to some of the fields in the Middle East. The exploitation of the massive oil deposits at Prudhoe Bay would allow the United States to supply the oil it needed to continue its post-war economic boom.

Yet before the oil could be drilled, major challenges had to be addressed. The first challenge was how the oil would be transported from the edge of the Arctic Ocean to refineries and markets in the Lower 48 ("Lower 48" is the term that Alaskans use to refer to the continental United States). During the winter that far above the Arctic Circle, the sun does not rise for a full two months. Temperatures easily fall to minus 60 or colder, with wind chills in the triple digits. Because of the extreme temperatures combined with Alaska's rugged terrain, there were not even any roads to Prudhoe Bay. In order to exploit the oil fields, the interested companies would have to create their own infrastructure to transport it to market.

The oil companies that wanted to drill at Prudhoe Bay formed a private consortium called Alyeska, from the Aleut (a tribe of Alaska Natives) word that means "Great Land." Through Alyeska, they could collaborate on how to legally and physically engineer the oil from Prudhoe Bay to the Lower 48. After some brainstorming and experimenting, they realized that the only way to transport the oil would be to build an 800-mile pipeline that would cut all the way through the frigid state, including across three mountain ranges and underneath hundreds of rivers. The pipeline would terminate at the southern city of Valdez, the country's northernmost port that is not frozen. From there, it could be taken to refineries in the Lower 48.

The original plan for the pipeline was for it to be buried underground, just like pipelines in any other part of the world. Yet the frozen Arctic tundra created a second challenge: permafrost. Permafrost is ground that is frozen for at least two consecutive years, and it can contain large amounts of ice. Much of Alaska has a layer of permafrost, usually ranging from two feet to six feet thick. However, sections above the Arctic Circle, including Prudhoe Bay, have areas of permafrost 2000 feet thick! If the ice in the permafrost melts, then the ground will collapse and create a massive sinkhole. The oil from Prudhoe Bay would flow through the pipeline at upwards of 100 degrees Fahrenheit; if it flowed underground, the heat would melt the permafrost and cause the pipeline to sink.

A third challenge was the high level of seismic activity in Alaska. In 1964, the Good Friday Earthquake measured 9.2 on the Richter scale, making it the second-largest earthquake ever recorded. The earthquake was so severe that it killed 131 people and permanently changed landscapes for hundreds of miles. When—not if, but when—an earthquake should shake the pipeline, millions of barrels of hot oil would flood Alaska's wilderness and cause irreparable harm.

Alyeska decided to do something that had never been done before by building the pipeline above ground. Propping it up several feet above the soil would keep the oil from melting the permafrost, and special joints would allow it to sway without breaking in the event of an earthquake. Alyeska was all set to begin construction in 1969 and even began stockpiling tens of millions of dollars' worth of steel pipe.

What the oil executives did not expect was the fierce resistance that the project would meet from the growing environmental movement. Groups such as the Sierra Club saw the proposed pipeline as the first major undertaking that could cause widespread ecological damage since the beginning of the environmental movement. How the federal government responded to the proposed pipeline would determine the direction of environmental policy for decades to come—whether the government would push for renewable energy or continue enacting policies that provided access to cheap oil.

Environmentalists also opined that scientists knew too little about the Arctic, its ecosystems, unique wildlife, and permafrost, and that more research was required to understand the impact of drilling in that area. There were also concerns about how the pipeline would affect the seasonal migrations of animals such as caribou; the proposed pipeline route cut through millions of acres of wilderness and would prevent animals from following their well-worn paths. Perhaps most importantly, drilling in Alaska would mean that the United States would continue in its dependence on oil instead of developing renewable energy sources.

And after Alaska, there would be no more frontier, no more untamed wilderness. Humankind and modern technology would have touched every corner of the country, and save for Antarctica, every corner of the world. Environmentalist groups feverishly lobbied Congress and filed lawsuits to prevent the pipeline from being constructed. Alyeska's pipeline came to a complete halt before it even began, and the stockpiled steel pipes began gathering snow.

To address environmental concerns, not only in Alaska but across the country, the United States government began enacting legislation to protect the environment and attempt to reverse some of the ecological damage caused by human activity. The National Environmental Policy Act of 1969, or NEPA, set forth nationwide goals for quality control on environmental issues. NEPA required that federal agencies complete environmental impact studies before approving any project and also created the Council on Environmental Policy to advise the president on issues related to the environment. The next year, the Clean Air Act of 1970 set guidelines for cutting carbon emissions, reducing ozone-damaging pollutants, and targeting the sulfur dioxide and nitrogen oxide emissions that cause acid rain. The Clean Water Act of 1972 specified how much pollution was acceptable in the nation's lakes and rivers. And the Endangered Species Act of 1973 provided for federal protection of habitats where endangered species—such as grizzly bears, which are common to Alaska—live. Each piece of legislation represented a victory for environmental groups and a delay for Alyeska in beginning construction of the pipeline.

But the victory for environmentalists would be short-lived, because an impending energy crisis would prove that the United States was addicted to oil.

GLOBAL: THE YOM KIPPUR WAR AND OPEC EMBARGO

Through the first half of the twentieth century, companies like Rockefeller's Standard Oil controlled much of the world's oil supply, to the extent that countries producing oil—such as Iran and Venezuela—had very little control over their own resources. In addition, Western countries, such as the United States and Britain, that were invested in oil-producing countries had deep interests in supporting companies like Standard Oil to ensure a steady supply of cheap oil. In 1960, the oil-producing countries of Iran, Iraq, Kuwait, Saudi Arabia, and Venezuela reacted against the interests of oil companies when they formed the Organization of Petroleum Exporting Countries, or OPEC; soon other oil-producing countries, such as Qatar and Algeria, joined. OPEC was a means of taking control of their own oil resources against Western countries and Western companies; OPEC countries would accomplish this goal by controlling levels of oil production so as to make sure that they maintain control over their own oil reserves. When OPEC was at the height of its power in the 1970s, it was able to control both the price of oil and the global supply of it. With many of the world's oil reserves in the Middle East and the vast majority of OPEC countries located in that region, trouble there would almost certainly mean an economic shock for oil-consuming countries, particularly the United States.

That trouble came in 1973 with the outbreak of the Yom Kippur War. The war began on October 6, 1973, when Egypt and Syria simultaneously launched offenses against Israel. The invading countries believed that Israel was acting with hostility towards them and other surrounding states and wanted to force it into diplomatic negotiations. The Egyptian and Syrian invasions marked the beginning of the fourth Arab-Israeli war since the forced expulsion of Palestinians in 1948; the leaders of those states hoped that the war would finally bring peace to the region by bringing Israel to its knees and forcing it into diplomatic negotiations. The Yom Kippur War lasted for less than three weeks, but it would have a profound impact on American life throughout the 1970s and beyond.

The Egyptian and Syrian forces were much more organized than they had been in previous wars against Israel, and they launched the 1973 offensive with fewer casualties and greater force than in earlier invasions. Soon, the neighboring countries of Iraq and Jordan allied themselves with Egypt and Syria. Israel quickly began to deplete its reserve supplies of munitions, so its prime minister, Golda Meir, urged the United States to intervene by supplying Israel with fresh arms. President Richard Nixon was hesitant to supply Israel, partially because its belligerent, Egypt, was an ally. Then the Soviet Union—which was deadlocked with the United States in the Cold War—came to the aid of Egypt and Syria, and Nixon immediately established a supply line to get arms to Israel. With the United States arming Israel and the Soviet Union arming the Arab states, the conflict quickly deteriorated into a flashpoint for the Cold War.

Nixon had a much-touted policy of détente with the Soviet Union, which meant that his goal was to reduce the tensions of the Cold War and thereby mitigate the threat of a nuclear attack. Now, with the conflict in the Middle East turning into a proxy war between the United States and the Soviet Union, the threat of nuclear war between the deadlocked countries became very real. Nixon's secretary of state, Henry Kissinger, flew to the Middle East and began engaging in "shuttle diplomacy"—he flew back and forth between the countries at war to try to negotiate peace agreements—as a protracted war in the Middle East could lead to a nuclear confrontation between the United States and Soviet Union.

The Soviet Union and United States never engaged in any direct combat, but all of the warring countries involved in the Yom Kippur War suffered heavy losses. On October 22, about two weeks after the fighting began, the United Nations adopted a resolution that would bring about an end to the war. The fighting finally came to a close on October 26, with the Arab states withdrawing from Israel and buffer zones established. Anwar al-Sadat, the president of Egypt, declared victory, but without a clear military success, the other Arab states were less optimistic about the war's outcome. And they were furious at the United States for arming Israel.

Syria and Egypt were not OPEC countries, but many of their allies—including Iraq—were. On October 19, a week before the war ended, OPEC declared an oil embargo on the United States, meaning that no OPEC country would export any of its oil there. Up until that point, though OPEC countries managed over half of the world's oil supply, they had had little success in achieving their collective goal of regulating the price of oil by controlling its supply. But when they all adopted an embargo on the United States, they quickly achieved their goal, as the cost of oil almost immediately quadrupled.

The effects of the embargo were swift and fierce. Cheap oil had fueled American economic growth since World War II, but now, the cost of gasoline skyrocketed so quickly that many people could no longer afford to fill up their cars. Drivers would wait in line for over three hours at gas stations, often to only be told that the station had run out. When winter set in, many families had no fuel to heat their homes. Not only was oil more expensive; it oftentimes was not even available.

The shock went beyond people not having a reliable source of fuel for their cars and homes. Many household goods contain oil, from plastics to car tires to synthetic fabrics. The cost of these goods increased, and they were often in short supply. Additionally, because oil is involved in transporting nearly all goods to market, the cost of everything went up dramatically.

These economic woes were exacerbated by government policies. When the cost of production increases, companies usually recoup the cost by raising the prices of goods. But in an effort to combat the out-of-control inflation, the government imposed price controls on many goods, meaning that companies could not raise their prices so as to ensure that they were at least breaking even. The only way for many companies to keep from going under was to lay off workers, so unemployment increased. Inflation went as high as 10%, but wages remained stagnant or even decreased while many lost their jobs. Hence the term "stagflation" to describe the American economy from 1973 until 1975.

OPEC repealed the embargo in March of 1974, about six months after it was imposed. But by then, the economic reverberations had pierced nearly every aspect of American life and caused a severe recession. Desperate for relief from the country's economic hardship, "the people" knew that America had to curb its dependence on foreign oil. But they were divided as to how they should proceed: environmentalists urged the development of renewable energy, while others—especially those interested in the development of Alaska's oil fields—wanted to see the United States invest in its own reserves of fossil fuels.

LOCAL: ECONOMIC MALAISE IN ALASKA

William Seward, secretary of state under President Andrew Johnson, purchased the territory of Alaska from the Russian czar in 1867. Though the purchase was a steal at only two cents per acre, many derided it as "Seward's Folly" or "Seward's Icebox." Few imagined that an American outpost in the Arctic would have any meaningful impact on the country. Yet Seward anticipated that the territory possessed immense natural resources, which it did.

Alaska was a United States territory for nearly a century before attaining statehood, and throughout its years as a territory, the federal government was responsible for Alaska's upkeep. With its proximity to Japan during World War II and to Russia when the Cold War began, Alaska became a military outpost from which the federal government protected the country from a Japanese or Soviet invasion. The federal government built military bases and funded the Alaska Communications System (ACS), which would enable contact with distant villages, and the Distant Early Warning (DEW) Line, which would provide an alarm in the event of a Soviet invasion. The government also funded schools, roads, and road maintenance, including snow plowing. Yet Alaskans wanted to have their own government and have representation on a national level, and those things could only happen if the territory became a state.

On January 3, 1959, 92 years after William Seward purchased Alaska, President Eisenhower signed the statehood proclamation. Beginning that day, the federal government no longer funded the services that it had been providing for decades. The state now had to pay for its own roads and for the cost of sending telegrams over ACS, but there was no strong economic base from which to collect state taxes. With few industries outside of fishing and the modest oil field in the Kenai to provide jobs for people, Alaska could barely afford statehood. If Alaska—one of the most financially impoverished areas of the country—was to become economically viable, it would need a major industry that it could call its own. Many Alaskans saw the pipeline as that industry.

Alaska Natives had been living off the land for millennia, hunting the wild animals that roam the lands and gathering the rich berries that grow every summer. Beyond the efforts of Russian and later American Christian missionaries to colonize them, Alaska Natives had, for the most part, not held down paying jobs or otherwise participated in the cash economy. But shortly after Alaska attained statehood, droves of white settlers poured into the new state, so many that they soon outnumbered Alaska Natives by four to one. Native ancestral lands, on which tribes had long lived subsistence lifestyles by hunting and gathering, were being choked out by the growth of

American-style cities and towns. Some Native villages, such as Matanuska—which lay between Anchorage and Wasilla—disappeared entirely. Continued American-style economic development in Alaska, which the pipeline promised, would continue to erode their lifestyles and communities.

In addition to environmentalists tying up the proposed pipeline in courts, the land rights claims of Alaska Natives were slowing down congressional approval. Alaska's state constitution, passed in 1959, stipulated that Alaska Natives could remain on their ancestral lands. However, a clause in the constitution said that the state could claim for itself any land deemed "vacant," and the state began acquiring for public use lands that Native tribes had claimed for themselves. Attempts to resolve tribal claims to the land resulted in numerous stalemates between the state of Alaska and the Native tribes. In 1968, with the discovery of oil at Prudhoe Bay, the issue of Native land rights became one of national concern, as it would have to be settled before the pipeline could be constructed.

Following the discovery of oil, many Alaska Natives, especially tribal leaders, were adamantly opposed to the pipeline. If the pipeline crossed their lands, it would cause irreparable harm to their subsistence lifestyles and force them to enter the cash economy. Their ability to hunt moose and caribou, which they relied on for survival, would be severely hampered. Furthermore, the broader ecological impact of the pipeline would desecrate the earth that they treasured and the land that they were fighting for. Alongside environmental groups, Native tribes filed lawsuits to thwart construction of the pipeline. If "the people" wanted the pipeline, then Alaska Natives were not of "the people."

In 1971, President Nixon, who supported the pipeline, signed the Alaska Native Claims Settlement Act (ANCSA) to guarantee land rights for tribes of Alaska Natives and compensate them for the land that they had lost. In return, the tribes could not claim land on which the proposed pipeline would run. Still, they continued to oppose its construction, while the settlers and pioneers who had come to Alaska wanted the pipeline built because it would bring jobs and economic viability to the state. Tensions between Alaska Natives and American settlers turned into stand-offs and sometimes violent confrontations. Between the environmentalists lobbying against the pipeline and the Alaska Natives opposing something that might destroy their way of life, the pipeline seemed doomed.

In a state desperate for economic growth, those who supported the pipeline maligned the Natives and the environmental groups. "The people" wanted a pipeline, and anyone who opposed it stood against the will of the people. Furthermore, in a vernacular that brought civil religion into the fray, some believed that the pipeline was God's will for the state so as to develop

Alaska's economy. If God supported the pipeline, then surely "the people" must submit to His will.

"The people" wanted the pipeline, but just who were "the people"? Were "the people" the Alaska Natives who had lived in the area for thousands of years? Or were "the people" the settlers who had come to the Last Frontier to stake out their land and find their fortunes? Were "the people" hard-working, Christian Americans who espoused capitalism as the means of preserving freedom against the communist threat? Or were "the people" the environmentalists who wanted the country to wean itself off of oil and develop renewable energy?

Behind the scenes, "the people" were far from a homogenous whole. "You must be an environmentalist," became the most banal insult that one could leverage against another person. Bumper stickers read, "Let the Bastards Freeze in the Dark," and "Sierra Go Home." Local newspapers in Alaska maligned environmentalist efforts to stall the construction of the pipeline. Any who stood in the way risked being ostracized from the community, losing their jobs, and even facing vigilante violence. Alaska Natives needed to be Americanized and Christianized so that they, too, would see that the pipeline was God's will. Environmentalists needed to repent of their earth worship and other pagan practices that caused them to value the natural environment over the supernatural will of God.

The OPEC embargo and ensuing oil crisis changed everything for the Forty-Ninth State. On November 16, 1973, less than a month after the embargo began, Congress passed the Trans-Alaska Pipeline Authorization Act, which immediately halted all legal challenges against the construction of the pipeline. No governmental agency, including the Environmental Protection Agency, the Alaska Department of Fish and Game, or the Alaska Department of Natural Resources, could impose any regulations on the project. On January 23, 1974, the oil companies involved in Alyeska signed an agreement with the federal government and then were able to begin work.

GLOCAL: BIG OIL AND THE REPUBLICAN PARTY IN ALASKA

> People who vote against this today are voting against me. I will not forget it.
> —Senator Ted Stevens, in a Senate speech regarding ANWR drilling

Long before the rise of Sarah Palin, Alaskans had a history of electing populist politicians to represent them. To appeal to Alaska's electorate, particularly in the state's early years, one needed to have a down-home feel, a strong connection to the land and the people, to be one of "the people." The needs of the politician had to be the same as the needs of the people, not only on a political level but also on a personal level. Politicians who lacked these qualities usually met their demise at the hands of an unhappy electorate.

One feature of populist movements is that they collapse the party's politics into the personality of a single charismatic leader. For many years in Alaska, that leader was Ted Stevens. What mattered was not so much the political views that "Uncle Ted" held—for example, he was pro-choice, while much of Alaska's population was (and still is) adamantly opposed to abortion—but rather how the man himself personified the state's frontier. Uncle Ted was Alaska, from the heavy wool parkas that he wore to a temper that mimicked an Arctic blast. And in a state that was barely financially solvent, he pushed for the pipeline that would solve, at least for a time, its economic woes. The symbiotic relationship between major oil companies and the Republican Party in Alaska is perhaps best seen in the life and political career of Ted Stevens.

Stevens was a Republican who began serving in the US Senate in 1968, the same year that oil was discovered at Prudhoe Bay. The next year, in 1969, the state of Alaska leased out land at Prudhoe Bay to major oil companies, including BP, Mobil, and Chevron, for a whopping $900 million. Whereas the state had been teetering on the verge of bankruptcy for a decade, it now had enough money to fund itself for four full years at 1968 levels. Yet it would not continue operating at 1968 levels, as the state had very limited infrastructure and few paved roads outside of Anchorage and Fairbanks. Some communities still did not have schools or electricity, so the state, flush with cash, quickly began using its petrodollars for the development of infrastructure. And advocating for the state at a national level was Senator Ted Stevens.

The Republican platform has long called for smaller federal government and states' rights, but Stevens was an anomaly among Republicans in that he pushed for more federal involvement in the state of Alaska, not less. He argued that with the state in its infancy, even with the influx of oil revenue, the federal government had an obligation to fund development projects. Sometimes hundreds of miles of roads separate the state's towns and cities, and in the "Alaskan bush," many villages were (and still are) only accessible by airplane. Stevens successfully advocated for tens of billions of federal dollars to get appropriated to the state of Alaska, much of it going to remote areas. "Stevens money" became so prolific that the senator would be bombarded anytime he appeared in public in the state, because people would appeal to him personally to ask for money for projects. But while many Alaskans cherished their Stevens money, those in the Lower 48 saw it as the height of pork-barrel politics.

Possibly Stevens' biggest contribution to the state was how he used his position in the senate to promote the development of Alaska's oil industry. As soon as he entered the US Senate in 1968 (initially appointed to fill a vacant seat before being elected), he began working on the Alaska Native Claims Settlement Act, which had to be resolved in order for the pipeline to be constructed. Once ANCSA was settled, he worked tirelessly to get congress to approve the pipeline. He also pushed for a second pipeline, one to transport natural gas from Prudhoe Bay to markets both in North America and other parts of the world. In return, oil companies gave hundreds of thousands of dollars—usually via political action committees (PACs)—to fund his re-election campaigns.

Later in his career, one of Stevens' focuses was to get congress to approve drilling in the Arctic National Wildlife Refuge, or ANWR. Like Prudhoe Bay, ANWR may hold large oil deposits under its permafrost; like Prudhoe Bay, the prospect of recovering its oil set off national environmental activism because it is the largest wildlife reserve in the country. Stevens never succeeded in getting drilling approved, though one of his bills passed both houses of congress, only to be vetoed by President Bill Clinton. Clinton's successor, the Republican president George W. Bush, supported drilling in ANWR, but congress prevented a bill from passing. When President Trump approved drilling in ANWR in December 2017, ostensibly because someone had told him that opening ANWR to drilling had long been a Republican goal, only a minority of Republicans across the country supported his move.

In 2008, Stevens' relationship with the oil industry would lead to his demise. He had failed to disclose on his financial statements hundreds of thousands of dollars' worth of gifts that he had received from oil executives, something that amounts to a criminal offense for public servants. Those gifts included a stained-glass window, discounted cars, home renovations, and a live sled dog. Stevens' trial became a national media event and threatened to derail the McCain-Palin campaign of that same year. In the end, the jury convicted Uncle Ted on seven felony counts. The same oil that marked the beginning of his political career defined the end of it.

A federal judge overturned the conviction on the grounds that the FBI, which had handled the investigation into Stevens' affairs, had withheld evidence that could have led to a "not guilty" verdict. But the damage was done, and when Stevens lost his re-election campaign, his 40-year tenure as Republican senator for Alaska came to an end.

Today many, though certainly not all, Alaskans remember Uncle Ted with fondness. He championed their isolated state at many critical junctures in its history, at times when the federal government may have let it fall to the wayside. Without him, Alaska's oil industry may have never developed into the mammoth that it is today, and its economy would have remained undeveloped. The populist leader represented everything that "the people" loved about Alaska. He was more than one of them; he was—and even after his death, still is—Alaska.

Chapter 3

The Rise of the Religious Right

If you spend enough time around the blogosphere, especially if you are trying to understand the Religious Right, at some point you will probably come across the term "dispensationalism" or "dispensational theology." Many people, from journalists to scholars of religion, have written about the effects of dispensationalism on Protestant fundamentalists and evangelicals in terms of how it shapes their political engagement. Yet few people take the time to explain what dispensationalism is and how its teachings helped mobilize conservative Christians into the voting bloc known as the Religious Right.

Granted, analysts of the Religious Right have pointed to numerous causes that mobilized it. Many have pointed to the pro-life cause, which became a primary concern of the nationalist preacher Jerry Falwell and ultimately became the raison d'etre of many people in the bloc. Yet the pro-life cause cannot tell the whole story, because the *Roe v Wade* Supreme Court decision, which legalized abortion in all 50 states, occurred in 1973, yet Falwell—who already had a public ministry—did not speak out against abortion until 1978.

Others have pointed to Israel's successes in the Six-Day War of 1968 and then the Yom Kippur War of 1973, events that caused fundamentalists and evangelicals to see Israel as a David, blessed by God in its war against the Goliath of the Arab states. These wars challenged conservative Christians to urge their government to support Israel. Yet this explanation falls short, as the United States had armed Israel in both wars and already had a vested interest in the country.

Other analysts point to the role of Big Business, which had been suffering legislative setbacks beginning with the socialized policies of the New Deal. Demands for workers' rights, such as a minimum wage, as well as welfare programs, such as unemployment payment and Medicaid, had eroded the laissez-faire capitalist system and led to a mixed economic system that included socialist policies. Furthermore, the communist threat stoked fears amongst everyday Americans, not just the country's largest business leaders, that their way of life and the freedoms they enjoyed could soon come to an end. Leaders allied themselves with the rising televangelists, such as Jerry Falwell and Pat Robertson, to promote public support for pro-business legislation. This explanation, too, falls short, as members of the Religious Right were more concerned with legislation to end abortion and bring voluntary prayer, along with the teaching of creationism, back into public schools.

Yes to all of the above. All of the above causes did mobilize the Religious Right. But there is an underlying ideology that ties all of them together and creates a coherent whole out of ending abortion, supporting Israel, and endorsing big business. That ideology is dispensationalism. Dispensational theology is the thread that runs through all of the above agendas and connects them to oil politics, the Republican Party, and American nationalism.

IDEOLOGY: DISPENSATIONALISM

> Then they gathered the kings together to the place that
> in Hebrew is called Armageddon.
> —Revelation 16:16, NIV

Dispensationalism is an approach to the Bible that is particularly common among Protestant fundamentalists. It is not generally considered part of evangelical theology (again, evangelicalism and fundamentalism are two separate religious phenomena), but it has shaped aspects of evangelical thought as fundamentalist movements have migrated in and out of evangelicalism. Dispensational theology comes in many different flavors, and there will probably be some dispensationalists who disagree with pieces of what follows in this section. In keeping with this book's topic on the relationship between faith and oil, this section focuses on the flavor of dispensationalism used by leaders of the Religious Right.

The term "dispensationalism" derives from the belief that God deals with humanity differently in different dispensations of history. A dispensation is more than a period of time that has a set beginning and a set end; it represents a covenant that God made with people and how God and people related to each other under that covenant. John Walvoord, a prominent dispensationalist teacher during the twentieth century, gave an apt description of this view of history:

> The Bible contains the history of the world up to the present time, including its creation, the beginning of the human race, and God's dealings with Israel and the nations of old. The New Testament adds its important account of the birth, life, death, and resurrection of Jesus Christ in His first coming. The teachings of Christ and the apostles gave the early church a system of truth that not only explained the past but also presented a prophetic panorama of events yet to come.[1]

Dispensationalism emerges from a literalist approach to the Bible, which is one of the five fundamentals that fundamentalists avow. Not only is the creation account in Genesis to be taken as a literal event, but so are many verses that dispensationalists see as describing events that have not yet happened and will occur in the future as part of the End Times. Because these prophecies must occur within history—as the Bible is historically literal—dispensationalists see current events as fulfillments of them and signs that the End is near. As such, dispensationalism refers to a literalist approach to the Bible that divides world history into different dispensations and stresses the apocalyptic nature of contemporary world events.

The first dispensation was that of creation and Adam and Eve in the Garden of Eden; dispensationalists believe not only that these events, as recorded in Genesis, are literal accounts of history but also that God dealt differently with Adam and Eve than He does with people today. A later dispensation was that of the covenant God made with the nation of Israel in the Old Testament, a covenant that only applies to the Jewish people. According to dispensationalists, we now live in a dispensation—known as the Church Age or Time of the Gentiles—which is wholly distinct from the ones that Adam and Eve or the ancient Israelites lived in.

John Nelson Darby was an Anglo-Irish theologian who, during the 1830s, preached throughout the British Isles and the United States about the Rapture of the church prior to a coming Great Tribulation. Darby interpreted the New Testament passage of 1 Thessalonians 4:13–18 to mean that at a certain point in history, Christians who are currently alive will be caught

---

1. John Walvoord, *Armageddon, Oil, and the Middle East Crisis: What the Bible Says About the Future of the Middle East and the End of Western Civilization* (Grand Rapids, MI: Zondervan, 1990 edition), 13.

up in the air and taken to heaven without dying; this event was the Rapture. Following the Rapture would be seven years of judgment on the world—in keeping with a literal interpretation of the book of Revelation, as well as Old Testament prophecies that have not yet literally been fulfilled in history—a period known as the Great Tribulation. Afterwards would come the Millennial Reign, during which he believed that Christ would reign on earth from a seat in Jerusalem for 1000 years. Darby's theology organized dispensationalism into the system that would be used by fundamentalists and leaders in the Religious Right. In the 1990s and early 2000s, this concept of the Rapture, Great Tribulation, and Millennial Reign became exceptionally popular through the *Left Behind* series, co-authored by dispensationalist thinkers Tim LaHaye and Jerry Jenkins.

Charles Ryrie, one of the most influential dispensationalists of the twentieth century, outlined what he saw as the three essential features of dispensationalism. The first of these essential features is that God deals differently with Israel than with the church; Israel's nation-ness (particularly the creation of the modern state of Israel in 1948) is more significant than its moral code or spiritual beliefs. The second is biblical literalism, in which the entire Bible must be taken literally from beginning to end, particularly in regards to the creation account in the Bible's first book, Genesis, and apocalyptic prophecies in its final book, Revelation. All of these prophecies must be grounded in actual historical events; if they have not yet literally occurred within world history, then they will occur at some point in the future. The third is a philosophy of history that views the glory of God, rather than the salvation of the world (as many non-dispensationalist Christians believe), as the ultimate goal of all things. That glory is the Millennial Reign.

The result of these three essential features is an approach to the Bible that equates contemporary world events with apocalyptic prophecies. Dispensationalists see the 1948 creation of Israel as the fulfillment of Amos 9:14–15 and Ezekiel 37:10–14. The formation of the United Nations is the one-world government prophesied in Revelation 13 and Daniel 7. The armies of Gog and Magog, which will march against Jerusalem as prophesied in Ezekiel 38 and 39, are the armies of Russia that will invade Israel. Furthermore, events that signaled that the End Times had come included the 1973 Yom Kippur War and OPEC embargo. To a dispensationalist, all of these events are signs that the End is near, and believers anticipate the impending Rapture of the church, Great Tribulation, and Millennial Reign.

One important component of dispensationalism is the Battle of Armageddon, as depicted in Revelation 16:16. Dispensationalism asserts that at the end of the Great Tribulation will come a final battle in which the armies of many nations will descend on Israel. The armies will be too great for Israel to defeat, but God will supernaturally defeat them in a slaughter that will be so great that blood will flow like a river and reach as high as the horse's bridle. This battle is the Battle of Armageddon, and dispensationalists believe that world events are being orchestrated by God to prepare the stage for this great slaughter. Dispensationalists in the 1970s saw the Yom Kippur War and ensuing OPEC embargo as God aligning the nations of the world in such a way that would lead to the Battle of Armageddon (see Chapter 5 for more). After Armageddon, the Great Tribulation will come to an end.

After the Great Tribulation will come the Millennial Reign, which is the final dispensation in history. In the Millennial Reign, the purposes of God in history will be fulfilled as God's glory is fully revealed throughout the world. Following this dispensation, the world will be destroyed by fire, an event that some dispensationalists believe will be a nuclear war. After this destruction, the world will end; all people will be judged and receive either everlasting life or everlasting damnation.

Because history is leading up to the Battle of Armageddon, dispensationalists believe that the world is continually getting worse and worse. There is no way to stop the destructiveness in the world—"wars and rumors of wars" are things that the Bible foretold and should be welcomed as signs that the Rapture is near—or the increase in sinful behaviors, such as children disrespecting parents, the widespread use of illegal drugs, and the legalization of abortion. For dispensationalists, wars around the world and social disintegration at home are signs that the End Times are at hand.

Many Christians believe that the history of the Bible continues to the present day and into the future through the church, both local churches and the global church, as well as the work of the Holy Spirit. What distinguishes dispensationalism is that it views the literal history of the Bible—the story that it began telling in Genesis 1—as the history of the world that is still unfolding, not only through the Holy Spirit's work in bringing people to faith but also in contemporary world events. While other Christians see biblical passages of apocalyptic events as figurative, dispensationalists see these passages as literal renderings of history that is written down before it happens. Critics of dispensationalism suggest that it is nothing more than a political agenda that has little to do with Christianity or how Christians have long interpreted the Bible; its emphasis on nations as being either good or bad causes dispensationalists to lose sight of the Bible's spiritual truth and moral teachings, such as loving one's neighbor and loving one's enemy.

This view of history, in which the Bible literally refers to apocalyptic events that must take place within world history in order for the glory of God to be revealed, formed the worldview of many leaders in the Religious

Right. Granted, dispensationalism is mostly limited to fundamentalists, and the Religious Right is an ecumenical movement that includes non-fundamentalist and even non-Protestant Christians—Orthodox, Catholic, Mormons, Jehovah's Witnesses, et cetera—as well as non-Christian groups, particularly Jews. But since its beginnings, the central leadership has been provided largely by fundamentalists, most of whom were dispensationalists or at least influenced by dispensationalism. The rise of the Religious Right was part of a broader evangelical movement that merged Christian and American nationalist thought vis-à-vis dispensational theology.

NATIONAL: BILLY GRAHAM AND THE COLD WAR REVIVAL

> When communism conquers a nation, it makes every man a slave. When Christianity conquers a nation, it makes every man a king.
> —Billy Graham

Billy Graham was an evangelist who traveled extensively to preach revivals, first throughout the United States and later throughout the world. He began preaching in the 1940s, and in 1949, a revival that he preached in Los Angeles lasted for an unprecedented eight weeks and drew the attention of the national media. From that 1949 Los Angeles meeting until his last public sermon in 2009, every time he preached, he drew enormous crowds and even larger radio and television audiences. Every sermon concluded with an invitation for people to give their hearts to Jesus, and as many as two million people responded to the invitation throughout his lifetime because of his preaching. There is no underestimating the cultural impact of so many people converting to Christianity under Graham's influence.

Estimates place over a billion people as hearing Graham's preaching during his lifetime, but his influence extended beyond radio airwaves and packed-out stadiums and straight to the White House, as he had a relationship with every United States president from Harry Truman (president from 1945–1953) to Barack Obama (president from 2009–2017). Perhaps ironically, 1949, the year of the Los Angeles revival, was the same year that the communist party took over China and declared the country a People's Republic. The struggle against communism during the Cold War would shape much of Graham's preaching from Eisenhower (president 1953–1961) through Nixon (president 1969–1974), as Graham used his national pulpit to declare that God was on the United States' side. His enormous influence helped shape the lens through which many people, including heads of state, viewed the Cold War: it was part of a dispensational struggle through which God was unfolding history.

Graham's influence helped spark a Cold War revival in the United States, particularly under President Eisenhower. While Eisenhower was campaigning for the presidency in 1952, Graham urged him to become baptized and join a denomination. Within two weeks of Eisenhower's inauguration in 1953, he had become a communicant of the Presbyterian church. In a display of civil religion, he went on to add the words "under God" to the Pledge of Allegiance and had the words "In God We Trust" added to the national currency. According to Nancy Gibbs and Michael Duffy, writing in *The Preacher and the Presidents*,

> Eisenhower needed for God to be on America's side, for that was how he framed the cold war. The essential difference between the American and Soviet systems was less economic or political than spiritual; they were "godless" while America was "chosen." Graham agreed completely and saw a clash of civilizations: "Either Communism must die, or Christianity must die," he wrote, "because it is actually a battle between Christ and anti-Christ." Eisenhower even made faith a weapon in the battlefield that counted most, where every single citizen could be called to arms. "Our forefathers proved that only a people strong in Godliness is a people strong enough to overcome... What is our battle against communism if it is not a fight between anti-God and a belief in the Almighty."[2]

In 1956, Graham began a journal called *Christianity Today* as a foil to the liberal journal, *Christian Century*. By the 1960s, *Christianity Today* had a circulation of over 250,000, making it a particularly influential arm of Graham's evangelistic ministry. The journal followed Graham's belief that the Cold War was a spiritual struggle that Christians should support as part of their patriotic duty to America. Indeed, Graham would declare at his revival meetings, known as crusades, that people could stand with Jesus and capitalism against the evils of communism and the Soviet Union and Red China. He believed that Americans giving their hearts to Jesus and converting to evangelical Christianity would strengthen the nation in its struggle against communism.

For Graham and *Christianity Today*, one of the greatest dangers of the growing communist bloc was the intentional efforts that communist

---

2. Nancy Gibbs and Michael Duffy, *The Preacher and the Presidents: Billy Graham in the White House* (New York: Center Street), 41–42.

governments made towards eradicating Christianity. Many Christians in communist countries, particularly the Soviet Union and Red China but also the tiny nation of Vietnam and surrounding countries, became political prisoners or were even killed as the communist party shut down churches and turned pastors into spies for the state. To prevent the complete collapse of Christianity in lands under threat by communist rule, Graham and the editors of *Christianity Today* supported the United States' military involvement in the Vietnam War and called on Christian citizens to support it, as well. To Graham, the Cold War was a spiritual struggle that was grounded into history, and Christian America had to stand on God's side in order to achieve victory.

Christianity Today posited that the capitalist United States did fight on God's side during the Cold War. In 1965, when the US Senate cast a vote to condemn Soviet persecution of Jews in the communist bloc, the journal claimed that the United States government effectively made a public declaration that it was on God's side. In contrast, the liberal foil to *Christianity Today*, *Christian Century*, condemned inhumane acts of communist governments and especially the persecution of Christians, but for its editors and readership, the Cold War remained an ideological struggle that could be resolved through diplomacy. For liberal Christians, the conflict was not a spiritual struggle, and nations were not God's eschatological actors. However, the circulation of *Christianity Today* was over ten times greater than that of *Christian Century*; coupled with Graham's massive public audience and access to the White House, the spiritual view of the Cold War became much more influential on the American public consciousness.

Meanwhile, tens of thousands of people were flocking to hear Graham speak at his crusades, some of which lasted for weeks, if not months at a time. His influence was so extensive that politicians, such as Richard Nixon, appeared alongside him as part of campaign rallies. This Cold War revival increasingly merged the United States and its engagement against the Soviet Union—and the broader communist threat, both worldwide and internally—with Christianity.

Under Graham's influence, the Cold War revival grounded "Christian America" into dispensational history. Graham was influenced by dispensationalism and believed that world events, particularly during the Cold War, were leading up to the great Battle of Armageddon, which he referred to as World War III. Graham was less keen than some of his contemporaries—such as John Walvoord and Tim LaHaye—to link world events with specific prophecies in the Bible. He took a more general approach to dispensational prophecies, such as when he wrote in 1981 that,

> There is no doubt that global events are preparing the way for the final war of history—the great Armageddon! As the earthly time clock ticks off each second and the world approaches midnight, this planet, according to the Bible, is going to be plunged into suffering too horrible to imagine or comprehend. As the top of Mount St. Helens blew off early in 1980 and became one of the great disasters of that period, so the Bible teaches in Hebrews 12 that God is going to shake the whole earth.[3]

Graham's evidence that the world was approaching Armageddon included the threat of chemical and biological warfare, the rise of terrorist groups, and the possibility of climate change; equally significant in the countdown was the decline of personal morality, demonstrated by increases in divorce rates, pornography, and the pervasiveness of drugs and alcohol. Graham believed that these evils existed in increasingly greater numbers because people have rejected God, exactly as prophesied in the Bible.

Dispensationalism shaped Graham's belief that the world is inexorably on a collision course that will lead to the Great Tribulation, which will find its completion in the Battle of Armageddon, followed by the Millennial Reign. Efforts to halt this collision course are futile, but people could find hope in the midst of it by placing faith in Jesus Christ. That faith would provide them with comfort as they faced trials—their personal armageddons—on earth, eternal security because they would go to heaven, and the assurance that the sufferings of the world would one day come to an end. Graham said,

> During Christ's [millennial] reign, political confusion will be turned to order and harmony, social injustices will be abolished, moral corruption will be replaced by integrity. For the first time in history the whole world will know what it is like to live in a society governed by God's principles. . . Man's dream for global harmony will be realized.[4]

For Graham, the spiritual reality of the Cold War was a sign that the End Times may be soon approaching. The ultimate fate of the world could not be avoided—it was prophesied in the Bible, and those prophecies must be fulfilled—but people could rest assured that they could be saved by placing their faith in Jesus. That faith would strengthen the United States as it faced off with the Soviet Union, as well as provide hope that the turmoils on earth would one day come to an end.

---

3. Billy Graham, *Till Armageddon: A Perspective on Suffering* (Waco: Word Books, 1981), 15.

4. Graham, *Till Armageddon*, 23.

GLOBAL: COMMUNISM THREATENS CAPITALISM AND CHRISTIANITY WORLDWIDE

Billy Graham's use of dispensational theology built on a long tradition of American civil religion. American civil religion posited that the divine hand of Providence favored the nation, that its democratic system enabled the people to ascertain the will of God via majority rule, and that the capitalist economy provided the people with biblical freedoms. Like William Jennings Bryan before him, Graham conflated the civil religion with Christianity; instead of appealing to a vague notion of "God" blessing America, he explicitly called on the American people to turn to Jesus. Graham saw America not only as a place of religious freedom but as a home for the Christian religion.

The American civil religion and Christianity are not the same thing, as Christianity has long existed outside of America. Christianity does not need a democratic political system or a capitalist economy in order to survive, and it thrives outside of the free world. In fact, Christianity has often proven itself to be strongest in countries where laws actively discriminate against Christian citizens and lead to their persecution. But Graham's fears about communism eliminating Christianity were well-founded, as Christians living in countries that fell to communism experienced severe state-sponsored persecution. Beyond this persecution, prominent dispensationalist thinkers in the budding Religious Right began claiming that biblical prophecies of the End Times relate to communist Russia and its coming destruction.

Karl Marx (born 1818, died 1884) was a Prussian (German) atheist who believed that class struggle between the bourgeoisie (elites) and the common, working proletariat (the people) was the root of society's problems. Like William Jennings Bryan in the United States, Marx championed the common people. However, he made a radical break with proto-populist thinkers by developing the idea of communism into a comprehensive political ideology. He believed that in the class struggle, the people would ultimately overthrow the elite and set up a utopian society of complete freedom and equality. Religion would not have a place in this utopia, as Marx saw it as a tool that elites used to keep the working people in oppression. Marx spent much of his life promoting the growing communist movements in Europe and advocating for armed revolt.

In 1917, the first successful communist revolution began when the Bolsheviks forced the Russian czar to abdicate the throne, murdered him and his family, and set up a communist state known as the Soviet Union. Soviet communism fundamentally opposed both capitalism and Christianity, and Christians in the Soviet Union soon faced an onslaught of state-sponsored persecution. Christians, along with members of other religious groups, were considered enemies of the state, and many were arrested as political prisoners. In the 1920s, the communist government imprisoned and tortured many leaders of the Russian Orthodox Church and only released them when they declared their loyalty to the Soviet state. By the end of the 1930s, the Russian Orthodox Church was no longer a viable institution because the state had systematically eliminated hundreds of thousands of Christians in the attempt to liberate the people from religion.

The tortures that Soviet Christians endured were severe. Government officials often rounded them up and shot them, then covered their bodies in mass graves. Once the system of forced labor camps, known as the Gulag, became operable, the government sent political prisoners—including tens of millions of Christians—to years of hard labor. Most of the people, including Christians, sent to the Gulag either died there or became so ill, crippled, and/or malnourished that they died soon after release. Female prisoners were frequently raped by both guards and male prisoners, and clothing during the brutal Russian winters was so scarce that inmates had to take the clothing from fellow prisoners who died. Alexander Solzhenitsyn, a Russian writer who won the Nobel Prize for Literature in 1970, survived nearly a decade in the Gulag. He wrote *The Gulag Archipelago* to tell the world of the horrors of the Soviet labor camps, which he described as a human sewage disposal system. As many as 20 million Russian Christians died under Soviet persecution during the years of the Soviet Union, from 1917 until 1991.

For many dispensational thinkers during the Cold War, the communist government of the Soviet Union embodied the biblical prophecies regarding Magog. Ezekiel 38–39 tells of the army of a man named Gog, from the land of Magog. Gog and the armies of Magog invade Israel and threaten to destroy the entire nation, but God supernaturally destroys them by causing earthquakes and raining down fire and brimstone. Dispensationalists interpret this passage as referring to a future event that must be fulfilled in exactly the terms explicated in Ezekiel. In the Cold War era, particularly with the rise in dispensationalist thought in America, dispensationalists arrived at a general conclusion that Magog is Russia and the present era is the End Times. A leader from Russia would amass an army that he would lead against Israel, only to be destroyed in the great Battle of Armageddon.[5] Many dispensationalists saw Russia's support of the Arab states in the Yom Kippur War as a prelude to the prophesied Russian invasion of Israel. The ensuing oil embargo demonstrated that the Arab states were allied with Russia and were opposed to God's people, the Jews.

---

5. Not all dispensationalists believe that Magog's invasion of Israel is the same as the Battle of Armageddon.

The significance of Israel—both the land and the Jewish people—within dispensational thought cannot be overstated, and before the systemic Soviet persecution of Christians, Russia had a long history of persecuting Jews. In fact, the word "pogrom," which refers in a general sense to a mass public assault, is a Russian word used to describe the violent riots in which people would kill Jews, burn Jewish homes, and destroy Jewish businesses. Under Russia's Romanov czars, the Jews were frequently targeted as the cause of all of the country's woes, and pogroms would sometimes last for years at a time. Russia's long history of antisemitism may have had a role in its support of Arab nations against Israel in the Yom Kippur War, and it strengthened the dispensationalist connection between Russia and Magog.

Prophecies about Gog and Magog became increasingly significant during the Cold War years. In 1972, Tim LaHaye (co-author of the megabestselling *Left Behind* series) published a book entitled *The Beginning of the End*, where he made a case for why Russia is the biblical land of Magog before claiming that

> History shows that atheistic Communism emanates from the political leadership in Russia and extends throughout their nefarious system all over the world. No nation in the history of the world has destroyed more flesh than Russia through the spread of Communism. This is true in her own land as well as in China, the eastern European satellite nations, Africa (particularly Congo and Biafra), India, Indonesia, and many other places.
>
> But her greatest sin has not been the destruction of flesh, as serious as that is. Her greatest sin has been the soul damnation caused by her atheistic ideology. This has been accomplished not only through Communist leaders in Communist countries, but through Communist infiltrators and dupes on university campuses of the free world. The Lord Jesus Christ's indictment of the Pharisees in Matthew 23 reveals the attitude of God toward the destroyers of men's souls—and it reveals his attitude toward Russia. Certainly no nation has done more to destroy faith in God than Communist Russia, thereby earning the enmity of God.
>
> Another factor that evokes the wrath of God against Russia and her leaders is their mistreatment of the Jews. . . Russia stands second only to Adolf Hitler in cruelty to Jews.[6]

LaHaye claimed that God is against Russia and will ensure that both its armies and land are destroyed. He also saw the passage of Ezekiel 38–39

---

6. Tim LaHaye, *The Beginning of the End* (Wheaton, IL: Tyndale House Publishers, 1972), 65.

as prophesying that Soviet spies who had infiltrated Western democracies would be supernaturally destroyed. "In one dramatic moment, God will solve the greatest internal threat to the security of the free countries of the world."[7]

During the Cold War years, biblical prophecies about Gog and Magog became politicized, as Christians in Russia were suffering severe persecution and Soviet intervention in the Middle East was causing a dramatic shift in oil politics. In fact, when Ronald Reagan was governor of California (1967–1975), he mentioned that Gog and Magog must refer to Russia and that the End Times are near.

LOCAL: JERRY FALWELL BEGINS THE MORAL MAJORITY

> No other nation on the face of the earth has been blessed by God Almighty like the people of the United States of America.[8]
> —Jerry Falwell

In 1956, the year that Billy Graham founded *Christianity Today* and when the threat of nuclear war with the Soviet Union loomed large, Jerry Falwell founded Thomas Road Baptist Church in the town of Lynchburg, Virginia. The church was small at its founding, with a congregation of just a few dozen people. But Falwell and his congregation quickly grew the church's numbers through efforts common to fundamentalists, particularly "soul-winning"—striking up conversations about faith with people, often by visiting them at home, to try to convert them to Christianity. The church quickly mushroomed in size and became the base of a nationwide ministry that blended the American civil religion with Christianity much more explicitly than Graham did.

The same year that Falwell began Thomas Road Baptist Church, he began airing its Sunday services in a weekly radio broadcast called *The Old-Time Gospel Hour*. The broadcast was styled after *The Old-Fashioned Revival Hour* of Charles Fuller, the fundamentalist oilman who founded Fuller Seminary. Falwell actually credited Fuller's radio broadcast with converting him to Christianity and, like Fuller, was an avid dispensationalist. In many ways, dispensationalism formed the basis of Falwell's political ideology, as he, like Graham, saw the Cold War as a spiritual struggle between the

---

7. Tim LaHaye, *The Beginning of the End* (Wheaton, IL: Tyndale House Publishers, 1972), 77.

8. Jerry Falwell, *Listen, America!* (New York: Doubleday Publishing, 1980), 117.

God-ordained system of capitalism and the evil, communist Soviet Union. He also saw the United States as having a special place in God's plan for history. He believed that the country's divine destiny could be fulfilled by conservative Christians engaging in political action, particularly by supporting Republican candidates for office, and taking the country back for God. From his local base in Lynchburg, Falwell organized the Religious Right when he and like-minded fundamentalist and evangelical leaders, along with partnering politicians and businessmen, created the Moral Majority in 1979. According to Falwell, the Moral Majority was pro-life, pro-family, pro-morals, and pro-American.

The Moral Majority was a grassroots organization that formed chapters when local churches created their own "Moral Action Committees." These local committees mobilized conservative Christians, many of whom had not previously even been registered to vote, into political activism. They supported conservative Republicans who campaigned for political office, along with some independents. Granted, for the organization to retain its tax-exempt status, it could not explicitly promote Republicanism; however, the candidates that the Moral Majority supported were almost exclusively conservative Republicans.

Prior to the rise of the Moral Majority, large numbers of fundamentalists and evangelicals did not concern themselves with the nation's political life; they were content to be left alone while the rest of the nation descended into the chaos of the Cold War. But with Falwell's preaching reaching millions of evangelical and fundamentalist Christians through *The Old-Time Gospel Hour*, they decided that their duty, as Christians and Americans, was to reverse what they saw as the nation's moral and spiritual decline by promoting political conservativism. In the 1980s, as many as one-third of American voters were part of the Moral Majority. The movement became so strong that it transformed the Republican Party into a political force that championed "traditional Christian values."

In keeping with the central debate between fundamentalist and liberal Christianity, Falwell and the Moral Majority advocated for creationism to be taught in public schools. Additionally, to protect schoolchildren from the corrupting influences of liberal society, Falwell advocated that the third time someone commits a drug-related offense, he or she should be given the death penalty. But his interpretation of fundamentalism went far beyond a fervent crusade against drugs and the creation-evolution debate that had separated the fundamentalists from the liberals a century before.

As a fundamentalist Falwell was a dispensationalist, and he applied dispensationalism to his beliefs about America, particularly regarding the Cold War and its God-given role in the Last Days. In 1980, the year after he formed the Moral Majority, he published a book called *Listen, America!* to communicate his beliefs about God's plan for America, particularly regarding the threat of communism during the Cold War. In the book he said,

> As a preacher of the Gospel, I must speak out against evil. Evil forces would seek to destroy America because she is a bastion for Christian missions and a base for world evangelization... I must speak out against godless communism, which would seek to destroy the work of Christ that is going out from this base of America... God will again bless us if we will turn back to Him as individuals and as a nation. There is power in the name of Jesus Christ, and it is the only power that can turn back godless communism. If God is on our side, no matter how militarily superior the Soviet Union is, they could never touch us. God would miraculously protect America. The destiny of America awaits our choice as to what we will do with God.[9]

Falwell believed that the United States is uniquely blessed by God to carry out a divine mission in the world within dispensational history. Its archrival, the Soviet Union, was not only the enemy of capitalism; it was the enemy of God. He saw liberal Democrats as weak on national defense and willing to cater to the communists. As such, the political goals of the Moral Majority included a strong military, which called for the stockpiling of nuclear weapons, to ensure the United States would be victorious in the Cold War. For Falwell, this victory was divinely ordained.

In addition to a strong national defense, the United States had a duty to fight any communist encroachment by ending all socialist policies. Falwell and his followers advocated for reductions in welfare and entitlement programs, as well as deregulation of private business, as government regulation and corporate taxes hampered the capitalist value of free enterprise. He saw free-market capitalism as both a Christian and an American value, and it was one way of keeping the country spiritually strong against the threat of communism.

Yet the role of dispensationalism in underlying Falwell's political goals extended beyond the conflict with the Soviet Union. He believed that the United States had a sacred duty to protect and defend the state of Israel, as Nixon did in 1973 during the Yom Kippur War (which became a proxy battlefield for the Cold War). In *Listen, America!* he said,

> I firmly believe God has blessed America because America has blessed the Jew. If this nation wants her fields to remain white with grain, her scientific achievements to remain notable, and

9. Jerry Falwell, *Listen, America!* (New York: Doubleday Publishing, 1980), 106.

her freedom to remain intact, America must continue to stand with Israel.[10]

Because the United States had a special place within dispensational history, Falwell believed, God's divine purposes for the nation could only be achieved if the people followed His principles. Yet liberation movements that gained nationwide traction during the 1960s, such as the gay rights movement and the women's liberation movement, contradicted a literalist interpretation of the Bible. There are verses in the Bible that condemn homosexuality, as well as verses that tell women to submit to men; Falwell's literalist reading of these verses concluded that the gay rights and women's liberation movements run contrary to the laws of God in the Bible. As such, these movements were sinful and invited God's judgment on America. In *Listen, America!* he said,

> The strength of America has been in her righteousness, in her walk with God. Now we see national sins that are permeating our nation, and we find that our citizens are without remorse, without regret or repentance, and we are not far from the judgment of God upon this great nation of ours. With our erosion from the historic faith of our fathers, we are seeing an erosion in our stability as a nation. We have already shown that we are economically, politically, and militarily sick because our country is morally sick.[11]

Falwell believed that the AIDS crisis, which struck the United States during the 1980s, was the beginning of God's judgment on the nation, not only because of homosexuality, but because liberal Christians were tolerating homosexuality. In *Listen, America!* he said,

> It [homosexuality] will not only have a corrupting influence upon our next generation, but it will also bring down the wrath of God upon America.[12]

But to Falwell, the greatest sin of America was that of abortion, which was legalized in all 50 states in 1973 through the landmark Supreme Court decision *Roe v Wade*. The cause of ending abortion proved to be the catalyst that would galvanize disparate groups of conservative Christians, from fundamentalists to evangelicals to like-minded Catholics, who had a longstanding tradition of opposing abortion, to come together to engage in conservative political activism through the Moral Majority. People in the

---

10. Jerry Falwell, *Listen, America!* (New York: Doubleday Publishing, 1980), 113.

11. Jerry Falwell, *Listen, America!* (New York: Doubleday Publishing, 1980), 119–120.

12. Jerry Falwell, *Listen, America!* (New York: Doubleday Publishing, 1980), 186.

Moral Majority refused to vote for any candidate who supported abortion; they became known as "values voters" or "single-issue voters."

As previously mentioned, Falwell did not preach his first sermon about abortion until 1978, a full five years after the *Roe v Wade* decision. However, Falwell placed abortion, too, within his understanding of dispensationalism, as it demonstrated the nation's moral and spiritual decline, which invited the wrath of God. The 1980 election cycle saw a slew of new politicians elected who had no political experience but were pro-life. Their goal was to reverse the country's moral decline—and by extension, curtail the wrath of God on America—by ending abortion.

The local groups of conservative Christians who organized committees in the Moral Majority felt that the government had ignored them and instead catered to the interests of the elites, liberal society, and the Soviet Union. From the bottom up, they expressed their anger at the establishment and the status quo and made their voices heard by electing new politicians that they saw as aligned with their populist agendas. They wanted to see America return to its Christian origins, and as Chapter 5 will show, this return required an approach to oil that grounded it into dispensational history.

GLOCAL: DISPENSATIONALISM IN ALASKA

Sarah Palin's long-time church in Wasilla, Alaska, Wasilla Assembly of God (now Summit Worship Center), holds to dispensational teachings, especially regarding the End Times. Its leadership and members believe that Christians will be raptured up to heaven prior to the beginning of the Great Tribulation; the Great Tribulation will then cleanse the world of evil and prepare it for the Millennial Reign of Jesus Christ. The state of Israel, which the United States—along with many, many patriotic and/or dispensational Christians—supports, will figure prominently in the End-Times drama until Israel fulfills its prophesied destiny during the Millennial Reign. As such, for Palin and like-minded Christians, including many with whom she has long shared Christian fellowship, support of Israel is both a patriotic and religious duty.

Due at least in part to the influence of Jerry Prevo, Jerry Falwell's colleague who led the Moral Majority in Alaska, many (though certainly not all) churches in Anchorage and the Mat-Su Valley are staunchly patriotic. This Christian patriotism does have the tendency to affect the teachings of local pastors and shape the theological views of Christians in Alaska. Many pastors, particularly in Alaska, have preached sermons on bringing Christian values back to American public life, why Christians should be patriotic and politically active, and how the Bible is the cornerstone of America. A strong sense of patriotism, blended into dispensational theology, helped shape the faith and politics of Sarah Palin, particularly regarding her views on Alaska's oil and the End Times.

Shortly before John McCain tapped Palin to be his vice-presidential candidate, the governor of Alaska gave an impromptu talk at Wasilla Assembly of God; the talk was firmly grounded in dispensational ideas about God's purposes within world history, local geography (including the state's natural gas reserves), and current events. The talk was at a Master's Commissioning service, at which the church commissioned people that it had trained in knowledge of the Bible and prophecy so that they could spread the gospel. While dispensational theology and Master's Commissioning are certainly not unique to Alaska, what is unique is how she and other Christian leaders in the area link Alaska to God's purposes in history. This view came out in her talk:

> Just be amazed, the umbrella of this church here and where God is going to send you from this church. Believe me, I know what I'm saying. God has sent me from underneath the umbrella of this church throughout the state. And Alaska is all over the world map right now. There's something going on in Alaska...
>
> Right now, we're the richest state in the Union in terms of natural resources, our oil, our gas, our minerals, the gold that we have under the ground. We're very, very rich. But our most important natural resource, of course, is our people... I can do my part in doing things like working really, really hard to get a natural gas pipeline, about a $30 billion project... I think God's will has to be done in unifying people and companies to get that gas line built, so pray for that.
>
> But I can do my job there, in developing our natural resources and doing things like getting the roads paved and making sure our troopers have their cop cars and their uniforms and their guns, and making sure our public schools are funded. But really, all of that stuff doesn't do any good if the people of Alaska's hearts aren't right with God. And that's going to be your job as I'm doing my job... We can work together to make sure God's will be done here...
>
> Pray for our military men and women who are striving to do what is right also for this country, that our leaders, our national leaders are sending them out on a task that is from God. That's what we have to make sure that we're praying for, that

> there is a plan and that that plan is God's plan. So bless them with your prayers...
>
> This is what I want to pray over you guys, that the God of our Lord Jesus Christ, the Father of glory may give to you a spirit of wisdom and revelation in the knowledge of Him, and that the spirit of revelation, also including the spirit of prophecy that God's going to tell you what is going on and what is going to go on. And you guys are going to have that within you...and it's going to pour out throughout the state of Alaska. Good, good things in store for the state of Alaska. Let us pray for God's will to be done here.

In Palin's talk, she communicated the idea that God's purposes within dispensational history included the American nation as well as the state of Alaska. God's will was enacted through America's military and the construction of a pipeline for natural gas, and people could discern this will through the spirit of prophecy (see Chapter 8 for more on extra-biblical prophecy). Following her talk, one of the church's pastors, Ed Kalnins, said,

> There are some things about the natural resources, about the state. There was some things that God wants to tap into to be a refuge for the Lower 48. And I believe Alaska is one of the refuge states...in the Last Days. And hundreds of thousands of people are going to come to the state to seek refuge. And the church has to be ready to minister to them. Amen.

Beliefs about the Last Days are not unique to dispensationalists, but they are particularly strong among dispensationalists. Between Palin and her pastor, ideas about the development of Alaska's energy resources were grounded into dispensational history as part of God's unfolding plan for the nations of the world. These ideas were particularly embedded into the role of the United States, and particularly Alaska, in the End Times.

For Palin, Alaska's pipeline and other energy reserves supplied more than the state's economic lifeline; they provided the means for the United States to no longer have to rely on foreign powers—many of which, such as OPEC countries, are seen negatively by dispensationalists—to supply its energy needs. Particularly because of the disastrous effects of the OPEC embargo, many see energy independence as a critical need for American national security. Two of the energy-supplying powers that she mentioned in other talks were Russia and Iran, both of which play significant roles in dispensational theology (for the role of Iran in dispensational theology, see Chapter 5). As she said in her talk at Wasilla Assembly of God, accessing the state's energy reserves, which could lead to energy independence for

America, was part of God's will for Alaska. This use of dispensationalism to communicate her beliefs about Christianity, America, and oil demonstrates one way that Palin's faith was shaped by oil politics.

Notwithstanding, local theologies that fitted dispensationalism into the pipeline and Alaska's oil-based economy were not particularly widespread. However, later movements, particularly the New Apostolic Reformation, which Wasilla Assembly of God is a part of, also shaped theological beliefs regarding the state's natural resources (for more on the New Apostolic Reformation, see Chapter 8). One result is a culture in which beliefs about the American nation and Christian faith are tightly interwoven into views about oil and other natural resources.

Chapter 4

Nationalism and Religion in the Moral Majority

Crafting the Identity Politics of the Religious Right

On the outskirts of Lynchburg, Virginia, adjacent to Jerry Falwell's Thomas Road Baptist Church, is Candlers Mountain, a 1200-foot peak that overlooks the city. In the 1960s, Falwell envisioned using the land on and around Candlers Muntain to build a world-class Christian college where professors would teach students from a Christian worldview.

Falwell framed Candlers Mountain and the school that became Liberty University in biblical terms. At a prayer rally in the summer of 1977, six years after Falwell's ministry began offering college classes, he urged his students and church members to pray that God would provide five million dollars in one month. The money was to purchase land on Candlers Mountain, which he renamed Liberty Mountain. He said,

> Our world is in trouble today. That is why you are here to train and prepare to minister in a world of more than four billion people who desperately need Jesus Christ. This summer we have experienced the constant threat of postal strikes, which has affected our offerings. The cost of our Clean Up America Campaign has been tremendous, but we could not, nor can we ever, stop proclaiming righteousness in our nation. Thus you see unfinished buildings that you desperately need. We serve a prayer-answering God. We have gathered on this mountain

today for a prayer meeting. We desperately need $5 million and have come to ask God to supply that need by September 24, which I have set apart as 'Miracle Day'. . .

The Jews had come through four hundred years of bondage. God delivered them from the Red Seat by the hand of Moses, and after forty years of wandering in the wilderness, delivered them from the river Jordan by the hand of Joshua. They had come far by faith, but now, having arrived in the Promised Land, they found the walls of Jericho immoveable. The inhabitants of Jericho had been reported to Joshua to be 'giants.' Everything seemed lost to the children of God. Defeat seemed imminent.

Liberty Mountain is our Promised Land. For many years we have prayed for this thirty-five hundred acres of sanctified property. After twenty-two years of miracles, we have arrived on Liberty Mountain. But now we find ourselves looking up at the high walls of bills and unfinished buildings. A miracle is needed.[1]

In the story from the Hebrew Bible, Joshua led the Israelite army in the Battle of Jericho through unconventional means. Jericho was a walled city in Canaan, the land that would become known as Israel, and the walls were so well-fortified that the Israelites could not hope to conquer the city. Joshua led the Israelites to march around the city for six days, and on the seventh day, they marched around Jericho seven times. They then blew their trumpets and made as much noise as they could, and the mighty walls of Jericho miraculously collapsed.

Falwell framed the miracle that he needed in terms of this story. A week before "Miracle Day," he drove his truck the 12 miles around Liberty Mountain—just as the Israelites had marched around Jericho—and prayed the whole time. On the seventh day, he drove around seven times before heading to the Sunday church service. In the one-month period between when Falwell made his appeal for five million dollars and "Miracle Day," he raised a total of seven million dollars. Surely, the walls of Jericho had miraculously fallen down.

IDEOLOGY: NATIONALISM AND LIBERTARIANISM

Nationalism and libertarianism both come across as rather simple concepts: nationalism is nothing more than what people believe about their nation,

---

1. Gerald Strober and Ruth Tomczak, *Jerry Falwell: Aflame for God* (Thomas Nelson, 1979), 79–81.

and libertarianism is a belief system that emphasizes personal liberty against government interference. Yet both ideologies are complicated in that they have no clear boundaries; defining a nation is a subjective matter, as is defining the limits of personal freedom and where government interference should begin. Jerry Falwell's use of dispensational theology in promoting American nationalism demonstrates how challenging the concepts of nationalism and libertarianism can be.

Jerry Falwell was an avid nationalist who believed that the American nation was inherently Christian, and he was fond of saying that he had three goals: to get people saved, to get them baptized, and to get them registered to vote. He often held rallies on the steps of state capital buildings, where members of his choir—dressed in red, white, and blue—would sing patriotic songs such as "I'm Just A Flag-Waving American." Members of the Moral Majority organized voter registration drives at their churches and distributed stickers that said "Vote," with the "t" enlarged to look like a cross. He believed that calling the American people to national duty and calling them to Christian duty were the same thing, and he often said that good Christians make good citizens.

Though nationalism comes across as a straightforward concept, understanding it becomes complicated by the difficulty in defining precisely what a nation is. Anthony Smith defined a nation as "a named human population sharing a myth of common descent, historical memories, and a mass culture, and possessing a demarcated territory, common economy, and common legal rights and duties."[2] Benedict Anderson's understanding of a nation is "an imagined political community—and imagined as both inherently limited and sovereign."[3] In other words, the idea of a nation exists in terms of how people see themselves and their cultural and ethnic relationship to the people around them. How people define a particular nation, or whether a nation exists at all, depends on subjective aspects of belief.

While one can look on a map and locate a country, one cannot necessarily locate a nation in purely objective terms that can be universally agreed upon. For example, one can point to the country known as the United States, but its place on the map does not designate what Jerry Falwell believed about the American nation. There were people who lived within the geographic borders of the United States and held American passports yet did not belong to what he saw as the American nation, as they did not imagine themselves as Americans the same way that he did. They may have been atheists, queer,

---

2. Anthony Smith, *The Antiquity of Nations* (Oxford: Polity Press, 2004), 42.
3. Anderson, *Imagined Communities: Reflections on the Origin and Spread of Nationalism* (London: Verso, 2016), 6.

or conscientious objectors to the draft, and these ideas did not align with his view of the American nation. For Falwell, America was a Christian nation built on biblical principles that had a divine destiny within dispensational history. Other people view the American nation differently, and some do not see it as a nation at all.

Dispensational theology understands Jewish nation-ness as central to God's plan in history. Dispensational beliefs about the nation of Israel begin in Genesis 12, when God called a man named Abram out of Ur, in modern-day Iraq. God told him to go to a promised land, what is now the land of Israel, and made him the forefather of the people of Israel, who would be a nation of His chosen people. God changed Abram's name to Abraham because he became the father of many nations, the most important of which—at least for dispensationalists—was the nation of Israel. The descendants of Abraham through the Israelite nation are known as the Jews, and dispensationalists believe that they are still God's chosen people with a divine destiny prophesied in both the Old and New Testaments.

Dispensationalists see the Old Testament as a historical account of God's dealings with Israel, both before the birth of Christ as well as prophecies about Israel for the End Times. Because Israel rejected Christ (who was himself a Jew), according to dispensational thought, history is right now in a "Great Parenthesis" known as the Church Age. During the Church Age, God is dealing with the church separately from how He deals with Israel, but this period will end with the Rapture. The creation of the modern state of Israel in 1948—the exemplification of Jewish nation-ness—is a sign that the End Times will soon come. The next event in prophetic history will be the Rapture of the church, after which the historical unfolding of God's plan will shift away from the church and back to Israel.

Falwell's interpretation of dispensational theology, which incorporated his beliefs about the American nation, claimed that the United States could only fulfill its divine destiny by unconditionally supporting the state of Israel. He saw Israel as having many enemies, particularly Russia and the Arab states (which supplied the United States' oil), that the United States had to stand against in events such as the 1973 Yom Kippur War. Part of his nationalist agenda was encouraging the United States to support Israel against Russia/Magog and the oil-producing Arab states, an idea that equated what he saw as American duty with Christian duty: Christian Americans could uphold their nation's divine destiny by supporting Israel against its enemies.

As a libertarian, Falwell promoted a free-market economy that is not hindered by burdensome government regulations. He saw the ownership of private property as a biblical value and capitalism as the economic system endorsed by the Bible; taxes that funded welfare programs impeded on personal liberty and undermined the capitalist way of life. In the Cold War era, when the threat of communism was ever-present, Falwell saw the duty of the American government as the protection of free-market capitalism, private property, and religious freedom. He promoted a military build-up, including nuclear weapons, so that what he saw as American, Christian freedoms—such as the right to own private property—would not be threatened by the Soviet Union. As such, he promoted what he saw as a biblical agenda for what he believed to be a Christian nation; his view of the American nation combined libertarian economics—free-market capitalism without government regulations on business or business taxes, especially taxes that funded welfare—with his interpretation of biblical morality as the basis for American national life.

In a break from libertarianism, though, he advocated harsh penalties for drug users, an ending of abortion, and nonrecognition of LGBTQ+ rights. Many libertarians endorse the decriminalization of drugs, access to abortion, and full rights regardless of sexuality, as these principles favor personal freedom. Falwell, however, saw them as incompatible with biblical morality; he believed that the economic and military might of the American nation would be undermined if the people tolerated LGBTQ+ lifestyles and that abortion is a national sin that will bring about God's wrath. He promoted economic libertarianism, in the form of free-market capitalism, while also promoting government interventions in personal areas such as sexuality; doing so, he believed, would preserve America's moral, Christian character in the face of Soviet aggression and also "stay the wrath of God" on the nation.

Falwell's beliefs about the American nation were certainly influenced by how he interpreted dispensational theology—like Billy Graham, he placed the nation into dispensational history—but perhaps equally importantly, so were his beliefs about other nations, particularly Russia and Israel. In Falwell's dispensationalism, Israel was God's chosen nation, and the United States had to support Israel unconditionally in order to receive God's blessing. Russia, the land of Magog, was the enemy of God's chosen people. In addition to choosing Israel, God had also chosen the American nation, and it had to promote free-enterprise capitalism while enforcing biblical morality as part of fulfilling its dispensational destiny.

Falwell's support of libertarian, free-enterprise capitalism and profound dislike of welfare policies also fit into his interpretation of American nationalism and dispensational theology, as these ideals opposed the Soviet communism that gripped the biblical land of Magog. He interpreted the Bible as describing Magog as evil and an enemy to Israel, its horrors culminating in the terrors of the Soviet regime and the impending Battle of Armageddon. Israel and Russia were nations that played a role in God's unfolding of history, and the United States had a divine destiny to protect Israel and repel Russian advances. That destiny came into stark focus with the Yom Kippur War, when the United States armed Israel to counter the Soviet arming of the Arab states.

The way that dispensationalism grounds the Bible into contemporary world events causes nationalism to become a major factor in how dispensationalists, such as Falwell, view history, including events of the past, present, and future. Nations are God's actors, and they will all collide at the Battle of Armageddon before the glory of God is fully revealed in the Millennial Reign. For Falwell, a libertarian ethos, in the form of free-market capitalism, combined with an enforcement of biblical morality were necessary requisites for the American nation to fulfill its destiny.

NATIONAL—THE 1925 SCOPES "MONKEY" TRIAL

The sociologist of religion Martin Marty commented on the importance of scripture to the development of fundamentalist movements. When holy scriptures become subjected to the same critiques that scholars apply to other ancient texts, people come to see the scriptures as historical documents rather than the revealed Word of God. The entire religion may face a crisis as the faithful must determine how they will approach scripture and whether the basis of knowledge comes from scripture or modern science. Fundamentalist movements often arise as an effort to reclaim the scriptures and uphold them as the literal and authoritative Word of God in the face of modernist, liberal critiques.

Fundamentalist movements often adopt an approach to scripture that affirms it as literally authoritative in terms of history and science. For Protestant fundamentalists in the United States, that approach led to the widespread adoption of dispensational theology, which supports a literal approach to the Bible throughout the entirety of the text. In order to protect the sacredness of the scripture, fundamentalist movements develop enclaves that have very rigid barriers to entry so that only people who affirm the same view of the scriptures are able to join the movement. These rigid barriers help preserve the sacredness of the scripture by ensuring that no one in a fundamentalist group will question the scripture's authority. For fundamentalists, this literalist approach to the Bible creates a conflict with modern science, a conflict that came to a head in the 1925 Scopes "Monkey" Trial.

In the United States, liberal Christianity emerged first in the big cities of the North. Liberal schools, such as the University of Chicago (which JD Rockefeller endowed), Yale, and Harvard taught higher criticism of the Bible by applying rigorous critiques to the ancient text. Ministers trained in these schools promoted, in their churches, a view of the Bible that saw it as an ancient text written by men rather than the literal and infallible Word of God. Among the liberal Christians who promoted the social gospel, many saw the Millennial Reign as a figurative rather than literal event; known as amillennialists (meaning that there would not be a literal millennium), they believed that the peace on earth that the Millennial Reign represented could be achieved by promoting the social gospel. They did not see prophecies as literal accounts of future events but rather as calls to work for justice.

The fundamentalist movement took hold most strongly among Baptists and Presbyterians in the North as a reaction against the rise of liberal Christianity. The Niagara Bible Conference, which began in 1875, emphasized the importance of biblical prophecy as something that would literally be fulfilled within dispensational history. The annual meeting of the Niagara Bible Conference led to the development of The Niagara Creed, a forerunner to *The Fundamentals*. The Niagara Creed emphasized a literal interpretation of the Bible, particularly in regards to creation, prophetic passages, and the coming Millennial Reign, in contradistinction to the idea that the Millennial Reign was a figurative event that the social gospel could accomplish. As such the fundamentalists and liberals came to represent two intractable lines of thought; between them, there could be no compromise.

Meanwhile, the higher criticism of elite northern schools did not penetrate the still-rural South until the Scopes "Monkey" Trial of 1925. The landmark trial in Dayton, Tennessee attracted nationwide media attention as it pitted fundamentalism and creationism against liberalism and evolutionism. The attorney who argued for creationism was none other than William Jennings Bryan, the populist who equated the American civil religion with Christianity.

For Bryan and like-minded fundamentalists, the social gospel was inadequate for addressing the ills of modern American society. America was sick because its people had rejected the authority of the Bible, not because newly arrived immigrants—most of whom were Catholic and Jewish, rather than Protestant—needed relief from the urban squalor of the late-nineteenth and early-twentieth centuries. For Bryan, an embrace of creationism and complete rejection of Darwinism, along with other elite ideas that caused people to question the Bible, would put America back on track. To help cure America, in the early 1920s, Bryan began campaigning throughout the South for laws prohibiting the teaching of evolution in public schools.

In Tennessee, a law passed in 1925 prohibited public school teachers from teaching any scientific views that were not consistent with a literal view of the creation account in Genesis.

John Scopes, the defendant in the Scopes Trial, taught high school biology in Dayton, Tennessee. When the American Civil Liberties Union (ACLU) wanted to challenge the new law that favored fundamentalism, he volunteered to teach evolution so that he would be arrested. The goal of Scopes and the ACLU was that following a trial, the law would be struck down. When the case went to trial, the ACLU hired the lawyer Clarence Darrow to represent Scopes in the attempt to get the law repealed. The trial was highly publicized, and people traveled from all over the country to see "the trial of the century."

When the trial began, what quickly became apparent was that what was at stake was not whether or not Scopes had broken the law or even whether or not the law was constitutional. What was at stake was whether creationism and biblical literalism were theologically sound. Darrow argued in favor of a liberal approach to the Bible, which he did not see as contradicting Darwinian evolution. Bryan represented the state and argued in favor of biblical literalism and creationism. Though John Scopes was the defendant for teaching evolution, creationism—and by extension, fundamentalist theology—was on trial. In the words of Clarence Darrow,

> The defense maintains that the book of Genesis is in part a hymn, in part an allegory and work of religious interpretations written by men who believe that the earth was flat and whose authority cannot be accepted to control the teachings of science in our schools. The narrow purpose of the defense is to establish the innocence of the defendant Scopes. The broad purpose of the defense will be to prove that the Bible is a work of religious aspiration and rules of conduct which must be kept in the field of theology.[4]

Bryan, on the other hand, argued from his unshakeable view in the authority of the Bible as the literal Word of God. For Bryan, God, not science, was the arbiter of all things and the source of all knowledge.

Scopes lost when the judge found him guilty of breaking the law. The fundamentalists won in what turned into the most humiliating victory of the century; they were derided in the national media and became a public laughingstock. Bryan died in his sleep a week later; whether or not he took his life in the wake of national embarrassment has not been proven.

---

4 "Scopes Trial Transcripts, 1925." From Hanover University archives. https://history.hanover.edu/courses/excerpts/111scopes.html, accessed on March 15, 2019.

Following the humiliation of the Scopes Trial, the fundamentalist movement seemed to retreat from the public scene. Fundamentalists were much less vocal; instead of debating with liberals, they built more of their own schools where a new generation of students could learn fundamentalist values. In addition to those already established, such as Biola and Moody, new Bible institutes included Bob Jones College (later Bob Jones University), Westminster Theological Seminary, and Dallas Theological Seminary. Many thought that the fundamentalist movement, which was no longer public, had disappeared entirely; then Jerry Falwell organized the Moral Majority, and fundamentalism regained its footing as a dominant force in American public life.

There was a bigger ramification to the Scopes Trial and creationism than the retreat of fundamentalists from public life. If the world was created in seven literal days approximately 6600 years ago—as many fundamentalists believe—then oil could not have been formed through millions of years of biological and chemical processes taking place inside the earth. Oil must have been placed inside the earth by God, and He placed it in certain geographic places to enact His purposes within history. Some creationists believe that oil was created as a result of the Great Flood, but how it ended up in particular parts of the world, such as Alaska, was a divine act. Palin, herself a creationist in a vein similar to William Jennings Bryan, claimed that God had put energy resources into Alaska's ground, and Alaskans had the responsibility to use them.

GLOBAL—THE RISE OF NATIONALISM

Falwell's American nation was both Christian and libertarian. As a Christian nation, America was the preserver of freedom in a world facing the very real threat (or, in some cases, the reality) of communism. Americans had to practice libertarian economics—low taxes, drastically reduced social spending, an end to the redistribution of wealth through taxes on the wealthy that fund programs for the poor, and reduced government regulations on businesses—to preserve the biblical freedom of owning private property and running private businesses. At the same time, people in this American Christian nation had to practice biblical morality in their personal lives, and the state had a duty to pass legislation regulating personal behavior.

Nationalism is nothing more than beliefs about a nation, and Falwell's nationalism was nothing more than what he believed about the American nation. To him, it was inherently Christian and blessed by God to be the preserver of liberty to the world. But it was also in danger of facing God's wrath for its sins, particularly its acceptance of LGBTQ+ lifestyles and the legalization of abortion. The rise of the Moral Majority in the United States did not happen in isolation; rather, it was one of the many nationalist movements that emerged across the world during the Cold War years of the 1970s and 1980s.

The period of nationalist-fueled violence in Northern Ireland that came to be known as "The Troubles" has a long history but ostensibly began in 1969. The Republic of Ireland has long been predominantly Catholic but the region of Ulster—"Northern Ireland," which became part of the United Kingdom in 1920—has a Protestant majority. Catholics in Northern Ireland have long wanted to be a part of the Republic of Ireland, while Protestants support British rule and want to remain part of the predominantly Protestant United Kingdom. A Protestant demonstration in the Ulster city of Derry in August of 1969 led to a riot in which seven people died; the violence quickly spread to the capital of Belfast, where Protestant nationalists, loyal to the United Kingdom, destroyed property owned by Catholics. The British Parliament sent in troops to attempt to restore order, and Catholic nationalists responded with the Irish Republican Army (IRA). Three decades of violence and bloodshed between Protestant and Catholic nationalists came to an end with the Good Friday Agreement of 1998, but nationalist tensions remain and threaten the stability of Northern Ireland.

Not long after The Troubles erupted in Northern Ireland, a 1973 revolution in Afghanistan, led by the Pashtun nationalist and former prime minister Muhammad Daoud Khan, sought to create a Pashtun state that would extend into the neighboring country of Pakistan. The Pashtuns are one of many people groups in Afghanistan, and Muhammad Daoud Khan had spent much of his political career promoting a nationalist agenda that would make Pashto the official language and bring the Pashtun tribes of Pakistan under Afghanistan's rule. His nationalist effort of turning Afghanistan into a Pashtun state came to an end in 1978, when a Soviet-backed coup led to his assassination and an ongoing civil war that has been raging since 1979.

In the 1960s and 1970s, the shah of Iran, Muhammad Reza Pahlavi, imposed a nationalist agenda that glorified Iran's pre-Islamic, Persian past. He erected monuments that celebrated Persian figures such as King Cyrus, who established the Persian Empire in in the sixth century BCE, and Abolqasem Ferdowsi, who wrote down the Persian *Book of Kings* around the year 1000; the *Book of Kings*, or *Shahnameh*, presented Persia's legendary past and the mythology of its ancient rulers. Yet he met resistance by Islamic clerics, who wanted Shi'a Islam to play a larger role in national life and who emphasized the importance of Islam in the history of Iran. Those tensions between the shah and Islamic clerics would erupt in a revolution in 1979 that would turn Iran into a theocratic state.

Other nationalist movements took place during the same time period in Cambodia, Vietnam, Nicaragua, Iraq, and countries all over the world. Not that nationalism began in the 1970s. Nationalism in Europe in the 1800s and early 1900s led to World War I and then World War II; nationalist movements in countries under colonial rule—such as India—following World War II led to their independence. What set apart the nationalist movements of the 1970s and 1980s is that they were essentially civil wars fought over the question of what the pure substance of the nation is. Was the pure substance of the nation to be found in Protestantism or Catholicism, as was the question for nationalists in Northern Ireland? In the Pashtun tribes or in visions of a unified Afghanistan? In the pre-Islamic past of the Persian Empire or in Iran's Islamic heritage? In the supposedly Christian faith of America's Founding Fathers or in the liberalism that separates church from state? While Falwell's nationalist movement would not erupt in a civil war or state-sponsored executions, it would cause the United States to become so divided that a populist surge in 2016 would lead to the election of Donald Trump.

LOCAL—THE CREATION OF LIBERTY UNIVERSITY

Many of the most prominent fundamentalist schools in America opened in the first half of the twentieth century. Biola, in Los Angeles, opened in 1908, while Fuller Seminary and Oral Roberts University opened after the Scopes Trial, in 1947 and 1963, respectively. Bob Jones University opened in 1927, two years after the Scopes Trial. Tennessee Temple University opened in 1946, and Baptist Bible College, which Jerry Falwell and Jerry Prevo (the leader of the Moral Majority in Alaska) both attended, opened in 1950. All of these schools have long taught science from an approach that affirms the creation account of Genesis.

Liberty University was a latecomer to the movement of fundamentalist schools opening in the wake of the Scopes Trial. Jerry Falwell had already opened up a private Christian school, Lynchburg Christian Academy, as a ministry of Thomas Road Baptist Church in 1967. His next foray would be into higher education by opening a fundamentalist college that taught American patriotic values alongside Christian ones. Lynchburg Baptist College—later Liberty Baptist College and then Liberty University—opened its doors in 1971 to train students in the nationalist and fundamentalist values that would shape the Moral Majority later in the decade.

Liberty University changed the face of the small town of Lynchburg, Virginia. As the school grew during the 1970s and 1980s, it not only became the town's largest employer; it transformed Lynchburg from a Southern hamlet hidden by mountains to the epicenter of the Moral Majority. Journalists from major newspapers, such as *The New York Times*, as well as national-level politicians, traveled from all over the country to visit Lynchburg and witness for themselves—as well as participate in—the transformation of American nationalism and Protestant fundamentalism that Falwell was spearheading. Lynchburg frequently played host to national-level politicians, including Ronald Reagan during his 1980 presidential campaign, Oliver North during the Iran-Contra Scandal, Vice President and later President George H. W. Bush, on to President George W. Bush and President Donald Trump. With the merger between nationalist and fundamentalist thought in the Moral Majority, giving a speech at Liberty University became a necessity for Republican politicians seeking the executive office.

For people in Lynchburg while these developments were beginning, Falwell was always the elephant in the room. Many townspeople did not approach the subject of Falwell, Liberty University, and the Moral Majority, as they did not know where other people stood. Many of the city's conservative Christians—evangelicals as well as fundamentalists—largely moved to the right with Falwell. On the other side of the divide, liberal pastors moved to Lynchburg to combat Falwell's movement. Some developed relationships with national-level journalists to provide first-hand accounts of the goings-on of the Moral Majority in the effort to halt Falwell's advances in American public life. Lynchburg split along liberal and conservative lines while becoming the seat of the transformation in America's faith and politics.

The split in Lynchburg was representative of the larger split that was happening throughout the United States. Liberal churches protested against using Christianity to promote a nationalist agenda, and in reference to the Islamic Revolution in Iran, pundits referred to Falwell and his cohort as "ayatollahs." Meanwhile, many evangelical Christians, who are not fundamentalist but have conservative theology, lauded the return of conservative values to American public life. From all across the country, evangelical parents sent their children to Liberty University so that they could receive a Christian education that would prepare them for adulthood as American citizens. Today, the debate about the relationship between Christian faith and American politics remains a contentious topic among both liberal and conservative Christians.

Nationalist and fundamentalist movements are both similar in that they see themselves as retrieving a pure version of the beliefs that shape the community. Nationalist movements see themselves as retrieving the pure version of the nation, as it existed in a "golden age" in the imagined past. This quest for purity can be seen in the appeals that conservative groups make to the nation's founding documents, the beliefs of the Founding

Fathers, and founding events such as the Boston Tea Party. To American nationalists, these images from the 1700s represent the pure substance of what the American nation is. Names of nationalist organizations, such as "The Heritage Foundation," appeal to the idea of returning to the ideals of this era of American history.

Fundamentalist movements see themselves as retrieving a pure version of the religion, which fundamentalists see as having been corrupted by secularization and liberalization. They also imagine a "golden age" in the religion's past—usually when the religion was founded—and seek to emulate it by bringing religious symbols from that era into the present. Those symbols are the fundamentals that define the fundamentalist movement. For fundamentalist Protestants, the goal is to recreate the first century of Christianity through an uncompromising adherence to a literal interpretation of the Bible; recognition of the virgin birth of Jesus; belief that the Bible is without fault; confidence in the bodily resurrection and future return of Jesus; and faith that his death on the cross was a substitutionary atonement for the sins of humanity. These symbols define the community and represent the minimal consensus of belief for one to join the movement. As such, both nationalism and fundamentalism use pre-modern symbols to appeal to the past; in doing so, they set the goals and aspirations for both the present and future.

Charismatic leaders—such as Jerry Falwell—who lead fundamentalist-nationalist movements, blend the nationalist and fundamentalist symbols so that the nation becomes indispensable to the religion, and the religion becomes indispensable to the nation. This blending of fundamentalism and nationalism can be seen in the name of his school, "Liberty University." "Liberty," or freedom, represents possibly the greatest American value, what those who fought in the Revolutionary War and in every war since were willing to die for. To not be in servitude to the government, to be able to determine where one wants to go to school or church, to not have to worry about state interference in personal matters. Possibly nothing in the American conscience is more important than liberty.

Liberty and freedom are also Christian values that are mentioned throughout the New Testament. John 8:32 (ESV) says, "And you will know the truth, and the truth will set you free." Romans 8:2 (ESV) says, "For the law of the Spirit of life has set you free in Christ Jesus from the law of sin and death." Whereas American freedom and liberty refer to not having state interference in private matters, Christian freedom and liberty refer to the ability to choose what is good because the soul is no longer bound to evil desires. But Jerry Falwell understood the American interpretation of liberty as being synonymous with the Christian interpretation. To him, the Founding

Fathers understood Christian liberty as referring to freedom of religion and being the cornerstone of their new nation.

By naming his school "Liberty Baptist College" and later "Liberty University," he seamlessly merged the Christian and American understandings of liberty to show that they both refer to the same thing—freedom of religion, particularly the Christian religion, particularly fundamentalist views about the Christian religion. On the entryway to the school's welcome center is the text of 2 Corinthians 3:17, which says, "Where the Spirit of the Lord is, there is liberty." The school's colors are red, white, and blue and, in the words of Jerry Falwell, "We teach patriotism here at Liberty Baptist College and Thomas Road Baptist Church as being synonymous with Christianity."[5]

Since its founding in 1971, Liberty University has grown from being the largest employer in Lynchburg to one of the largest Christian schools in the world. In addition to a sprawling campus, Liberty has developed an online program that has nearly 10 times as many students as those who attend on campus. It continues to teach a causal relationship between American and Christian values, alongside creation science and other fundamentalist values that hearken back to William Jennings Bryan, the Scopes Trial, and the early fundamentalist movement. It remains a necessary stop for Republican politicians who are campaigning for office, and an endorsement from the Falwell family and Liberty University often leads to the electoral support of the Religious Right.

GLOCAL—FUNDAMENTALISM AND NATIONALISM IN ALASKA

When the Religious Right first emerged in the 1970s, many saw it as an extremist movement for the way that it merged Christianity with American nationalism and championed illiberal social policies. Those policies aimed to counteract the women's rights movement, the gay rights movement, and the children's rights movement (particularly the United Nations Year of the Child in 1979). Additionally, the Religious Right presented an identity of American-ness that left little room for racial minorities, including Native Americans and African Americans, as well as immigrants and their children, whether or not they were citizens. Ultimately, the identity politics of the Religious Right promoted an ideal of purity and homogeneity among both the American and Christian people, as it left little room for those who did not conform to its rigid ideas of who is an American and who is a Christian.

5 "Our Citizenship As Americans," preached on March 7, 1976. Acquisition number OTGH 179.

At the time that the Religious Right was gaining traction, debates about the construction of the Alaska pipeline had already been settled. It underwent construction from the years 1974 until 1977, a mere two years before Jerry Falwell formally established the Moral Majority. During the critical pipeline years of the 1970s, Jerry Prevo used his pulpit in Anchorage, as well as the many churches throughout the state that he helped establish, to promote the fundamentalist nationalism that was beginning to reshape the country. That fundamentalist nationalism took root in the burgeoning oil culture of Alaska so that by the time of Sarah Palin's rise, fundamentalism, nationalism, and oil were firmly intertwined.

In 2012, a professor of anthropology at a college in Alaska wrote an opinion piece for the *Anchorage Daily News* that highlighted the relationship between libertarian, free-enterprise capitalism and the teachings of Falwell's colleague in Alaska, Jerry Prevo. The article said,

> The most prominent prosperity theology church in Alaska is the Anchorage Baptist Temple headed by Rev. Jerry Prevo... The thinking goes: God has chosen people, both in human and corporate form, to be wealthy. We should seek wealth to seek God's blessing. We should honor that blessing by reducing taxes and other restrictions on the rich and their corporations. It's God's will people are rich and secular governments should not impede on God's will. Taxation is tantamount to sin...
>
> In Alaska the multinational oil companies' wealth is a sign to prosperity theology adherents of God's blessing, and the demand for lower oil taxes has God's blessing as well. Resource development, if not sacred, is close to it. By implication, those who would channel Alaska's wealth into public use such as roads, schools and communications infrastructure via oil taxes must be the devil's consorts.
>
> Some of the harshest critics of prosperity theology are Pentecostal fundamentalists who call the idea that God blesses through wealth blasphemy. They would note, for example, Matthew 6:19–21: "Do not store up for yourselves treasures on earth... For where your treasure is, there your heart will be also."[6]

(For more on prosperity theology, see chapter 7.)

Along with the Moral Majority's call for libertarian economics, with low corporate taxes and not funding social programs, is the call for biblical morality to be legislated. In 1977, the Anchorage Assembly passed a city ordinance that would prohibit discrimination of LGBTQ+ individuals in areas

---

6. Alan Boraas, "'Prosperity theology' embraces wealth," in *Anchorage Daily News*. April 14, 2012.

such as education, employment, and housing. The mayor, George Sullivan, vetoed the ordinance in favor of allowing discrimination to continue. When the ordinance went back to the city assembly, Jerry Prevo organized a campaign for the veto of the LGBTQ+ rights measure to be upheld. With Prevo's campaigning, the city assembly was unable to garner the votes necessary to overturn the mayor's veto, and discrimination against LGBTQ+ individuals remained legal in Anchorage until 2015. In a pamphlet that Prevo disseminated for the Moral Majority, he explained his reasons for promoting discrimination against the queer community:

> Our country is rapidly turning into a twentieth century Sodom and Gomorrah because we have permitted a few amoral humanists to take over the most influential positions in our nation. Humanism, with its moral emphasis on no absolutes and situation ethics, challenges every moral principal upon which America was originally founded. Advocates of abortion on demand, recognition of homosexuals as a bona fide minority, pornography, prostitution, gambling, free use of drugs and much, much more are destroying this country.[7]

Like other Protestant fundamentalists, Prevo took a literal approach to the Bible, particularly in regards to science and history. The school that he established as part of Anchorage Baptist Temple taught a dispensational view of history, including creationism, to its thousands of pupils, many of whose parents worked on the pipeline. Under Prevo's influence, if there was a failure on the pipeline that the mechanics could not fix, workers would gather around and pray for God to miraculously fix the fault. After all, the pipeline represented God's plan for Alaska and His supernatural provision for the state's economy. For Prevo's followers, God had given ownership of Alaska's oil resources to Christians, and their duty was to reclaim both the American nation and Alaska's oil for God. Success on the pipeline was evidence of God's favor, and to not extract the state's natural resources meant defying the will of God.[8] Meanwhile, during Prevo's church's services, he told the people in his megachurch's congregation that they had a God-given duty to vote for Republican candidates.

As governor of Alaska, Palin took much of Jerry Falwell's fundamentalist nationalism, vis-à-vis Jerry Prevo, and made it state policy. In a state dominated by oil, where relations between oil companies and the

---

7 Wallace Turner, "Group of Evangelic Protestants Takes Over the G.O.P. in Alaska." *The New York Times,* June 9, 1980.

8 Prevo may not have preached this view specifically, but it was reflected in anecdotal accounts from people, particularly pipeline workers, that he influenced.

government define much of the political agenda, she promoted private enterprise without government interference. Her promotion of capitalism and free enterprise in Alaska's oil-based economy further embedded oil politics into conservative Christianity and American nationalism, as she effectively gave the oil companies more power by deregulating the industry in the name of Christian and American values.

During her tenure in Juneau, Governor Palin signed a proclamation stating that in public schools, creation science should be taught alongside biological evolution, thereby answering the central question of the fundamentalist-modernist controversy that began a century and a half earlier. In April 2008, a few months before the John McCain campaign nominated her to be his vice-presidential candidate, she made a proclamation that May 1, 2008 would be the National Day of Prayer in Alaska. A "day of prayer" invites people from any religious background, not only Christianity, as long as their faith encourages prayer. But the year before, in 2007, she had made a proclamation exclusive to Christianity, stating,

> WHEREAS, since the earliest days of our democracy, Americans have turned to the Bible for divine guidance, comfort, and encouragement.
> WHEREAS, the Bible has profoundly influenced art, literature, music, and codes of law.
> WHEREAS, the Bible has motivated many to acts of compassion, humanity, and charity.
> WHEREAS, the Bible continues to provide motivation, inspiration, hope, and comfort for countless Alaskans.
> WHEREAS, the National Bible Association reminds Alaskans and people of all faiths of the Bible's unique place in American life.
> NOW, THEREFORE, I, Sarah Palin, Governor of the State of Alaska, do hereby proclaim November 18–25, 2007, as Bible Week in Alaska, and encourage interested citizens to participate in this observance.[9]

That same year, she also made a proclamation creating "Christian Heritage Week" in Alaska when she signed an official notice, saying,

> WHEREAS, the celebration of Christian Heritage Week reminds Alaskans of the role Christianity has played in our rich heritage. Many truly great men and women of America, giants in the structuring of American history, were Christians of caliber and integrity who did not hesitate to express their faith.

---

9. Alaska Governor's Office: Press Release, "Bible Week," October 17, 2007.

> WHEREAS, the Preamble to the Constitution of the State of Alaska begins with, "We the people of Alaska, grateful to God and to those who founded our nation..."
> WHEREAS, George Washington enunciated, "Animated alone by the pure spirit of Christianity... we may enjoy every temporal and spiritual felicity."
> WHEREAS, James Madison, father of the United States Constitution, advocated, "The diffusion of the light of Christianity in our nation" in his Memorial and Remonstrance.
> NOW, THEREFORE, I, Governor Sarah Palin, do hereby proclaim October 21–27, 2007, as Alaska's 9th Annual Christian Heritage Week in Alaska, and encourage all citizens to celebrate this week.[10]

For Palin, none of these proclamations affected freedom of religion; rather, they enhanced it. She saw herself as exercising freedom of religion while occupying the highest position in the state, and people who followed different religions were under no obligation to commemorate events such as Christian Heritage Week or Bible Week. To her and like-minded nationalists, people who opposed these proclamations did not want freedom of religion but rather freedom from religion. Along with Jerry Falwell and Jerry Prevo, she believed that being a patriotic American meant valuing the nation's Christian heritage. And the truest exercise of American and Christian values was seen in free enterprise, which, in Alaska, means deregulation of oil.

---

10. Alaska Governor's Office: Proclamation, "Christian Heritage." September 14, 2007.

Chapter 5

Oil Politics and the Cold War

Alaska's Glocalized Economy Intersects With International Affairs

In 1862, President Abraham Lincoln enacted the Homestead Act to encourage people to move away from the urban centers on the East Coast—such as Boston, New York City, Philadelphia, and Washington DC—and settle the country's western frontier. People could stake out a tract of 160 acres, build a house on it, and live on it for five years; once the five-year term ended, they could obtain legal rights to the land, making it their private property. In 1898, legislation extended the Homestead Act to the newly purchased territory of Alaska to bring pioneers to the northern frontier.

When people move to the frontier, they have a reason for doing so. Some pioneers have headed west—and later north, to Alaska—because they are looking for a simpler life away from the hustle and bustle of overcrowded cities. Some have looked for the opportunity to explore and live an adventurous life out in the wild, where they must forge their own way. Others have looked to the frontier as a place where they can build a community of believers whose faith is not widely accepted by the mainstream religious community. What many frontier pioneers have long had in common is the desire to live on the fringes, away from government interference in their lives.

People have headed to Alaska for all of the above reasons and, in the nineteenth and first half of the twentieth centuries, shaped a frontier culture where hard-working individuals, not the government, must carve their own paths. Many Alaskans, both Democrats and Republicans, see themselves as libertarians who do not want the government to intervene in business or personal matters (though a notable exception is abortion, as many Republican libertarians in Alaska want to outlaw abortion).

Today, homesteading and the pioneer experience are largely relics of the past. Many of Alaska's original homesteads have been sold to developers and turned into subdivisions; others are now parts of growing towns and cities, whose residents have electricity and running water (with some exceptions, as in some parts of Alaska, the frozen ground prevents the development of public works, especially running water). Yet the libertarian ethos of the state's pioneer days lives on, particularly in the widespread belief that the government should not tax or regulate businesses, including the state's oil industry, especially if those taxes will fund social programs.

Libertarian ideas about the Alaska pipeline are reinforced by dispensational theology. Many dispensationalists are also adherents of the prosperity gospel and believe that through free-market capitalism, God will bring wealth to those who work hard. They believe that part of God's blessing on the American nation is the biblical free-enterprise system; the fact that modern capitalism is fueled by oil is evidence that oil is a divine resource that Christians are to use to build a society based on private businesses and private property. Dispensational beliefs about oil and capitalism became particularly important during the Cold War, particularly when the Yom Kippur War and OPEC oil embargo led to the construction of the Alaska pipeline.

IDEOLOGY: DISPENSATIONAL THEOLOGY AND OIL POLITICS

This book has already demonstrated how the fundamentalist movement was, at the turn of the twentieth century, funded by the oil industry. It has also shown that fundamentalism is very closely linked to nationalism, as both ideologies rely on appeals to recreate a glorious golden age. Yet Protestant fundamentalism is about more than a past golden age; it is about a future one, as well. The future golden age to which fundamentalists aspire is the Millennial Reign of Christ, an event that, according to dispensational theology, represents the culmination of history and the full revelation of the glory of God.

The throne from which dispensationalists believe that Christ will rule during the Millennial Reign is the throne of David in Jerusalem. At present, Jerusalem is the most contested city in the world, as it is the geographical center of two faiths (Judaism and Christianity), as well as the third-holiest site in Islam. Instead of being peacefully shared among adherents of the three Abrahamic faiths, Jerusalem lies at the nexus of much of the conflict in the Middle East, particularly the ongoing Palestine-Israel conflict. Jerusalem is critically important in dispensational theology; in fact, all of the conflicts in the Middle East that have been raging since World War II are seen by dispensationalists as the harbingers of the End Times. Because so many of the conflicts there are related to oil, some dispensationalists believe that oil is a divine resource whose importance to the global economy has been used by God to fulfill End Times prophecies.

In 1974, the year after the 1973 OPEC oil embargo began, John Walvoord published a book entitled *Armageddon, Oil, and the Middle East Crisis: What the Bible Says About the Future of the Middle East and the End of Western Civilization*. At the time, Walvoord was a professor at Dallas Theological Seminary, which was and remains a leading institution for dispensational teaching, and he later became the school's chancellor. He was also associated with the Moral Majority, having received his second doctorate from Liberty University in 1984 and later serving on its board. Walvoord published many books on dispensationalism, particularly on biblical prophecies regarding topics such as the Rapture and the Great Tribulation, and they sold millions of copies during his lifetime. *Armageddon, Oil, and the Middle East Crisis* presented a dispensational view of the Yom Kippur War and the larger conflicts surrounding it, namely the Cold War and disputes over oil. For Walvoord, though, the greatest conflict was the eschatological one in which God was using the Cold War and oil politics to fulfill biblical prophecies about the End Times.

In a revised 1990 edition of the book, following Saddam Hussein's invasion of Kuwait in the Persian Gulf War, Walvoord posed the question, "Are the immense resources of oil in the Middle East part of the divine plan to make the Middle East the theater of end-time events even as it was in the history of the ancient world?"[1] He answered his question by saying,

> Though the conflicts in the Persian Gulf are not the immediate subject of prophecy, they fit into the general pattern of end-time events that picture cataclysmic events leading up to the second coming of Christ, including a final world war that will feature its major battles in the Holy Land of Israel.[2]

1. John Walvoord, *Armageddon, Oil, and the Middle East Crisis: What the Bible Says About the Future of the Middle East and the End of Western Civilization* (Grand Rapids, MI: Zondervan, 1990 revised edition), 48.

2. John Walvoord, *Armageddon, Oil, and the Middle East Crisis: What the Bible Says About the Future of the Middle East and the End of Western Civilization* (Grand

Walvoord believed that the 1973 OPEC oil embargo represented a shift in global power from the West to the Middle East, thereby paving the way for the impending Battle of Armageddon. Arab states, which were for the most part opposed to Israel, control the vast majority of the world's oil reserves. In *Armageddon, Oil, and the Middle East Crisis*, Walvoord claimed that "the prosperity of the world depends on some mechanism to guarantee peace and a continued flow of oil from the [Middle East] region. This is precisely what biblical prophecy predicts."[3] When the OPEC countries flexed their muscles through the 1973 embargo, they showed that they could manipulate the world's economy by controlling the price of oil. Because dispensationalists, such as Walvoord, believe that the prophesied events of the End Times will take place in the Middle East and center on Israel, they claim that the region must once again become central to the global economy. Global power has long been concentrated in the West, but with the 1973 oil embargo, it shifted to the Middle East; some dispensationalists believed that this shift meant that the End Times will soon come and the world scene will soon be staged for the Battle of Armageddon.

For Walvoord and like-minded dispensationalists, the conflicts in the Middle East, particularly those over oil, are signs that the End is near. In the book he claimed,

> The providential presence of oil explains why the Bible makes the Middle East the center of world attention for prophecies of the last days. It will be the scene of the Battle of Armageddon and the end of Western civilization as we know it. The Bible clearly outlines exactly what will happen leading up to the second coming of Christ.[4]

In a different book published in 1999, one of Walvoord's colleagues at Dallas Theological Seminary, Dr. Charles Dyer, wrote about the significance of Iraq's oil reserves in fulfilling biblical prophecies regarding the End Times. Dyer described the ancient city of Babylon, as depicted in the Old Testament, as being built as an act of rebellion against God and a place that represents human wickedness any time that the Bible mentions it. He went so far as to claim that Babylon is where evil began and that it must be destroyed in order for Israel to be fully restored. He claimed that, as of 1999, Babylon, located in modern-day Iraq, has yet to be fully destroyed.

Rapids, MI: Zondervan, 1990 revised edition), 48.

3. John Walvoord, *Armageddon, Oil, and the Middle East Crisis: What the Bible Says About the Future of the Middle East and the End of Western Civilization* (Grand Rapids, MI: Zondervan, 1990 revised edition), 15.

4. Walvoord, *Armageddon, Oil, and the Middle East Crisis*, 12.

In fact, Saddam Hussein, then the president of Iraq, was attempting to rebuild the ancient city, imagining himself as the archetypal Babylonian king, Nebuchadnezzar.

Dyer pointed to prophecies about Babylon as being fulfilled by the global oil economy, as Iraq held 12% of the world's proven oil reserves before Saddam's invasion of Kuwait in 1990. Had he successfully taken over Kuwait, he would have wielded control over 25% of the world's oil reserves and thereby controlled the world's economy, just as Babylon is, according to a dispensationalist perspective, prophesied in Revelation 17 and 18 as being a global economic powerhouse. Like Walvoord immediately following the Yom Kippur War and 1973 oil embargo, Dyer believed that oil is God's providential resource for ushering in the End Times. For Dyer and like-minded dispensationalists, the way that the global oil economy fuels perpetual crisis in the Middle East can only mean that the End Times prophecies are being fulfilled.

But the conflicts are about more than oil; they are also about the state of Israel and Russian intervention, as demonstrated during the 1973 Yom Kippur War. Walvoord believed that Gog and Magog in the Bible refer to the Russian people and the land of Russia; in a Cold War context, particularly regarding the Yom Kippur War, he believed that the Russian army was being used by God to prepare the world for the Battle of Armageddon. For dispensationalists, the Yom Kippur War, especially with the Soviet (Russian) intervention, seemed like it may be a fulfillment of End Times prophecy.

In other words, for dispensationalists, these conflicts are not things to be resolved. They should not be resolved, as they are divine instruments to bring about the fulfillment of End Times prophecies. In speaking about the Egypt-Israel peace treaty of 1979, Jerry Falwell said,

> In spite of the rosy and utterly unrealistic expectations by our government, this treaty will not be a lasting treaty. . . We are certainly praying for the peace of Jerusalem. . . But you and I know that there's not going to be any real peace in the Middle East until one day, the Lord Jesus sits down upon the throne of David in Jerusalem and rules and reigns for 1000 years on this earth. We call this the Millennial Age, the Golden Age, the Age of our Lord and Savior, Jesus Christ.[5]

Conflicts over oil, Israel's relations to the surrounding Arab states, and Russia's shipments of arms to the region cannot have solutions. They must be intractable in order for the End Times prophecies to be fulfilled. And because

---

5. Jerry Falwell, "1980 Update on Bible Prophecy, Part I," from cassette series *Dr. Jerry Falwell Teaches Bible Prophecy*. (Lynchburg, VA: *Old-Time Gospel Hour*, 1979).

these prophecies were decreed by God, they must be literally fulfilled at a future time within world history.

Dispensational theology, particularly with its assertions about Russia/Magog, was uniquely suited to address the Soviet threat and the fears that were part of everyday life. John Walvoord saw the proposed Alaska pipeline as providing a solution for America's energy needs without causing it to continue its entanglements with countries that opposed Israel. Energy independence, which included construction of the Alaska pipeline, would mean that the US would be free to support Israel without getting caught up in the Soviet and Middle East oil politics that were leading to Armageddon. American Christians could oppose the enemies of God—the Soviets and the Arabs—by supporting the construction of the pipeline; if environmentalists or anyone else opposed the pipeline, they were opposing God, the Christian people of America, and His chosen nation of Israel.

Oil politics and Protestant fundamentalism are all but inseparable. Fundamentalism is built on dispensational theology, and dispensational thinkers have, for at least half a century, been tying their interpretations of End Times prophecies to conflicts related to oil. One should not be surprised that the Alaska pipeline, which carried the promise of energy independence for the United States following the 1973 Yom Kippur War and OPEC oil embargo, had resonances among dispensationalists.

NATIONAL: MILITARY PRESENCE IN ALASKA

Prior to World War II, most Alaskans engaged in primary-sector jobs that contributed to a subsistence lifestyle. They were largely fishers, farmers, and foresters, along with a few teachers and bank tellers. Gold mining had been a profitable industry, such as in the Independence Mine near Wasilla, but most gold mining came to an end around World War II. But World War II and the Cold War sparked such an enormous shift that by 1952, over 25% of the population of Alaska was employed by the US military; many of these soldiers were not born in Alaska but rather had come up with their families for military service. This number does not include contractors, civil servants, or family members of those in the military, which may have put the percentage of those in Alaska associated with the armed forces upwards of 50%. In other words, World War II and the onset of the Cold War transformed Alaska into a massive military outpost. Between World War II and the construction of the Alaska pipeline (1974–1977), the US military was the largest employer in the state.

During the Cold War, Alaska's military bases found new use as the new enemy of the United States, the Soviet Union, was only 50 air miles away. Seismographs placed in Alaska could measure nuclear tests being conducted in the Soviet Union, and soldiers who trained in the territory's polar weather would be better equipped for combat in Russia's frigid climate. And because Alaska was still a territory until 1959, the federal government did not have to negotiate with a state in order to bring in more soldiers and military equipment. The militarization of Alaska, due to its proximity to Japan and the Soviet Union, contributed to the fundamentalist nationalism that became embedded in the pipeline and America's faith-based oil politics during the 1970s.

The militarization of Alaska brought about one change in particular that has never been reversed: Whereas before World War II, there was about a 1:1 ration between Alaska Natives and white settlers who had come up from the Lower 48, by 1950, whites outnumbered Alaska Natives by four to one. There were also African-American military units stationed in Alaska, as well as some multiracial units. The state would retain an image of subsistence, pioneer lifestyles and a vast frontier, but the reality behind that image was quickly becoming irrevocably modernized. Still, the state was very sparsely populated, with only about 138,000 people living there in 1950.

Most military bases were concentrated around Anchorage and Fairbanks, so with the influx of military personnel and their families during the 1950s, both cities mushroomed so that they roughly doubled in size. Additionally, a number of veterans from World War II moved up to Alaska to get a fresh start. These military families were not looking to stake out land and homestead it, as so many had done prior to World War II. Rather, many of them wanted the amenities of modern life, from electricity and running water to refrigerators and washing machines. In short, the "Alaska experience" was becoming a very cold version of the American military experience. The desire for modern industry and conveniences in Alaska, rather than a frontier experience on a homestead, would be one motivation for many people supporting the construction of the pipeline while it was under debate from 1968 until 1973.

To defend Alaska from a possible Soviet invasion, beginning in 1959, the military installed Nike missile stations in the mountains around Anchorage and Fairbanks. When Soviet planes flew into Alaska's airspace, as they often did, the silos holding the missiles would open and the missiles would come out. The Nikes were never fired, but their presence served as a constant reminder throughout the 1960s and 1970s that if there was going to be a nuclear confrontation between the Soviet Union and United States, it would probably happen in Alaska. In response to the threat, Alaskan civilians, including "Eskimo Scouts," volunteered their services to do nighttime reconnaissance by keeping watch for Soviet planes overhead. Civilians took their job so seriously that some even built observation watchtowers onto their homes. The Soviet threat was such an ever-present reality for Alaskans that when the 1964 Good Friday Earthquake hit, some people initially thought that the Soviets were bombing Alaska.

The climate of fear caused many Alaskans to turn to the fundamentalist nationalism promoted by the likes of Jerry Falwell and Jerry Prevo. These pastors framed the Cold War in spiritual terms that assured victory for Christian America against the evil communist empire. To them, the nuclear threat called for fervent prayers and a symmetrical nuclear buildup that would prevent the Soviets from striking first (Mutually Assured Destruction). "Peacenik" pastors, who supported a nuclear freeze and disarmament, scarcely even had a right to pray to the Almighty for deliverance, as they were both un-Christian and un-American. Falwell and Prevo assured their congregations that God was against the Soviets and on the side of the United States and that a nuclear war would not happen as long as God's people ensured a strong national defense.

The tensions in Alaska regarding the Soviet Union continued well into the pipeline years. By that time, the pipeline had overtaken the military as the largest employer in the state, and the military had begun dismantling the Nike missiles stationed around Anchorage and Fairbanks. Yet as the pipeline was being constructed from 1974 until 1977, Soviet planes frequently flew overhead in what may have been reconnaissance missions. Shots were never fired, but the fear was real. That fear was compounded when events connected to the Cold War and oil politics erupted in Central Asia with the 1979 Islamic Revolution in Iran and the Soviet invasion of Afghanistan.

GLOBAL: THE ISLAMIC REVOLUTION AND SOVIET INVASION OF AFGHANISTAN

> The kings of the earth set themselves,
> and the rulers take counsel together,
> Against his Anointed, saying,
> "Let us burst their bonds apart
> and cast away their cords from us."
> —Psalm 2:2–3, ESV

Despite Richard Nixon's policy of détente, during the 1970s, the Cold War intensified, particularly in Central and Southeast Asia. The Vietnam War, where American troops fought alongside the South Vietnamese in the attempt to prevent a communist takeover of the country, did not end until halfway through the decade. Coupled with the Watergate scandal that took down Nixon in 1974, the Vietnam War caused many Americans to lose faith in their government. They burned flags instead of waving them, deciding that they did not want to see their military intervene in other countries by bombing and massacring civilian populations.

Yet the United States still had a strong military presence in Central Asian countries that bordered the Soviet Union, particularly Iran and Afghanistan. American officers trained Iranian and Afghan tribal militias as guerilla fighters in the event of a Soviet invasion, while the American government ardently supported Iran's shah. Trouble would begin in Iran in 1979, with a populist revolution that would oust the shah and bring in Ayatollah Ruhollah Khomeini as the leader of the new Islamic Republic. To prevent the revolution from spreading, that same year, the Soviet military invaded Afghanistan and sparked a decade-long war that devastated the country. In the United States, the facts of the turbulent events in Central Asia became lost as news outlets broadcasted sensationalized stories and preachers like Jerry Falwell invoked the crises as events prophesied in dispensational history as part of the End Times.

Iran, a country whose fields have been flowing with oil since 1908, was for decades exploited by Western countries, particularly Great Britain, that wanted steady access to the country's oil. The Anglo-Iranian Oil Company (now British Petroleum, or BP) became the most prolific British business interest in the world, as Great Britain effectively owned all of the oil underneath Iran's ground and only had to pay a paltry royalty to the country. In 1951, an Iranian nationalist named Muhammad Mossadegh became the country's prime minister and had the goal of bringing control of the oil fields into the hands of Iranians. Mossadegh promoted a model of secular democracy against both the dictatorship of the shah and the heavy influence of Iran's Shi'a clerics; though he championed an ideal of democracy that is highly valued by Western countries, his nationalization of the country's oil was too much for Great Britain and its ally, the United States. In 1953, the British prime minister, Winston Churchill, and the American president, Dwight Eisenhower, organized a coup that overthrew Mossadegh and gave greater powers to the shah. Afterwards, many Iranians saw the shah as a puppet for Western powers, particularly the United States.

The modern country of Iran is the heartland of what was once the ancient Persian Empire. The Bible mentions the Persian Empire in positive terms, as its founding ruler, Cyrus, allowed the Jewish people to return from exile to the land of Israel. 2500 years later, the United States had strong diplomatic relations with Iran's shah, Muhammad Reza of the Pahlavi dynasty. Dispensationalist thinkers who merged America's civil religion with Christianity—such as Jerry Falwell and Tim LaHaye—saw this relationship as one that God blessed. Like the United States, Iran supported the state of Israel, with the shah believing that Israel would help restrain the influence of the Arab states. Yet the shah became increasingly unpopular among his own people, especially after the coup of Mossadegh, as his Western-backed modernization projects forced many to leave their traditional, subsistence lifestyles, and his secret police (SAVAK) silenced those who dissented against him. He exiled and even executed people who disagreed with him and used the military against protests, many of which were peaceful, causing many people to die.

The populist revolution in Iran began with Ayatollah Khomeini, a radical cleric who had been exiled to the Iraqi city of Najaf and later to Paris, writing and preaching against the American-backed shah. He advocated creating an Islamic government modeled after Islam's final prophet, Muhammad, and his successor, 'Ali, and disseminated his ideas through a series of tracts and sermons that came to be known as *Vilayat al-Faqih*. With popular dissent against the shah growing, Khomeini became the central figure who was able to galvanize the disparate movements of political discontents into a cohesive force that would overthrow the shah. Street gangs, many led by mullahs, began roaming the streets of Tehran and shooting foreigners and those associated with the shah. Soon, the violence became so great that the shah had to leave the country, along with nearly all Americans and many other foreigners. When Ayatollah Khomeini returned from exile in February of 1979, "the people" of Iran welcomed him home as a hero. He became the Grand Ayatollah who oversaw the entire government of the new Islamic Republic of Iran.

Despite how the events occurred on the ground, Jerry Falwell preached to millions of people that the Islamic Revolution in Iran happened because the United States had betrayed its ally, the shah. He claimed that Khomeini was a communist who was actually allied with the Soviet Union and that the revolution had been prophesied in the Bible as part of the End Times. In 1980, the year after the Islamic Revolution, he preached that the ancient Persian Empire had to form an alliance with Russia/Magog to wage war against Israel in the lead-up to Armageddon.

In Iran's neighboring country of Afghanistan, a coup in 1978 led to the overthrow of the Pashtun nationalist Muhammad Daoud Khan and the instatement of Nur Muhammad Taraki as the president of Afghanistan. Like Iran's shah, Taraki instated a series of Westernizing reforms while also silencing dissent of groups and individuals that opposed him. He was overthrown in late 1979 by Haffizullah Amin, and leaders of the Soviet Union—which shared a border with Afghanistan—feared that President Amin would seek an alliance with the United States. They also feared that the Islamic Revolution in neighboring Iran would spread to Afghanistan and disrupt their power base in Central Asia. On December 24, 1979, the Soviet military invaded Afghanistan, deposed the president, and instated a Soviet loyalist as the new leader of Afghanistan. While Soviet forces quickly gained control of Afghanistan's major cities, such as Kabul, the United States armed mujahideen forces of Afghan Islamist fighters, who controlled the countryside and tribal areas. The Soviets remained in Afghanistan for nearly a decade, withdrawing in 1988, and their invasion caused Afghanistan to deteriorate into a civil war that continues to this day.

At the same time as these tumultuous events in Central Asia, the United States was in the process of ratifying the SALT II treaty with the Soviet Union. SALT II, the successor to the SALT I treaty, would impose limitations on the nuclear build-up that both countries were engaging in, as part of an attempt to prevent a nuclear war. President Jimmy Carter signed SALT II in the summer of 1979, provoking the anger of Jerry Falwell and his growing movement of conservative Christians. Falwell saw SALT II as the United States signing a deal with the devil, effectively placing itself at the mercy of the Soviet Union. In fact, opposing SALT II was one of the first goals of the Moral Majority.

Because—in Falwell's view—the Cold War signaled the End Times, he also saw the Soviet invasion of Afghanistan as a harbinger of the Last Days. The Soviets needed oil to fuel their energy needs, so he projected that Soviet the invasion of Afghanistan was part of a larger project to take over all the oil fields of the Middle East. These events could not be stopped, as they had been prophesied thousands of years before in the Bible. Rather they should be welcomed, not only because they meant that the Rapture would soon happen but also because they were God's answer to the prayers of American Christians. According to Falwell, because Khomeini was supposedly a communist agent and the Soviets had mercilessly begun a brutal war in Afghanistan, these events divinely demonstrated to the American people why they should not ratify SALT II. The turbulence in Central Asia represented God's deliverance of America, which Falwell saw as in danger of also falling to communism. Even the Iranian hostage crisis, in which 52 American diplomats were kidnapped in Tehran and held hostage for 444 days, was part of this deliverance of the American nation, as it demonstrated the necessity of American sovereignty as a Christian imperative.

The Islamic Revolution did mean that the United States no longer had access to the Iran's vast oil resources, thereby threatening another oil crisis. Further, the Islamic Revolution and Soviet invasion of Afghanistan did prevent congress from ratifying the SALT II treaty, so it never went into effect. Throughout the next decade, the Reagan years, Falwell's Moral Majority attained national prominence, and Falwell frequently appeared alongside the president and claimed him as a personal friend. During those years, the United States began investing again in nuclear weapons, effectively restarting the arms race with the Soviet Union, in order to protect Christian America against the wave of godless communism that had swept Central Asia.

LOCAL: THE MORAL MAJORITY IN ALASKA

For the supporters of the Moral Majority, the answer to the compounding international crises of the 1970s was a stronger national defense for the United States and the reinstatement of biblical morality. If the American people stopped tolerating homosexuality, feminism, abortion, and other national sins, then God would once again look with favor on the United States and cause it to prosper. And to protect American democracy, which was emblematic of both American and Christian freedom, against the threat of the Soviet Union, the United States had to maintain a strong national defense, including a nuclear arsenal. That national defense would also protect God's chosen nation of Israel against any Arab or Soviet threat.

In Alaska, the back door through which Soviets could gain access to the United States, Jerry Prevo began the state's chapter of the Moral Majority in December of 1979. The timing was such that oil money had only recently begun filling the state's coffers. Fundamentalism and nationalism had already become firmly embedded into the state's oil pipeline via interpretations of dispensational theology; the state's heavy military presence and proximity to the Soviet Union further solidified those ideological relationships. Despite the state's small population, Alaska may have had the most dramatic developments regarding the Moral Majority, and Jerry Prevo emerged as a national leader in the movement.

The Moral Majority in Alaska organized quickly and had a swift effect on the state's politics. One Republican representative in the state legislature, Ray Metcalfe, reported on how Jerry Falwell and Jerry Prevo walked into his Juneau office and introduced themselves as the "conservative wing of the Republican Party;" they went on to tell him that they wanted to change the state's primary election system so that they could better push forward their moral agenda. The primary system changed from one in which any registered voters could vote to one in which only registered members of the party could vote; in turn, Republicans loyal to the Moral Majority pushed through inexperienced candidates who professed Moral Majority-type values. By

March of 1980, three months after Prevo began the Moral Majority in Alaska and six months before the election of Ronald Reagan, approximately two-thirds of Fairbanks's and Anchorage's delegates to the state's GOP convention were members of or supported by the Moral Majority. Established Republican politicians, including Metcalfe, suddenly found themselves left behind as newbies, many of whom had no political experience but were adamantly pro-life, were elected into their spots.

Members of the Moral Majority began sending out "report cards" on candidates, assessing them not on their political experience but where they stood on moral issues—the traditional family as opposed to LGBTQ+ rights, ending abortion as opposed to supporting women in the workplace, support of Israel as opposed to kowtowing to the oil-producing Arab states, and a tough national defense as opposed to nuclear disarmament. As the Moral Majority represented a surge of populism, both in Alaska and the United States, there could be no compromise between the politicians that "the people" of the Moral Majority supported and the established "elite" who now had to contend with them. Any compromise would be seen as moral bankruptcy and earn that politician a failing grade on his or her report card. Many voters decided who to support based on the Moral Majority's report cards.

In Alaska's 1980 caucuses, the Moral Majority effectively usurped the state's GOP, indicating that the moral values of the organization's members now dominated the party. "Establishment" Republicans such as Metcalfe, who believed that the government should not legislate on matters regarding the personal lives of citizens, wondered why these new "conservative" Republicans were more concerned with people's private lives than with issues of corruption and bribery between the oil industry and the Republican party. Meanwhile, Moral Majority leaders, such as Prevo, believed that Christians had to engage in political activism to protect freedom of religion, which he believed was being eroded by the establishment politicians, particularly the secular humanists, in government. In the summer of 1980, Prevo was featured in *The New York Times* for the group's success in ensuring that all 19 of the state's delegates to the RNC supported the nomination of the ultra-conservative (and arguably populist) Ronald Reagan. Reagan was not a devout Christian, but he advocated the strong national defense and traditional family values that the Moral Majority championed. Several other national media outlets, including CBS News and ABC News featured Prevo to discuss the success of the Moral Majority, the importance of the Bible in American life, and Republican politics. In 1984, he appeared alongside Jerry Falwell at the Republican National Convention, where both were interviewed on national television.

In March of 1980, the same time that the Moral Majority was taking over Alaska's GOP, Frank Murkowski began his bid for the Republican nomination to serve as United States Senator alongside "Uncle Ted" Stevens. The Moral Majority successfully campaigned to secure his nomination, and Murkowski ousted the Democrat Mike Gravel at the same time Reagan was elected. His lengthy career in the US Senate lasted for 22 years and came to an end when he was elected governor of Alaska in 2002. As senator, Murkowski promoted the federal government handing over public lands for private businesses to develop in order to access mineral and energy resources, and he spoke about how the "elite" opposed what seemed to be common-sense energy and economic policy. From 1995 until 2001, he chaired the US Senate Committee on Energy and Natural Resources, where he promoted further development of Alaska's land and energy resources, particularly its oil. The effects of the Moral Majority would continue to be felt while he served as governor and thereafter, when Sarah Palin unseated him in 2006. There existed almost a straight line between the rise of the Moral Majority in Alaska and the rise of Sarah Palin.

The Moral Majority remained so influential in Alaska's politics that in 1988, it was one of only four states to nominate the televangelist Pat Robertson in the Republican presidential primaries. Prevo's influence on Alaska's Republican Party did not end with the dissolution of the Moral Majority in 1989; in 2010, the national publication *Politics Magazine* listed him as one of the 40 most influential individuals in Alaska. When Uncle Ted Stevens died in 2010, his funeral was held at Prevo's church, Anchorage Baptist Temple. Having served in the US Senate for four decades, he had a state funeral that many national and politicians attended. In presiding over the funeral, Prevo preached to a crowd of 4000 people that consisted of former heads of state, current and former congressmen and women, and other key political players.

Prevo's national influence, though diminished in the years after the Moral Majority, took on new significance when Sarah Palin, whose hometown of Wasilla is 35 miles from Anchorage and who is in many ways a product of the movement that he helped construct, effectively succeeded Falwell in 2008 as the galvanizer of the Religious Right. While progressive reforms, such as pro-gay and pro-choice legislation, had been transforming the Lower 48 since the dissolution of the Moral Majority, Prevo helped ensure that Alaska remained a stronghold of nationalist "traditional values" and fundamentalist oil politics. When Palin could emerged onto the national scene, she took those values with her.

GLOCAL: ESTABLISHMENT OF THE ALASKA PERMANENT FUND

If there was a massive military presence in Alaska during the 1970s, one might have expected soldiers to provide some semblance of law and order to the boomtowns of Fairbanks, Anchorage, and Valdez while the pipeline was being constructed. And if there was an emphasis on Christian morality as an American virtue that became connected to how Alaskans viewed their oil resources, one might have expected better conduct by those working on the pipeline. Tens of thousands of workers and their families flooded Alaska beginning in 1974, looking for work with the Alyeska company. Fairbanks, located in the state's interior about halfway between Anchorage and Prudhoe Bay, was the center of much of the pipeline frenzy; its population exploded so much that upwards of 50 people would sleep in one two-bedroom house. And they were the lucky ones, as many slept outside in sub-zero temperatures. Just like with so many other boomtowns throughout history, during the years of the pipeline's construction, Fairbanks saw a spike in drug use, theft, arson, and the world's oldest profession, as prostitution increased by as much as 5000%. Arson became so commonplace that the fire department stopped investigating when fires broke out.

The population explosion was so severe that Alaskans joked that their favorite sight was an Okie leaving with a Texan under each arm. Some who had been in Alaska before the construction began thought that the state had already paid too great a price for the oil that would soon flow, not because of how the pipeline had disturbed the natural environment but rather because of how much crime and frenzy had come with the building of the pipeline. There were also concerns about how the state would cope with a rapid exodus of the very same workers who had flooded in a mere three years earlier. But when the first drops of oil began to trickle through the pipeline in June of 1977, everything changed. While the rest of the United States was in a recession caused largely by a volatile global oil market, the state of Alaska quickly soared to such economic prosperity that it became one of the wealthiest states in the country. And with the concurrent rise of the Moral Majority came the prevailing belief that God had shown special favor to Alaska by blessing it with oil.

In 1969, when the state first leased out its public lands at Prudhoe Bay to the private oil companies to develop, it received a windfall of $900 million. The state might as well have won the lottery, and as with any massive influx of cash, no one could agree on what the state should do with the money. Some thought it needed to fund better schools, while others wanted to use it to begin paving roads. One Alaskan economist, Arlon

Tussing, suggested that it be distributed equally among Alaska's residents so that they could spend it as private citizens. Many people balked at this idea, including the citizens who would have received a check. In the end, the cool billion quickly evaporated without leaving a noticeable mark on the state's economic development.

By the time oil began flowing in 1977, the state once again became awash with cash and once again had to decide how to spend the money. The governor at the time was a Republican named Jay Hammond. Hammond was from Bristol Bay, an area dominated by the fishing industry. Many of the fishermen there were not from Alaska and took their paychecks out of the state; the payrolls in Bristol Bay were not going to local residents, and the money was not circulating in the local economy. Hammond wanted to prevent that situation from happening statewide with oil, so he devised a plan to make sure that oil money stayed in Alaska and fueled Alaska's economy. He proposed the establishment of a Permanent Fund with some of the oil money, which would be set aside for Alaska's posterity, particularly in the years after oil stopped flowing. Each resident of Alaska would get an annual dividend check, which represented a portion of the interest that the Permanent Fund earned.

In 1976, Hammond's administration established the Permanent Fund, into which a minimum of 25% of oil revenues would be invested, as a means for promoting economic development in Alaska outside of oil. He intended for it to be re-invested in renewable industries, such as timber and fishing, that could sustain Alaska after the oil stopped flowing. As such, Alaska's economy could diversify while getting the immediate cash injection it needed from the oil industry. The Permanent Fund was not to finance any of the government's budgetary needs; rather, it was to promote long-term and sustainable economic development. However, the actual purpose of the Permanent Fund was never codified, so there is no clear legislation on exactly how the money should be used.

The only aspect of how the Permanent Fund should be used was in the annual payment of dividend checks—the Permanent Fund Dividend, or PFD—to Alaskan residents. At first, the idea of a PFD did not go down smoothly. Some Alaskan economists expressed concerns that the money needed to get re-invested in infrastructure and in developing an economy that was not solely dependent on oil. Others were concerned about how the rest of the United States would react when people learned that the state of Alaska was giving money away to individual citizens. But when Alaskans began receiving dividend checks in 1980—$1000 for every man, woman, and child who lived in the state—the money played into the libertarian belief, firmly rooted in Alaska, that the people, rather than the government, should be able to determine how to spend the money. Many came to see the purpose of the Permanent Fund as being the generation of money for the PFD.

Ultimately, the PFD fit in squarely with the Moral Majority's populist mindset. The people of Alaska, rather than the elite oil companies and the government establishment, owned the state's oil resources and should be the ones to benefit from them. The government merely had the responsibility of managing those resources, while the people determined what to do with the money generated. Today, the PFD—which has made annual payments of as much as $3000 to every single eligible resident of Alaska—is one of the most contentious policies in the state. Many Alaskans vote for politicians based on promises that they make about PFD payments, and debates about how the government should use the Permanent Fund—whether it should fund state budget deficits or be used as Hammond originally intended, to diversify Alaska's economy—have caused political earthquakes.

Despite Hammond's intention of using the Permanent Fund to diversify Alaska's economy away from oil, the opposite has happened. Approximately 90% of the state's government is still funded by oil money; meanwhile, because of the PFD payments, many people came to Alaska so that they could receive PFD payments instead of having to work. In fact, despite the state's oil revenue, unemployment in Alaska is often double the national average; even though the Permanent Fund is one of the biggest investment accounts in the country, many markers of poverty—such as homelessness, long-term prospects of aged-out foster youth, unemployment, and percentage of people receiving welfare—point to Alaska today as being one of the poorest states in the country. And because the Alaska pipeline still supplies 10% of the country's oil, it figures significantly in the national economy. Many Alaskans fight every election cycle to ensure that they continue receiving their PFD payments and that the American economy remains dependent on Alaskan oil.

PFD payments would also take local beliefs about the state's oil resources beyond the fundamentalism and nationalism that became commonplace in the 1980s. God's blessing on Alaska was about more than Cold War fears and complex global oil politics; it was about overcoming the wildness of the land and gaining control over its natural resources through capitalism and drilling for oil. The PFD would actually tie oil—both in Alaska and all over the world—to Christian dominionism, an ideology that asserts that Christians must exert dominion over all their spheres of influence (for more on Christian dominionism, see Chapter 9). In other words, through oil and the Permanent Fund, God had not only blessed Alaska; He had blessed the people for being Alaskan. They had to preserve that blessing by promoting policies that not only favor oil companies but also make sure that they continue seeing prosperity through their annual PFD checks.

Chapter 6

The Price of America's Addiction to Oil

The Alaska pipeline serves as a mirror to turbulence in the Middle East and Central Asia regarding how American Christians—particularly those in the Religious Right—view those events. Congress did not approve the pipeline's construction because oil companies found massive reserves at Prudhoe Bay; rather, congress approved the pipeline because the United States' involvement in the 1973 Yom Kippur War led to the OPEC embargo and an energy crisis. While many Americans—including a number of conservative Christians—wanted to see the country move away from oil, Jerry Falwell and like-minded fundamentalist leaders saw America's oil-based prosperity as evidence of God's blessing on the nation. With oil flowing from Alaska, there was no need to reduce the country's dependence on black gold. Instead, the United States could pass oil-friendly legislation that included a stronger presence in the Middle East and Central Asia, particularly countries that exported oil to the United States. That fundamentalist leaders viewed those countries as part of End-Times prophecies meant that the United States should continue to procure oil from them, as they saw oil as God's means of driving the world towards the great Battle of Armageddon.

One of those countries was Iran, formerly the seat of the ancient Persian Empire and, until 1979, under the rule of a shah who catered to American interests. When Khomeini's populist revolution in 1979 dethroned the shah and ended all exports—including oil—from Iran to the United States, many feared that another energy crisis loomed. Yet the oil that had just begun flowing from Alaska prevented an oil deficit and convinced many that oil would continue to be a stable means of fueling America's economic system.

IDEOLOGY: AMERICAN EXCEPTIONALISM

From infancy on, children are often told that they are special. They learn how to crawl, stand, and walk with parents telling them how wonderful they are. They learn how to ride a bike and run footraces with their friends, believing that they have the necessary "oomph" to finish in first place. Yet while a healthy dose of self-esteem is important for children's growth and development, only a minority of children truly are exceptional. "Exceptional" refers to those who stand out among their peers in a way that no one can compete with them—the coding whiz who begins developing computer programs for Silicon Valley companies while still in elementary school, the piano virtuoso who plays to a packed-out audience at only eight years old. All parents should believe that their children are special, but children who attract the praise of critics, rather than only the praise of their parents and close relations, fall into the category of "exceptional."

American exceptionalism is basically the belief that America is special, over and above nativist claims about "our nation." It is not only special because it is "our" nation; it is special as being better than other nations. God has favored it more than other nations. God has blessed it more than other nations. And just as with critical praise that may be lauded onto exceptional children, American exceptionalism is more than a healthy dose of nationalist self-esteem; it is the belief that the United States has a unique role to play in the world and cannot fail in its mission.

There are some ways that the American nation is indeed exceptional. It was the birthplace of modern democracy, beginning with the town hall meetings of colonists during the seventeenth and eighteenth centuries and on to the representative form of government created by the constitution in 1787. With the very notable exception of slavery and Jim Crow laws, the United States has never had a rigid class system that people are born into. The constitution guaranteed freedom of religion at a time when state churches still exerted large amounts of power over European countries. And following World War II, the United States used its industrial and military might to help repair countries, including enemy countries, that had been devastated. In these ways and more, America truly does stand out among its peers and deserves the applause of its critics.

In Sarah Palin's book *America By Heart*, she wrote about how America's exceptionalism reflects Matthew 5:14, in which Jesus told his disciples, "You are the light of the world. A city set on a hill cannot be hidden." The Puritan leader John Winthrop applied this verse to America's Massachusetts colony in 1630 when he declared that the Puritan settlement would be a city on a hill for all nations to ponder. Ronald Reagan, in his 1989 farewell address, quoted directly from Winthrop when he said,

> For we must consider that we shall be as a city upon a hill. The eyes of all people are upon us, so that if we shall deal falsely with our God in this work we have undertaken, and so cause Him to withdraw His present help from us, we shall be made a story and a byword throughout the world.[1]

Palin sees America as a nation that has its flaws but has, since the first Puritan settlers came over, ultimately been a force for good, both within its own borders and throughout the world. And beyond its acts of goodness, its beacon of light shines for all to see.

Throughout the nineteenth and most of the twentieth centuries, many pondered America's exceptionalism in terms of its diversity and ability to accommodate a plurality of views under the aegis of democracy. France gifted the Statue of Liberty to the United States on its centennial to honor its commitment to freedom; the poem "The New Colossus," displayed on a bronze plaque inside the statue, commemorates the country's zeal for immigrants, who could build for themselves a better life within its shores. John F. Kennedy (president 1961–1963) called the United States a nation of immigrants; it was a multicultural melting pot where people who could not succeed in their own countries, due to systemic marginalization and widespread poverty, could find prosperity through hard work and opportunity. The belief that America was exceptional was strengthened by its victories in not one but two world wars and found new grounding in the idea that it could halt the spread of communism in other countries. Ergo, the wars in Korea (1950–1953) and Vietnam (1955–1975).

The advent of television had a profound impact on beliefs about American exceptionalism. On the one hand, the new medium showed the unlimited capacity of American ingenuity and hard work, as many of those associated with the invention of television were from the United States. The country could lead the world with technological innovation and make invaluable contributions to the future of humanity and global connectivity. On the other hand, with televisions in people's homes, they could see

---

1. President Ronald Reagan's Farewell Address. January 11, 1989.

footage from the Civil Rights Movement, which included police officers using water cannons and attack dogs on peaceful marchers. Shortly thereafter, people began seeing horrific images from the Vietnam War, including the My Lai Massacre, in which over 500 civilians were murdered—many also raped and mutilated—by US soldiers.

By the time of the Vietnam War, American exceptionalism included the belief that the United States could fight another country's war—and win. As registers of American soldiers killed in the war mounted and especially when images of American forces bombing civilian populations appeared on the news, people began to protest both the war and the belief that the United States had an exceptional mission to the rest of the world. It was not only fighting a losing war; it was using its exceptional power to oppress some of the most vulnerable people in the world. Particularly among the emerging New Left, American exceptionalism became a euphemism for American arrogance.

The New Right that emerged with the Moral Majority reacted against this derogatory view of the American nation and American exceptionalism. For Jerry Falwell and his associates, America was not only great because of its commitment to democracy and freedom; America was great because God had made it great. God had created America with a divine destiny in mind, and American Christians had to rise up in order to reclaim and fulfill that divine destiny. Half of the world's Christian missionaries were either sent out from and/or funded by American churches, so for Falwell, world evangelization would not be possible without God's blessing on America. Furthermore, American support of Israel ensured that the Soviet Union and Arab states did not push God's chosen people into the sea. Being a Christian, in Falwell's view of the American nation, meant seeing one's patriotic, national duty as coextensive with one's Christian duty.

As such, Falwell supported the country's engagement in foreign wars, as they were part of its divine destiny to be a city on a hill. This version of American exceptionalism carried over into the Reagan administration (1981–1989), as Falwell had a public relationship with the president and was a frequent guest at the White House. He supported the CIA operations in Central America that attempted to prevent communist takeovers of countries such as El Salvador and Nicaragua, as well as operations in the Middle East and Central Asia, where Iran was locked in a decade-long war with Iraq and Afghan mujahideen were fighting the Soviets.

Yet liberals, along with conservatives who did not conform to the norms of the Moral Majority, decried how this form of exceptionalism was destroying the environment and dispossessing indigenous peoples of their local cultures. They saw America as not using its industrial and military might to empower vulnerable nations but rather to control them. Liberal Christians in particular protested the belief that God had blessed America in such a way that it could exert force and dominance over the global poor.

Today, American exceptionalism is not only about the American nation being better than other nations; it is about America being the exception to the rule. Other countries may have to choose between a powerful military and a thriving economy, but America can have both. Other countries may need to divest from fossil fuels and develop an infrastructure based on renewable energy, but America can continue drilling for new oil reserves and further deregulate its oil industry. America is not only special to the people who call it home; just like an exceptional child who has no equal, America is great because God has made it so. It must train itself daily, just like an exceptional child must train to develop his or her own innate talents, but its exceptionalism is something that God gave to it.

NATIONAL: ELECTION OF RONALD REAGAN

In 1973, the Supreme Court voted in *Roe v Wade* to remove the authority of the states in determining whether or not a woman could have an abortion; a woman's right to abortion was now a federal matter, and states could not pass legislation banning it. Though the cause of overturning *Roe v Wade* became the galvanizing force for much of the Religious Right later in the decade, at first, the pro-life movement was somewhat anemic. In fact, two years before *Roe v Wade*, the Southern Baptist Convention passed a resolution declaring that its members will work for legislation to "allow the possibility of abortion under such conditions as rape, incest, clear evidence of severe fetal deformity, and carefully ascertained evidence of the likelihood of damage to the emotional, mental, and physical health of the mother."[2] Catholics, who had long opposed abortion, organized against *Roe v Wade*, as they see abortion—along with other social ills, such as poverty and capital punishment—as a life issue, and the Catholic faith has long taught that all life must be treated with dignity. However, for some conservative Protestants, the landmark decision was something of a victory.

But in the tiny European country of Switzerland, an American fundamentalist missionary named Francis Schaeffer had been building a ministry based on shaping what he called a "Christian worldview," underpinned by Judeo-Christian values. In the late 1970s, he and his son, Frankie, decided

---

2 Southern Baptist Convention, "Resolution on Abortion,"(Southern Baptist Convention, 1971), http://www.sbc.net/resolutions/13/resolution-on-abortion, accessed April 7, 2017.

that if people are made in the image of God, then to abort a child in the womb was to commit murder. Heads of state, including American presidents, had already been guests at the Schaeffers' chalet, L'Abri, so when Francis and his son decided to take up the anti-abortion cause, people listened. They found an audience with Jerry Falwell, who preached to thousands of people all across the United States every week through his *Old-Time Gospel Hour* radio broadcast. Falwell took up the anti-abortion cause, and in 1978—five years after *Roe v Wade*—he preached his first sermon on abortion.

At the time that Jerry Falwell took up the anti-abortion cause, the Democrat Jimmy Carter was president. Conservative fundamentalists and evangelicals had helped vote the Southern Baptist peanut farmer into the highest office, not because he opposed abortion but because they thought he would help restore the dignity of the presidency after Nixon's Watergate scandal. Personally, Carter opposed abortion, but as a politician, he believed that his duty was to uphold the authority of the Supreme Court and its decision in the *Roe v Wade* case. Yet with the tide of the Religious Right turning into a crusade to end abortion, leaders such as Jerry Falwell and Tim LaHaye decided that they had a God-given duty to put in the White House someone who would uphold the dignity of human life. For them, that person was Ronald Reagan.

Falwell and like-minded conservative Christians believed that if politicians who supported their views got elected, their beliefs would become law and the country would once again be a moral, Christian nation. Throughout the election cycle, he traveled the country preaching a stump sermon entitled "America Can Be Saved." In it he said,

> Somebody asked me recently, 'Who are you going to vote for?' I'll tell you. I will quickly vote for the man who stands before the television cameras and says to the American public, 'This is a Christian nation. And I am a Christian, a follower of the Lord Jesus Christ. We're glad to have all the non-Christians in our borders with first-class citizenship, enjoying all the luxuries of the American way of life. But this is a Christian nation, and I am a Christian. And as long as I lead this nation, I will lead it as a Christian under orders from his Lord.'[3]

Though an evangelical Christian—Jimmy Carter—currently occupied the White House, the Religious Right did not consider him a true Christian leader because he supported the right of the Supreme Court to issue a ruling in favor of abortion. But Ronald Reagan declared that life begins at conception and that if elected, he would try to pass a "Human Life Amendment"

3. Jerry Falwell, "America Can Be Saved." Undated.

that would ban abortion at a constitutional level. He would also support a "Voluntary School Prayer Amendment" that would ensure the right of children to pray in public schools in such a way that even the Supreme Court could not rule against it. To show their support of Reagan's candidacy for the White House, conservative Christians held rallies—everywhere from on the steps of state capitols to massive convention centers and stadiums—where they wore red, white, and blue and sang patriotic songs.

Churches held voter registration drives, often as part of their weekly Sunday services, because many fundamentalists and evangelicals were not even registered to vote. As part of their campaigning, members of the Religious Right distributed stickers that said "Vote," with the "t" enlarged to look like a cross; a 1980 edition of *Newsweek* magazine even featured a cover image of the "vote" emblem to show how powerful the Religious Right was quickly becoming. Churches could not explicitly endorse a political candidate, as doing so could cause them to lose their tax-exempt status. Reagan fixed this problem by declaring, to thousands of fundamentalists and evangelicals gathered at Reunion Arena in Dallas on August 21, 1980, "I know that this is a bipartisan event, and you can't endorse me. But I want you to know that I endorse you." What he said may have been the most famous line in the history of American evangelicalism.

Up until that moment at Reunion Arena, the American public had not paid much attention to evangelicals. In fact, when Jimmy Carter campaigned in 1976 and said that he was a born-again Christian, he had to tell reporters what the term "born-again Christian" meant because most Americans had never even heard it. By telling the members of his born-again audience that he endorsed them, Reagan was saying that he took them seriously and understood their concerns. At the gathering in Reunion Arena, he went on to tell his audience that if he was on a deserted island and could only have one book, he would undoubtedly bring the Bible. He also said that life begins at conception and that he would try to overturn the fateful *Roe v Wade* decision; he had to stop speaking numerous times because the applause was so loud that no one could hear him. Following his speech, he received a 10-minute standing ovation.

And Jerry Falwell, the leader of the movement, was no longer seen as a backwoods Baptist pastor in a small town in Virginia. He was being featured in articles in national publications for how he and his cohort were mobilizing the "silent majority," "the people" in a revolution that would ensure that conservative Christians would have a say in the direction that the nation would take. When election results were called on November 4, 1980 and Ronald Reagan was declared the next president, commentators credited Falwell and the mobilization of the Moral Majority.

In retrospect, historians today are hesitant to give the Moral Majority and broader Religious Right much credit in Reagan's 1980 landslide victory. Jimmy Carter's failed policies, which included advising people to wear sweaters to stay warm because the price of oil was so high, made him so unpopular that Reagan would have probably won marginally without the Religious Right. But what the 1980 election season did show was that the fundamentalists, who had been in a self-imposed exile from public life since the humiliating Scopes Trial, were now a force to be reckoned with.

GLOBAL: THE IRAN-CONTRA AFFAIR

While abortion was the piece de resistance of the Religious Right, legalizing voluntary prayer in America's public schools was one of the goals professed by the Moral Majority. During the Cold War revival of the 1950s, schoolchildren across the country daily recited a prayer that acknowledged their reliance on God and asked for His protection. A group of Jewish parents in Long Island, New York felt that their children being required to recite a prayer every day violated the separation of church and state and took their case to the Supreme Court. The 1962 ruling in *Engel v Vitale* said that requiring children to pray in school did violate their constitutional rights, and the following year's ruling in *Abington School District v Schempp* said that public school teachers could not organize prayer or scripture reading at school.

A generation before, William Jennings Bryan believed that the nation's embrace of Darwinism was the cause of its social ills; in the 1970s, Falwell began saying the same thing about school prayer. He believed that children were engaging in crime, including experimenting with drugs, and families were disintegrating because children were not allowed to pray in school. For Falwell, electing a president who would bring back school prayer would fix many of the nation's problems. Yet following Reagan's election, he proved to be lukewarm on the issues of the Religious Right, such as when he appointed to the Supreme Court Sandra Day O'Connor, a woman who voted to uphold *Roe v Wade*. And though a constitutional amendment legalizing school prayer was drafted, Reagan never tried to push it through congress. However, the Moral Majority's support of the president did not waver, as seen in Falwell's response to the Iran-Contra Scandal.

Following Iran's 1979 Islamic Revolution, Saddam Hussein—president of the neighboring country of Iraq—invaded Iran and began a decade-long war that would have a million casualties on each side. Iran needed arms to fight the war, and in return, it had something that the United States desperately wanted: American hostages (not the same hostages that were kidnapped from the American embassy in 1979). In August 1985, under direction from the Reagan administration, government officials covertly arranged for missiles to be sold to Iran in exchange for both money and the release of American hostages. Those holding the hostages were terrorist organizations, so the Reagan administration was effectively sending missiles to terrorists. To complicate the scandal, Reagan had publicly declared that he would not negotiate with terrorists, and the United States had a complete trade embargo with Iran; part of this trade embargo meant that the United States could not import any Iranian oil. One goal of some officials involved in the selling of arms to Iran was to reopen trade so that Iran would continue to supply oil to the United States; the cost of this hoped-for oil was sending arms to terrorist organizations.

The same year as the Islamic Revolution, in the Central American country of Nicaragua, communist rebels known as Sandanistas launched an insurgency that Americans feared would bring communism ever closer to their shores. A paramilitary group known as the Contras was fighting the Sandanistas, but because the Contras were funded primarily by cocaine money, the American government could not lend support to them. By forming a series of off-shore shell companies, the Reagan administration funneled the money from the weapons sold to Iran to fund the Contras. When the illicit arms sales to terrorist groups and money laundering came to light, members of the Reagan administration lied to congress and the American public about their involvement. The affair, known as the Iran-Contra Scandal, called into question both the ethos of the executive branch as well as the idea of America's exceptional mission to the world.

Lieutenant Oliver North, who served on the National Security Council and was heavily involved in the scandal, shredded a series of incriminating documents the day before the attorney general had a scheduled visit. He and other officials involved, including National Security Advisor John Poindexter, deceived congress and independent investigators in order to cover up their involvement. When the facts of the scandal began to become clear, North proclaimed that he had been acting in the best interests of the American hostages in Iran and that he was proud of his actions. Yet serious ethical issues arose, including when (if ever) an official should intentionally deceive the government and American public. And was America really so exceptional that its government could engage in back-door deals with terrorists and illicit rebel groups?

Yet for Falwell, the leadership of the Religious Right, and the students and staff of Liberty University, the issue was not whether or not members of the executive branch had broken the law. The issue was whether the United

States had an obligation to support those fighting against the communist regime in Nicaragua. As the scandal unfolded, Liberty's student newspaper, *The Liberty Champion*, regularly featured articles about Iran Contra, but the paper's student reporters said almost nothing about the government funneling arms to terrorist groups in Iran. Rather, they focused on whether or not the United States had an obligation to support the rebel Contras in their fight against the communist Sandinista government in Nicaragua. An opinion article from the March 30, 1988 edition of *The Liberty Champion* said,

> As an American, I support the efforts of North and others to supply military aide to the Contras. I believe America should come to the aide of its allies whenever they need help... Morally, as a Christian, I believe America should support freedom fighting countries because they are as brothers who are in need.[4]

The article also featured an opinion that opposed American aid to the contras, but this section appeared as an edited interview rather than an op-ed. The interviewer used loaded terms, such as "freedom fighter" in describing the Contras, and asked loaded questions, such as, "If this is not a civil war, what are the Freedom Fighters fighting for and what are the hundreds of thousands of Nicaragua refugees fleeing from?" The discourse between the interviewer and interviewee was reactionary, and the article did not allow for a full profile of an opposing view.

For Falwell, in spite of the Iran-Contra Scandal, America was still exceptional, and the officials involved were national heroes. North told a reporter regarding the investigation, "Read the eighth beatitude of Matthew 5."[5] The verse to which he was referring says, "Blessed are they which are persecuted for righteousness' sake, for theirs is the kingdom of heaven." (KJV) In making this statement in connection to the investigation of Iran-Contra, North was effectively claiming that the administration was acting in God's own interests, even though the administration's actions were illegal. Jerry Falwell did not disagree that the Reagan administration was acting righteously. He invited North to speak at the 1988 commencement ceremony for Liberty University and claimed that North was a true American hero. He even compared North to Jesus when he said, "We serve a Savior who was indicted and convicted and crucified."[6]

---

4 Michael Wilson, "Contras: should the U.S. send aid?" *The Liberty Champion* (March 30, 1988).

5 Frances Fitzgerald, "Reagan's Band of True Believers," *New York Times* (May 10, 1987).

6 Donald Baker, "Falwell Defends North, Compares Him to Savior," *Washington Post* (May 3, 1988).

In Jerry Prevo's Alaska, support of members of the Reagan administration who were involved in the Iran-Contra scandal revealed how deeply embedded the Moral Majority had become in local faith and politics. In February 1991, while North was appealing his felony convictions and the United States was involved in the Persian Gulf War, he delivered a sermon at Prevo's church, Anchorage Baptist Temple. Don Young, Alaska's long-time Republican congressman in the United States House of Representatives, introduced North to the congregation by calling him a "true hero." North's sermon spoke of the need for Christians to be involved in government affairs and called for prayer to be brought back to public schools. Bringing prayer back to public schools, he said, would solve many of the country's problems and prepare children to become national leaders. He claimed that he felt that he was being persecuted by his own government and that Christians had a role in bringing biblical truths to bear on those in power. Following his sermon, the congregation gave him a standing ovation, and many asked him to sign their Bibles. Yet outside the church, a group of demonstrators protested against North's crimes in the scandal and called for him to be fairly prosecuted.

Poindexter, North, and others involved in the scandal had hoped that the arms-for-hostages scheme in Iran would help stabilize relations between the Islamic Republic and the United States and allow Iranian oil to once again help fuel America. They did not accomplish that goal, and the rift between Iran and America's ally, Saudi Arabia—fueled as much by oil as by sectarian differences between the Shi'a Iranians and the Sunni Saudi Arabians—would soon increase when Saudi Aramco glutted the world's oil supply and caused oil prices to tumble. The 1980s oil glut would reveal how much Alaska's economy was dependent on events in the Middle East.

GLOCAL: ALASKA'S OIL BOOM AND CRASH

During the Reagan years, Alaska was flush with oil money. After the completion of the pipeline in 1977, employment dropped and many of the migrant workers who had come to Alaska for a pipeline job had to return to the Lower 48. Boomtowns saw a rapid population decline, but statewide, the economy entered a period of unprecedented prosperity. The state could now afford to pay public school teachers a living wage and build roads that connected rural communities to urban hubs, such as Anchorage and Wasilla. And with the beginning of the PFD payments in 1980, homesteaders and Alaska Natives who had not been not part of the cash economy now had an influx of money.

Some of the changes that came with the oil money were welcome, while others were not. People in rural communities, such as Trapper Creek on the south end of Denali National Park, now had jobs working on the state's new roads, but the fact that there was now a road to Trapper Creek meant that it was no longer the libertarian haven it had once been. State troopers regularly patrolled the area and destroyed illegal marijuana farms, and people working in government-funded positions—such as road workers and public school teachers—were subject to government oversight. With the state now able to afford welfare payments, people moved out to rural communities—where the cost of living was much lower than the national average—where they could live off of welfare and the PFD. In urban areas, the effects of the new oil-based economy were much more pronounced, as real estate exploded, new colleges opened, and the University of Alaska vastly expanded in size. Many Alaskans, including politicians, thought that the oil bonanza would last forever, and they became reliant on petrodollars. But when oil prices tanked in the late 1980s, the entire Alaskan economy went down, too.

Following the 1973 OPEC embargo, oil prices soared while global demand stagnated. In order to keep prices high, OPEC countries—including Iran, which soon became embroiled in the Islamic Revolution—restricted their oil output over the next decade. Saudi Arabia, home of the state-run Aramco oil company, bore the brunt of these restrictions, as it had to reduce its output by 60%. When oil began flowing through the Alaska pipeline in 1977, prices were still high from the effects of the embargo and restricted output, peaking from $21.59 a barrel in 1980 to $34 a barrel in 1982. But Saudi Arabia protested how much it had to restrict its production relative to other OPEC countries and, in 1986, increased its oil exports by 25%. The price of oil collapsed to $12 a barrel, and then less than $10, as the increase in Saudi oil exports caused the global supply to far outpace the demand.

Between 1980 and 1985, about 36,000 new homes were built in Alaska, a number that is higher than it sounds given the state's relatively small population. But the population was growing so rapidly—it grew by over 35% during those same years—that the influx of new homes did not cause home prices to drop; on the contrary, prices rose, along with interest rates that hit 17%. Companies located in the Forty-Ninth State bought up luxury artwork to display in their offices as a display of their newfound wealth, and the government built roads, schools, and other infrastructure to support the massive economic growth. The state, real estate companies, and local markets built all of this growth on a foundation of oil and petrodollars. When oil prices dropped in 1986, that foundation bottomed out so that while the rest of the country was watching coverage of reports on the Iran-Contra Scandal, Alaskans now struggled to survive.

Production on the North Slope remained constant, but with oil prices in a free fall, the state quickly went from a budget surplus to a $3 billion deficit. When people who had been buying up all of the new houses began to default on their mortgages, they often had no choice but to leave Alaska and move in with family in the Lower 48. Many left behind all of their furniture because they could not afford to take it with them, and entire housing developments became vacant. By the end of the decade, Alaska's population had decreased by approximately 44,000 people. So many houses went into foreclosure, with no new buyers on the market, that over half of the state's banks failed (by comparison, during the Great Depression, one-quarter of America's banks failed).

Mainstream dispensational thinkers, such as John Walvoord and Tim LaHaye, did not have much to say about Alaska's economic collapse, though it was very much connected to OPEC and events in the Middle East. In fact, the rest of the United States benefitted from the fall in oil prices, as it could resume its economic growth fueled by cheap oil. The price drop only had a negative effect on oil-based economies, such as OPEC countries, the Soviet Union (which had increased its oil production to become a leading world supplier during the 1970s), and Alaska. While national-level dispensationalists may not have paid much attention to the economic recession that hit Alaska, local Alaskans—in particular, Jerry Prevo—had a lot to say about it. Like John Walvoord, he believed that oil was the resource God was using to draw the nations of the world towards the Middle East and towards the prophesied Battle of Armageddon. With its role in the United States' supply of oil, Alaska would be a significant player in that apocalyptic buildup. For Prevo, the oil-based economies of OPEC, the Soviet Union, and Alaska were being drawn together as part of the End-Times drama.

Oil prices began to recover in 1990, when new troubles in the Middle East led to the Persian Gulf War. Saddam Hussein led the Iraqi military to invade Kuwait, with gaining control over the tiny country's massive oil fields a primary goal. Following the intervention of the United States in the war, which began on January 16, 1991, pastors across Alaska, particularly in the urban center of Anchorage, spoke about the war and the duty that Christians have. While many Alaskan pastors took a somber tone and called for peace, Prevo celebrated the war as another step towards fulfillment of End Times prophecies. In his sermon the Sunday after the war began, he called the war "righteous" and spoke of how America's engagement against Iraq aligned with biblical prophecies. To exemplify why support of war was a necessary component of the Christian life, he said,

> We can pray all we want to for peace, but we aren't going to stop the wars in this world. As we know from the Bible, wars have been with us since the beginning of time and Adam and Eve's first sin. And according to his own words, God's going to come down and make his own war someday. And he's going to do what he wants because God doesn't need the support of Congress or the United Nations or any allied forces. And we, as Christians, can support a war when the war is right.[7]

Sure enough, the Persian Gulf War did stabilize global oil prices so that Alaska's economy was able to recover.

Prevo's views were far from comprehensive for all of Alaska. He was arguably the most controversial figure in the entire state, and pastors and Christians from Anchorage and beyond routinely staged peaceful protests that called for acknowledgment of the biblical call to love your neighbor. But despite being controversial, he was incredibly influential, having relationships with not only national-level leaders in the Moral Majority, such as Jerry Falwell and Tim LaHaye, but also state- and national-level politicians, including the beloved Uncle Ted Stevens. His rhetoric that bashed liberals—in October 1994, his church hosted a "Scare the Liberals Sunday," in which his guest speaker caricatured liberals as nonintellectual elites with PhDs—and supported the American military's involvement in the Middle East was reflected by Sarah Palin when she ran alongside John McCain and then emerged as the leader of the Tea Party movement.

In the meantime, Alaska did not diversify its economy—the state's finances remain, to this day, almost exclusively dependent on its oil industry—but it did begin aggressively investing money into its Permanent Fund in the event of another economic downturn. Meanwhile, the oil companies on the North Slope began exploring and drilling in more fields and building new refineries to make sure that Alaskan oil continued to flow.

LOCAL: THE *EXXON-VALDEZ* OIL SPILL

> And now we just pay more for the fuel,
> The cost has been passed down, we learn
> And the helpless anger that I feel,
> It could make these waters burn.
> —Geoff Bartley, "The Wreck of the *Exxon-Valdez*"

---

7. Jay Blucher, "Congregations Pray For Peace, Victory," in *Anchorage Daily News* (January 21, 1991).

Environmental groups had feared the dire potential that the Alaska pipeline held for immense ecological catastrophe, and those fears found fulfillment in the early hours of March 24, 1989. The captain of the supertanker *Exxon-Valdez*, which was bound for refineries in California, steered the ship out of the normal shipping lanes and caused it to run aground on Bligh Reef. Just a few minutes after midnight, eleven million gallons of crude oil began to flow from the tanker into the pristine waters of Prince William Sound in what was, until 2010, the largest oil spill in United States' history. The effects of the spill made some question whether the environmental and economic price of Alaskan oil was worth what they had to pay.

Because of the environmental lawsuits that had been brought against the pipeline before congress approved its construction, the Alaska pipeline has some of the most stringent environmental regulations in the world. In addition to it being constructed in such a way that has minimal impact on local wildlife, the oil companies had to have a contingency plan in case of an oil spill in the water. The contingency plan was supposed to provide an immediate response in the event of a spill so that the oil would be rapidly cleaned up and the damage as small as possible. Yet an immediate response did not happen when the *Exxon-Valdez* struck Bligh Reef. The captain did not place a phone call informing anyone of the spill until 20 minutes after it happened, and though the spill began at midnight, a response team did not arrive until late in the afternoon.

Communities immediately affected by the spill considered Exxon's slow response to be a failure. On the day of the spill and for a few days afterwards, the waters of Prince William Sound were so calm that the oil could have been sectioned off and then drawn out of the water. However, personnel and equipment to begin working on the spill did not arrive until three days later. Local fishermen, frustrated by Exxon's slow response and fearful of what would happen if the oil spread to areas where they fished, used their own boats and equipment to try to contain the oil. On the day that an Exxon crew arrived to begin a clean-up effort, a storm with 70mph winds blew the oil so far and wide that the slick could not be contained. Without Exxon leading an organized effort to halt the oil's spread, the slick continued to move until it filled up all of Prince William Sound and began a journey that would cover 1200 miles of Alaskan coastline.

The oil decimated the wildlife of Prince William Sound. Nearly every animal in the immediate vicinity of the spill died; dead whales washed onto oil-soaked beaches, and so many birds died that volunteers had to throw hundreds of bird carcasses into bonfires. With annual migrations that occur in the spring bringing more animals into the area, volunteers had to organize to prevent more wildlife from paying the ultimate price for the oil spill.

They captured birds, otters, sea lions, and other animals to wash off the oil that accumulated on their skin and under their feathers, then released them into areas that had not been contaminated. However, animals continued to die at rapid rates because of how drastically the oil had permeated the food chain. Over 30 years later, the wildlife of Prince William Sound has not recovered.

Dotted along Prince William Sound are villages of Alaska Natives, who have long lived subsistence lifestyles and rely heavily on fishing. Many became sick, both from the toxic oil fumes in the air and from the contaminated waters. At the time of the spill, approximately 85% of their diet came from what they could harvest from the sea—salmon, snails, halibut, clams, octopus, and seals—as well as wild birds and deer. When the oil from *Exxon-Valdez* contaminated their waters, their marine harvesting came to a complete halt. Exxon sent in barges of food to the villages, but the processed foods and red meat that Exxon delivered were far from what the Natives were accustomed to eating. Furthermore, having to eat food that had been shipped in instead of harvested by the community interrupted their subsistence lifestyles. Some Natives, eager to return to eating habits that connected them with nature, resumed fishing in areas that were still heavily contaminated so that they could continue eating the fresh food that they craved. Many became sick as a result.

The contamination of the local food supply was not the only disruption that Native populations faced. Throughout the summer, as part of Exxon's clean-up effort, it hired Natives to work at the eye-popping rate of $16.99 per hour (adjusted for inflation, that amount is $35 per hour in 2020). Villages that had been mostly outside of the cash economy quickly became dependent on oil money, and competition over high-paying jobs disrupted longstanding traditions of sharing and generosity. To this day, many Native villages that entered the cash economy because of the oil spill have lower levels of subsistence and traditional practices. They also have higher levels of stress and trauma from how much their way of life was disrupted.

One ironic result of the oil spill is that it helped pull Alaska out of the recession caused by the drop in oil prices. Many who were out of work and facing the prospect of foreclosure, even bankruptcy, could spend the summer working to clean up the coastline. So many people took clean-up jobs, enticed by the high rates of pay that Exxon offered, that there were labor shortages in cities such as Anchorage. The rapid influx of cash allowed many families to avoid foreclosure and continue buying food and household essentials; it also demonstrated that in spite of the detrimental effects of the spill, the state's economy could not break its dependence on oil. Because of how many people came to work on the spill, the oil industry remained the largest employer in the state.

Yet despite the massive clean-up effort, headed by volunteer organizers as much as by Exxon executives, the oil spill has still not been cleaned. Chemical dispersants that Exxon used to clear the slick did not eliminate the oil; they only pushed it down to the sea floor. Today, one can walk down beaches in Prince William Sound and still see oil underneath rocks. The long-term effects of the spill raise the question that environmentalists raised prior to the pipeline's construction: Can oil and wildlife co-exist?

For Sarah Palin, the answer is a resounding yes. Wildlife live on the North Slope, alongside the oil wells that pump black gold from the earth and into the pipeline. Areas that have offshore drilling also have high populations of whales, walruses, and sea lions that have not been harmed by oil. In fact, she and other Alaska politicians—particularly Ted Stevens and Frank Murkowski—promoted drilling in ANWR and allayed ecological concerns by pointing to the stringent environmental regulations on Alaskan oil. For Palin, Stevens, and like-minded politicians, the *Exxon-Valdez* spill demonstrated the potential that oil has for harming the environment but did not point to oil and wildlife as being incompatible.

Others disagree with this view. Environmental activists claim that as long as oil continues to flow, oil spills will continue to happen. They may not happen in Alaska—the 2010 BP oil spill happened on the other side of the country, in the Gulf of Mexico—but America's insatiable appetite for cheap oil means that oil spills and their long-term effects will remain a feature of American life. Furthermore, climate change, which scientists have long pointed to as being caused by burning fossil fuels, is also harming wildlife in ways that scientists are only beginning to understand. For many environmentalists, the only way that American society can co-exist with wildlife is for the country to get off of oil.

But American exceptionalism means that the country does not need to get off of oil. The American nation is uniquely blessed by God, and part of that blessing is access to the oil that fuels the capitalist system. Accessing that oil may mean flouting the country's laws, as in the selling of arms to terrorist groups in Iran, but this law-breaking was justified in the name of America's God-given prosperity and divine mission to the world. Alaska's economy may intersect with the oil-based economies of the Middle East, but for dispensationalists, this paradigm cannot be avoided, as it is part of the unfolding of the End Times. Yet Alaska can ensure that the United States maintains access to oil when events in the Middle East, such as Iran's Islamic Revolution, cut off parts of the United States' oil supply. Despite the Iran-Contra Scandal and the *Exxon-Valdez* oil spill, the Alaska pipeline means that America can remain exceptional and remain addicted to oil.

Chapter 7

The First Bush Years

Wasilla, the Alaskan town where Sarah Palin grew up and served as mayor, was formed in 1917 as an outpost for the Alaska Railroad on the way to the gold mines of the Talkeetna Mountains. During the Great Depression of the 1930s, the federal government relocated about 200 families from failed farms in the Midwest to the Mat-Su Borough, the county that Wasilla is in, but the area remained sparsely populated and economically undeveloped for decades. After World War II, veterans that had been stationed in Alaska during the war headed to the Wasilla area to settle on homesteads, where many pumped their own water and had no electricity. In contrast to the post-war boom that the Lower 48 experienced, electricity did not arrive in the Mat-Su Valley until the 1950s, and by the time Alaska gained statehood in 1959, Wasilla had a population of only 150 people.

All of those things changed when oil was discovered at Prudhoe Bay. During the construction of the oil pipeline, from 1974 through 1977, the northern city of Fairbanks and southern city of Valdez turned into boomtowns. The sudden influx of jobs and wealth created an explosive growth of population and crime, from prostitution to money laundering. Arson and murder became so common in Fairbanks that café owners and shopkeepers openly carried guns to work. Many families who had come to Alaska to find work on the pipeline settled in the quieter, more provincial town of Wasilla, which saw a slower but steady boom to its population and economy.

Wasilla today looks vastly different than it did before the construction of the pipeline, and its local culture is integrated with the oil industry that brought about its prosperity.

People in Wasilla and the surrounding area thanked the oil dollars that came in for the new modern conveniences in their area, from better schools to paved roads to full-service shopping centers. Oil also provided high-paying jobs in an area that had been economically depressed; many, including Sarah Palin's husband, Todd, secured high-paying jobs on the pipeline. But the sudden development came with a heavy price, as the opening of Wal-Marts and Targets spelled the beginning of the end of the pioneering spirit and a loss of the area's pristine, frontier innocence. People no longer had to rely on friends and family as they struggled through the severe Arctic winters. Soon families, municipalities, and the state government became dependent on oil money and the prosperity that it brought.

IDEOLOGY: THE PROSPERITY GOSPEL

Oil and an ideology known as the prosperity gospel have gone hand-in-hand since the first oil boom of the late 1800s. "Prosperity gospel" is a very broad term that does not refer to one strand of theology in particular (such as dispensational theology) but rather the general belief that God wants humans, especially believing Christians, to prosper in every area of life.

In the early fundamentalist movement, which coincided with the nineteenth-century oil boom, one prevailing belief was that oil was God's blessing on the United States to bring the country to a place of prosperity in the world. This view was iterated by the Reverened E. W. Hutter in 1865, when he claimed,

> Wine and milk continue to be derived by ancient methods from ancient sources. But oil, of a kind most valuable for use, is flowing from unexpected quarters. For thousands of years, it may be, in secret laboratories, the plastic hand of God has been compounding it for us. Only now it is being elicited, and that in incalculable abundance. Thus a new element of individual and aggregate wealth stands disclosed to our astonished gaze, at a juncture in our national history most opportune. To private and public enterprise a fresh stimulus is imparted. Now, oh, how wonderful oil is drawn from overflowing wells, almost as copiously as water, and exported by the cargo to foreign lands, in exchange for their commodities! Who so blind to the providence of this invisible Power,

that sits enthroned in the heavens, as not to discern herein fresh proofs that 'God has not dealt so with any nation?'[1]

In addition to the idea that God had blessed the American nation with oil, another prevailing belief was that Christians should harness oil for both its economic potential and for funding Christian missions. One fundamentalist oilman who held to this idea was Patillo Higgins, the "prophet of Spindletop." He embarked on what he saw as a divine mission to find the oil that he knew lay under the surface of Beaumont, Texas, with the intent of finding the wealth that would make him rich as well as further the Kingdom of God on earth. Higgins' one-time business partner, Anthony Lucas, succeeded in striking oil at the famous Spindletop geyser; unable to profit from the find, Higgins drilled on land he had leased around Spindletop and found his fortune.

Others looked to oil's industrial potential for creating a more Christian society. Almost immediately after the oil strike at Spindletop, the small enclave of Beaumont exploded into a boomtown. One of Higgins' partners, George Carroll, sought to use the oil platform that was bringing so many to Beaumont to turn the town into a "city on a hill." In addition to winning Beaumont's many lost souls to Christianity through revival-style preaching, he wanted the town to industrialize in such a way that it heralded the Kingdom of God on earth. Carroll believed that oil represented the potential for peace on earth and prosperity in life.

The relationship between oil and the prosperity gospel has remained constant for the century and a half since the first oil boom that financed the early fundamentalist movement. Indeed, the Zion Oil Company today—financed by Christians who believe that God will reward their faithfulness—is drilling for oil in Israel; its cohort is driven by firm belief in the promises of God regarding His chosen people, the Jews, through a dispensational view of history that includes hope for oil to be found in Israel. The prosperity gospel has also been closely intertwined with the Religious Right, particularly during its formative years.

The rise of the Religious Right during the 1970s and 1980s concurred with the rise of what is called the Electronic Church. The Electronic Church refers to the surge in televangelism, as fundamentalist and Pentecostal pastors such as Jerry Falwell, Jimmy Swaggart, Pat Robertson, and Benny Hinn broadcasted their church services and studio-recorded shows—such as Robertson's *The 700 Club*—across national television networks. The rise of the Electronic Church marked a shift in how people viewed church; it

---

1. "Oil in the Pulpit," in *American Phrenological Journal* Vol. 43 Issue 4 (October 1865): 109.

was no longer just a building that Christians attended on Sundays but was a culture that permeated the airwaves and had increased relevance on the day-to-day lives of the faithful. It also marked a shift in how Christians viewed spiritual leadership, as televangelists came to have more influence on the lives of believers than their local church pastors did, even though many televangelists did not have formal theological training. Their sermons lacked theological depth and relied more on the charisma of the personalities involved than on two millennia of Christian thought.

In addition, the Electronic Church marked a shift in how Christians gave to churches. Most church finances come from donations given by members of the local congregation, but the Electronic Church had national, rather than local, congregations. And the congregations were not composed of members but rather of viewers—many of whom also had a local church—watching from home. The televangelists appealed for funds from viewers, but rather than asking that viewers support the televangelists' ministries instead of local churches, they asked that viewers give out of the abundance that God has promised them.

Many of these televangelists not only had ministries on television but also in third-world countries, where they provided food, education, and medical care for the world's poorest people. The televangelists promised their congregations of viewers that God would bless them for sowing a seed into the ministry. Viewers could use their money, over and above what they gave to their local churches, to spread the Kingdom of God across the airwaves of America and to the farthest reaches of the earth. In return, the televangelists claimed, God would bless donors for the money given in faith with the miracle that they needed. Many of the televangelists diverted the funds that viewers gave in order to finance their own lavish lifestyles, and several—including Jim and Tammy Bakker (whose scandal hit the national media at the same time as the Iran-Contra Scandal) and Benny Hinn—went to prison for fraud. Jerry Falwell never served time in prison, but his financial practices invited the scrutiny of the Securities and Exchange Commission (SEC) and nearly led to the collapse of Liberty Baptist College (before it became Liberty University) and Thomas Road Baptist Church.

Falwell's prosperity gospel was more tied to the American nation than to the "seed sown in faith" of viewers that other televangelists promoted, as he believed that God had uniquely blessed America more than any other nation on earth. Oil underpinned the nationalist prosperity gospel preached by the early fundamentalists, who saw the resource as God's means of making American the greatest of all nations. Though Falwell did not preach about oil the way that E.W. Hutter did, he linked the favorable economic conditions brought about by cheap oil during the 1980s to God's blessing on the American nation. And today, particularly in a state whose entire economy is completely dependent on the flow of oil, it is both the evidence of God's favor and a repository of apocalyptic thought.

NATIONAL: THE MORAL MAJORITY DISBANDS

The Iran-Contra Scandal did not cause the Religious Right to lose faith in President Reagan or his administration. Rather, the scandal showed the extent of the evangelical and fundamentalist support of the Reagan White House; he held the office of president because God had put him there, and if members of his administration had acted on God's behalf, they should not go to trial for breaking the law. In the wake of the Iran-Contra Scandal, Falwell and the Moral Majority threw their support behind Reagan's vice president, George H.W. Bush, when he campaigned for the Oval Office in 1988. His win marked another victory for the Religious Right.

But the 1988 election of George Bush came with less fanfare than the 1980 election of Ronald Reagan. There was no great moment at Reunion Arena in which the Republican candidate announced his endorsement of the religious voters gathered. The "Vote" stickers with the "t" enlarged to look like a cross were leftovers from the 1980 season. Part of the Religious Right's lackluster support was due to differences of opinion regarding the candidacy of Pat Robertson, a televangelist who also sought the presidency. But much of it was due to the fact that the Republican Party had shifted so that the Religious Right had become mainstream.

The televangelist scandals of the 1980s, particularly that of Jim and Tammy Faye Bakker, severely tarnished the reputation of the Moral Majority in the latter part of the decade. In 1966, the Bakkers began their televangelism ministry alongside Pat Robertson on *The 700 Club* before launching *The Jim and Tammy Show*, which aired on Robertson's *Christian Broadcasting Network*. They went on to begin their own television network which featured their own variety show, *The PTL Club* (PTL stands for "Praise the Lord"), which had guests such as Billy Graham and Oral Roberts, as well as secular stars, such as Mr. T. They went on to build their own theme park, Heritage USA, which became the destination of choice for Christian vacationers and was surpassed only by the Disney resorts for popularity. To support the massive business empire, alongside a missionary outreach in third-world countries, Jim and Tammy Faye appealed to viewers for funds, promising that in return, God would grant them health, wealth, and victory.

Their empire began to crumble in 1982, when a report issued by the Federal Communications Commission revealed that the Bakkers had diverted $350,000 that had been donated for their overseas missions, in order to fund the theme park. The report also revealed that they had used donated funds for personal use to finance their own exorbitant lifestyles. Everything unraveled in 1987, when an investigation revealed that Jim had paid hush money to his church secretary to hide the fact that he had had a sexual encounter with her; the secretary claimed that both Jim and his associate had drugged and raped her. The scandal hit the national media with such intensity that it may have actually pulled public interest away from the Iran-Contra Scandal, which was being exposed at the same time.

Jim and Tammy Faye were of a substream of evangelicalism, Pentecostalism, which is similar to fundamentalism in its emphasis on biblical literalism and dispensational prophecies of the End Times. They had been leaders in the Religious Right and, like Falwell, promoted American nationalism as part of Christian faith and praxis. Instead of handing their business empire over to a fellow Pentecostal leader, they handed it over to Falwell. He only held onto it for a few months, but the scandal was so severe that with Falwell now in charge of the PTL ministry empire, donations to the Moral Majority dropped precipitously. Shortly after stepping down from PTL in 1987, Falwell announced that he would no longer chair the Moral Majority.

Carl Henry, the moderate evangelical theologian who had helped Billy Graham begin *Christianity Today* three decades earlier, declared that despite millions of dollars spent, the Moral Majority had not accomplished a single legislative goal. Notwithstanding the almost unanimous support of the Moral Majority for Ronald Reagan, he appointed the pro-choice justice Sandra Day O'Connor to the Supreme Court; during the 1992 *Planned Parenthood v Casey* case, she voted to uphold a woman's right to abortion, as set by *Roe v Wade*. There was no Reagan-era legislation that said marriage is between a man and a woman, though Falwell did help make sure that the government issued nearly no funding for the AIDS crisis, which plagued LGBTQ+ communities, for nearly a decade. No legislation for teaching creation science or allowing for voluntary prayer in public schools, though—to Falwell's approval—Reagan did take an aggressive stance against the Soviet Union. Despite being exceptionally vocal, Falwell and the Moral Majority had actually accomplished very little in terms of public policy.

In the summer of 1989, a few months after the inauguration of George H.W. Bush, Falwell announced that he was disbanding the Moral Majority on the grounds that the group had accomplished everything it had set out to do. Its success had not been with legislative victories, which were practically nonexistent. Rather, its success was in how conservative Christians across the country had been mobilized into political action. Millions of American fundamentalists and evangelicals—as well as a handful of Catholics,

Orthodox, and non-Christian groups, such as Jews—now saw engagement in national politics as part of their religious duty. Pastors, including those who had been party to the 1971 Southern Baptist Convention resolution to support a woman's right to have an abortion, now used their pulpits to decry abortion as murder.

Furthermore, the 1988 Republican Party platform revealed that the conservative values of the Moral Majority were now mainstream. The platform supported a human life amendment that would ban abortion at a constitutional level and teaching abstinence as the best form of birth control. In 1992, the platform included support of continuing to ban homosexuals from joining the military, and in 1996, it supported the right of states to ban gay marriage. The hard right turn that the Republican Party took as a result of the Moral Majority's influence can still be seen in its platform today. Even though Falwell disbanded the Moral Majority in 1989, the Religious Right was here to stay.

GLOBAL: THE PERSIAN GULF WAR

From the time that Billy Graham began preaching in the Cold War Revival until Jerry Falwell disbanded the Moral Majority, containing the Soviet Union and the spread of its communism was at the forefront of the political agenda for the Religious Right. Oil politics were always under the surface—and in Alaska, above the surface (literally, as the oil flowed through an above-ground pipeline)—yet following the 1973 Yom Kippur War and OPEC embargo, many, including Falwell, saw the real nemesis as the Soviet Union, not oil-producing countries such as Iraq, Saudi Arabia, and Iran. Even with the Islamic Revolution in Iran, the taking of hostages in Tehran, and the Iran-Contra Scandal, the Religious Right was not overly concerned with the Middle East. The bloc's focus was Magog—the Soviet Union—and preventing a communist takeover of America.

Symbolic of the divide between the communist East and the capitalist West was the Berlin Wall, a structure built to prevent East Germans—who lived under the rule of the Soviet Union—from crossing into capitalist West Germany. Just a few months after Falwell disbanded the Moral Majority, the Berlin Wall fell on November 9, 1989. Its collapse signaled the breakup of the Soviet Union, which quickly disintegrated into countries such as Hungary, Poland, Russia, Georgia, and Ukraine. Reagan's presidency had been marked by an aggressive stance towards the Soviet Union, and with the empire no longer in existence, Bush's would be marked by a war in the Middle East that would make oil politics a primary concern for the Religious Right.

The Persian Gulf War marked a shift in the political engagement of the Religious Right, away from fighting communism and to turning dispensationalism into a much more widespread theology of oil. That theology of oil was the mirror image of the prosperity gospel.

While the Alaskan economy was in a severe recession due to the drop in oil prices, Iraq's economy was destroyed. Saddam Hussein had just led his country through an eight-year war against Iran, so Iraq was heavily in debt; now, with oil prices at an all-time low, Iraq had no way of paying off its wartime debts. It had a long-standing border dispute with Kuwait, and Saddam began claiming that Kuwaiti oil companies were drilling Iraqi oil. Further, he claimed that Kuwait's government was using the country's immense oil reserves to control the global market in such a way that kept Iraq in debt. When Saddam invaded Kuwait on August 2, 1990, his actions threatened to destabilize the world's economy—the West had been so focused on the Soviet Union and the Cold War that it did not realize how volatile the Middle East, the global supplier of oil, was becoming.

President Bush advocated to the United Nations that the use of force be approved against the Iraqi military that was occupying Kuwait. The UN responded by giving Saddam from November 29, 1990 until January 15, 1991 to withdraw. By January 16, the Iraqi military was still occupying Kuwait, with Saddam seeing the UN threat of force as a bluff. The US military, chiefly the Air Force, descended upon Saddam's forces in an aggressive UN-backed campaign to expel them from Kuwait. The entire operation took about six weeks, though most of Saddam's military had been ousted in less than one week. Yet despite this short timeframe, the Persian Gulf War signaled a massive change in international relations, US foreign policy, and oil politics: the world's eyes had gone from the Soviet Union to the oil-rich Middle East.

The war also signaled a turning point for dispensationalism, as dispensational theologians saw the world events that warned of the impending apocalypse as now much more heavily grounded in the oil-based economies of the Middle East. John Walvoord, the dispensational theologian based at Dallas Theological Seminary, revised his book *Armageddon, Oil, and the Middle East Crisis* to show how Iraq's invasion of Kuwait fulfilled biblical prophecy. The 1990 revised edition made stronger claims than the original 1973 edition did about oil being a divine resource that is drawing the nations of the world towards the Battle of Armageddon. And people bought the book—within 10 weeks, the 1990 edition sold one million copies, twice as many as the original, and it was even featured in major newspapers, including *The New York Times*. *Armageddon, Oil, and the Middle East Crisis* sat on the front shelves of bookstores alongside titles such as *The Rise of*

Babylon, written by Walvoord's colleague, Dr. Charles Dyer; *The Last Days Handbook*, written by another one of Walvoord's colleagues, Robert Lightner; and *One World Under Antichrist*, written by Peter LaLonde, whose company, Cloud Ten, would produce the *Left Behind* movies. Even Johnny Cash wrote a song, "Goin' By The Book," that tied the Persian Gulf War into fears of Armageddon. Dispensationalism was no longer relegated to Protestant fundamentalists; with the Persian Gulf War, dispensationalism and its view of oil politics became front-page news.

Yet the tone was different for Arab Christians in the Middle East, as well as non-evangelical Christians in the West and evangelicals who did not support a war fought over oil. An article from Billy Graham's magazine *Christianity Today*, entitled "Leaders Wrestle With Faith And War," expressed the views of many Christian leaders towards the Persian Gulf War. While Pat Robertson, the televangelist and former presidential candidate, saw the war as part of the buildup to Armageddon, others insisted that matters of the American government, military strategy, and international relations do not fall within the purview of biblical interpretation. The Mennonite leader Myron Augsburger commented, "The world needs to know that we are concerned about justice, not simply about oil and economic issues that meet our American interests."[2] For many of the Christians who opposed the war, the question was not about the End Times but whether the United States had the right to wage a war over oil. Oil and the economic prosperity that it had brought to the country for more than a century had long fed the prosperity gospel, and they saw the cost of the prosperity gospel as being further destabilization in the Middle East and deteriorating relationships between Christians and Muslims. Further, they raised concerns over the environmental cost of the prosperity gospel, as oil fumes were polluting the air, oil spills were killing wildlife, and production of consumer goods and military supplies was taxing the earth's resources. Christians who opposed the war saw the relationship between oil and the prosperity gospel as something that crippled a biblical faith built on trust in God and justice for the poor; instead of social justice, the prosperity gospel proclaimed health, wealth, and victory, built heavily on a foundation of oil.

The intense focus on the End Times that became public during the Persian Gulf War continued far beyond the war's end. In 1995, the prominent dispensational theologian and colleague of Jerry Falwell, Tim LaHaye, began writing with Jerry Jenkins the *Left Behind* series. The series is a fictional account of End Times events as LaHaye saw them prophesied, beginning with the Rapture, on to the Great Tribulation, and ending with the

---

2. "Leaders Wrestle With Faith And War," *Christianity Today*. February 11, 1991.

Second Coming of Jesus. By the time the first book would be made into a movie in 2000, tens of millions of copies would have already been sold. The opening scene of the movie could not better demonstrated dispensational beliefs about Magog and the Persian Gulf War: Arab and Russian planes attacked Israel in a surprise air raid.

For dispensationalists who supported the Persian Gulf War, oil was not the goal but rather the proxy that was leading up to Armageddon, a worldwide battle that could not be prevented. By the time President George H.W. Bush's son, President George W. Bush, would deliberate an American-led invasion of Iraq in 2003, the refrain among people in the Religious Right was already familiar. Wars and rumors of wars, trouble in the Middle East, the rise of Babylon, all these things had been prophesied in the Bible. The United States was getting involved in events that had been divinely foretold, but the question for evangelical and fundamentalist Christians was not whether they had a prophetic mandate to control the world's oil. Rather, the question was if they were ready for the Rapture. Meanwhile, the question for Christians who opposed the invasion of Iraq was about whether the cost of the country's oil-based prosperity was one they were willing to continue paying.

LOCAL: SARAH PALIN BEGINS HER POLITICAL CAREER IN WASILLA, ALASKA

By 1996, the year that Sarah Palin ran for mayor of Wasilla, the Moral Majority had been dissolved for nearly a decade. However, its impact on Alaska—and particularly the state's most conservative region, the Mat-Su Valley—was such that its values became embedded into the local culture. Valley Hospital, located in Wasilla's neighboring town of Palmer, became ground zero in the struggle to end abortion; the hospital provided abortions, but concerned citizens—many of whom were aligned with the Moral Majority—made the ending of abortion there a personal crusade.

In the early 1990's, pro-life advocates campaigned to be on the hospital's board so that they could vote for a hospital policy that restricted abortions. The abortion debate overwhelmed the hospital boardroom, where administrators had to redirect board members—who were solely concerned with ending abortion—to the governance challenges of running a nonprofit hospital. The debate over abortion in the Mat-Su Valley became so severe that some pregnant women chose to deliver their babies in Anchorage, nearly an hour away, at hospitals that did not provide abortions; at least one baby died en route. Following passage of the restricted abortion policy, in the mid-1990s, the Mat-Su Coalition for Choice sued the hospital. The court ruled in the Coalition's favor and prevented the hospital from enforcing the policy. Valley Hospital appealed the judgement all the way to the Alaska Supreme Court, which decided in 1997 that Valley Hospital had to perform abortions and that pregnant women had a right to the procedure. This environment was the one in which Sarah Palin ran for mayor of Wasilla in 1996, and her small-town politics blended the pro-life, pro-libertarian capitalist values of the Moral Majority with an oil-based economy.

When Palin ran for her first political office in 1992, a seat on the Wasilla City Council, revenue from the pipeline funded almost all of the state's budget. Despite Alaska's economic downturn of the late 1980s, the state income tax had been abolished, and many municipalities, including Wasilla, did not even have a sales tax; the oil-based economic development, particularly with the annual PFD payments, brought about the mindset that the people could—and should—rely on oil money rather than taxes to fund their state.

When Palin began her 1992 campaign to be on the city council, Wasilla still did not have a local police force but had grown large enough that the state decided it should provide one for its residents. To compound the issue, the oil bust of the late 1980s had led to a sharp increase in local crime. But funding a police force would mean running against a culture that had come to rely on oil revenue to fund its economic development: the city of Wasilla would have to levy a sales tax. To make the idea of a sales tax more palatable, those running on a pro-tax platform combined the sales tax with a lower property tax rate. In 1992, Palin campaigned for a seat on the city council—and won—with a platform in favor of implementing a 2% sales tax, lower property taxes, and a local police force. Despite the new sales tax, her campaign for lower property taxes caused a plurality of locals to see her as anti-tax and in favor of Moral Majority-style libertarian capitalism. That she was adamantly pro-life added to her appeal, even though a pro-life stance is not usually considered libertarian.

By the time Palin began her rise in local politics, the Mat-Su Valley had transformed into what some locals call the "Bible belt of Alaska." Not only were chain stores beginning to open in Wasilla—in keeping with the libertarian capitalism of the Moral Majority and the oil money that poured into the state—but during the years of the Moral Majority, Mat-Su Valley voters began taking up the anti-abortion cause on a much larger scale. In her 1996 mayoral campaign, she spoke as much about opposing abortion—what critics saw a as national- and state-level issue—as she did about fixing local roads and how to spend the newly imposed sales tax.

During that election season, local politics took a highly partisan turn, particularly regarding the mayoral contests in Wasilla. The Republican

Party sponsored a fundraiser that featured Palin, though the money went to Republican districts rather than to her campaign. Full-page ads featured her alongside state-level Republicans, and some voters complained that the involvement of the Republican Party detracted from local, nonpartisan issues. John Stein, the incumbent mayor seeking a fourth term, led a campaign that emphasized his experience and the good that he had brought to Wasilla. Palin's campaign motto was "A Time For Change," and she characterized Stein as a "good ole boy" who had lost touch with the people. She did not have the political experience of Stein, but Wasilla voters saw that quality as a reason to support her. As a populist, she promised to listen to "the people" in a way that the incumbent was no longer able to. Shortly after the election, she compared her win to the tenacity and drive that helped her take her high school basketball team to the state championship in 1982. Mayor Sarah was a down-home favorite whose primary appeal was that she was one of the people, and she carried this appeal into her two terms as mayor, from 1996 until 2002.

As mayor of a small town, Palin was unable to make any changes to legislation about abortion. Yet she embodied other conservative values of the Moral Majority, including cutting the size of the government and reducing her own salary by 10% upon taking office. Yet her term got off to a rough start when she spoke with a local librarian about how to ban books that some of the people thought were inappropriate; the librarian refused to comply, and Palin later cut the library's budget so severely that the library nearly closed. She cut funding to the city museum, which also nearly closed, as well as numerous other public services. She drew fire at the beginning of her term when she requested all city department heads to hand in resignation letters and banned them from speaking with reporters unless they received permission from her first. The editor of the local newspaper, *The Frontiersman*, called the ban a gag order.

After the rocky start, Mayor Sarah earned favor among Wasillians by further cutting property taxes and also cutting business taxes, thereby enabling Wasilla's oil-induced boom to accelerate. Tax revenue increased because of the new businesses that opened, yet so did the size of the government; despite Palin's libertarian appeal among those who supported her lower taxes, the city's government grew by over 30% while she was mayor.

In attempting to ban books, close city institutions, and make abortion the center of her campaign, opponents felt Palin was bringing state- and national-level issues to bear on what should be a nonpartisan matter of running a small town. The mayor of a town of less than 5000 people cannot issue legislation about abortion, yet in the Valley, the issue became a litmus test of whether or not someone had the moral qualifications to serve in a government position. At the end of her second term, her mother-in-law, Faye Palin, ran for mayor. Sarah could not support her mother-in-law's bid, not because she disagreed with her on local issues, but because she was pro-choice.

The mayorship of Sarah Palin marked a decisive turn in the small-town politics of the Mat-Su Valley. Voters came to see national issues, particularly those advocated by the Moral Majority, as being of primary importance in local elections. For many, the views that a candidate for city council had on abortion became as important as how that candidate planned to spend the city's oil and tax dollars. Furthermore, Palin's rise from city council to mayor to governor and then vice-presidential nominee revealed that one's stance on abortion in a local election could have immense significance later on. Many mayors in the Mat-Su Valley, before the rise of Palin but certainly thereafter, have set their ambitions on state and national positions, where they hope to enact stricter abortion laws and maybe even outlaw the practice altogether.

GLOCAL: SARAH PALIN EXPOSES CORRUPTION IN ALASKA

At times Mayor Sarah's stance on abortion may have overwhelmed small-town politics, but being pro-life is not unusual for an Alaskan politician. Neither is being opposed to gun control, as the state has some of the most lenient gun laws in the country. As McCain's vice-presidential candidate, when she promoted drilling in ANWR and further development of Alaska's oil resources, many saw her as awkward and out of tune with environmental concerns; however, what may have been an unpopular stance on a national stage was a commonplace one in Alaska. What made Sarah Palin stand out among other Alaskan politicians was not her stance on abortion and gun control, nor her approach to drilling and building up the state's oil industry. Her positions in those areas may stand out on a national level, but on a state level, they were necessary for one to even be elected. What made her stand out was that she stood against the corruption and cronyism between politicians and oil companies, most famously in the 2004 scandal involving Randy Ruedrich, the chairman of the Alaska Republican Party.

The central challenges of state-level politics in Alaska are how one should understand the relationship between the oil companies and the government and what the government's obligations are to the people, particularly in terms of how it manages the state's natural resources. The Mineral Leasing Act of 1920 prohibited a rush of oil companies from staking claims and drilling haphazardly in Alaska, as they had previously done in the Lower 48 before Standard Oil took control of the oil industry. The Act said that individuals or companies could not profit from the commercial use of the natural resources, even on private property, without special approval. When oil was discovered at Prudhoe Bay in 1968, the companies involved could not buy up large tracts of land and drill. Instead, they have had to lease the land from the government, which, in turn, manages the development of the oil in the best interests of the people. The government uses the money from the land leases and taxes on oil to fund itself and the Permanent Fund, as well as to develop the state's infrastructure. As such, relationships between multinational corporations—namely, oil companies—and the government, and between the government and the people, are different in Alaska than in any other part of the country.

Companies do not always function according to ethical and transparent principles, and the government does not always act in the best interests of the people, especially when hundreds of millions of oil dollars are involved. Whistleblowers in Alaska are constantly raising concerns about back-room deals between oil executives and politicians, such as in the relationship between Ted Stevens and the VECO oil company that came to light in 2008. Sarah Palin built her reputation as a state-level politician who represented the people's interests over the oil companies when she exposed an unethical relationship between Randy Ruedrich, government officials, and oil executives.

Following Palin's two-term tenure as mayor of Wasilla, in 2003, Governor Frank Murkowski appointed her as one of three commissioners and ethics supervisor on the Alaska Oil And Gas Conservation Commission. The AOGCC is a government body tasked with managing the state's oil resources and overseeing the oil companies' production. In her book *Going Rogue*, Palin claimed that the state's oil is the issue that she cares about most, both for the state and the entire country.[3] The appointment to the AOGCC gave her the opportunity to develop what she saw as the state's God-given resources in a manner consistent with her Christian principles.

Randy Ruedrich, a former oil executive, served alongside Palin on the AOGCC while also working as chairman of the Alaska Republican Party. In the 1990s, he had been involved in a cover-up in which the oil companies BP and Doyon were illegally disposing of hazardous materials down oil wells to save money. While on the AOGCC, he used his position as chairman of the Republican Party and his relationship networks among the state's

---

3. Sarah Palin, *Going Rogue* (New York: Harper Collins, 2009), 93.

Republican politicians to solicit oil dollars—essentially bribes—to fund the party in what amounts to a severe ethical violation.

Palin tried multiple times to resolve Ruedrich's ethical lapses from within the AOGCC by going up her own chain of command, as far as the governor. When Governor Murkowski refused to take the issue seriously, she realized that in order to take on the corruption within the AOGCC, particularly involving Ruedrich, she would have to take on the entire Alaska Republican Party. She turned over incriminating evidence about how Ruedrich was engaging in back-room deals with oil executives to funnel money into the state's Republican Party. She then resigned her position in disgust at how much Alaska's government was being run by cronyism and bribes between oil executives and public servants. Ruedrich pleaded guilty to ethical violations and had to pay a $12,000 fine. However, he remained the chairman of the Alaska Republican Party.

In exposing how Ruedrich had used his government position to make deals with oil executives to fund the Alaska Republican Party, Palin earned the ire and enmity of established Republican bosses. Her role in uncovering the scandal would transform her from a small-town mayor, who campaigned on an anti-abortion platform, into a political outsider who championed "the people" over the "elite" oil executives and established politicians.

That populist persona became her brand as she moved into the governorship of Alaska in 2006, became McCain's vice-presidential candidate in 2008, and emerged as the leader of the Tea Party in 2009. And the persona was something she had rightfully earned, because she had taken on some of the most powerful people in the state in order to recover ethical oversight of Alaska's oil resources. Her brand of populism promised to bring oil-based prosperity back to the people of Alaska instead of letting it become locked up among elites engaging in unethical dealings.

Chapter 8

The Second Bush Years

Populism, Oil, and the Prosperity Gospel

In 2004, a leader in a growing movement among evangelical Christians purchased the land and buildings of what had once been Jim and Tammy Faye Bakker's Heritage USA resort. Rick Joyner, the director of Morningstar Ministries and an apostle in the New Apostolic Reformation, believed that God had commissioned him to restore the derelict buildings, and even more importantly, the derelict reputation of the church that came with the televangelism scandals of the 1980s. Like the Bakkers and other televangelists, the New Apostolic Reformation embraces the prosperity gospel; it also encourages Christians to seek "kingdom wealth" so that they can further God's kingdom on earth.

Many Christians did not support Joyner's plan to remake Heritage USA, and some were horrified to find that he was now broadcasting his church services from the same site as Jim and Tammy Faye Bakker in the 1980s. As a growing number of American Christians learned about the New Apostolic Reformation, they rejected the movement completely. However, the influence of the New Apostolic Reformation grew so immensely at the turn of the twenty-first century, and into the 2010s, that many Christians who denounced it accepted some of its lighter, less-controversial teachings.

Joyner's purchase of Heritage USA came the year after American troops, under the direction of George W. Bush, invaded Iraq. The purchase came four years after evangelicals helped bring him to the highest office in the land and two years before Alaskans elected Sarah Palin as governor of their state. While Bush may not have been party to the New Apostolic Reformation, many of its leaders supported him, along with evangelicals, whose votes put him into office. Palin has been a longtime follower of the New Apostolic Reformation, and the movement became particularly strong in Alaska.

Oil politics and prosperity theology became further intertwined in a symbiotic relationship through the New Apostolic Reformation, particularly under the influence of Bush and Palin. Though many Christians opposed (and still do oppose) the movement, the War on Terror, particularly in Iraq, and subsequently high oil revenues in Alaska helped embed this relationship in the public consciousness.

IDEOLOGY: NEW APOSTOLIC REFORMATION

Fundamentalism today does not look the same as it did when the movement first began in the latter part of the nineteenth century. The goal of fundamentalism remains much the same as it has throughout the history of fundamentalism—that goal being the recreation of the first-century church—but ideas of what the first-century church looked like and how one should recreate it have changed. For the early fundamentalists, recreating the first-century church meant believing in the five fundamentals: that the Bible is inerrant, that Jesus was born of a virgin, that He died a substitutionary death, that He came back to life and will one day return, and that the Bible offers a literal account of the events it records. According to the early fundamentalists, believing these five points set one apart from liberal modernists and made one a true Christian, in continuity with the early church.

Fundamentalism today still holds to the five fundamentals, but its focus has shifted to growing and replicating churches in a manner consistent with how the earliest Christians grew and replicated their churches. Church growth and replication has been a feature of Christian practice throughout the history of Christianity, to varying degrees; what sets the current church-growth movement apart and qualifies it as fundamentalist is the way its leaders see themselves as recovering the methods used by the first-century church. The New Apostolic Reformation uses what its leaders see as first-century models for church growth with the goal of transforming secular government.

The architect of the New Apostolic Reformation was C. Peter Wagner (1930–2016), a church-growth specialist who worked at Fuller Seminary from 1971 until 2001. He viewed the New Apostolic Reformation as a movement that broke with traditional denominationalism—separating different groups of Christians into categories, such as "Catholic," "Protestant," or "Orthodox," based on their beliefs and worship practices—in such a way that revived the New Testament, first-century office of the apostle. The New Apostolic Reformation bypasses cumbersome denominational structures, such as boards and committees, in favor of church congregations placing trust directly in the pastor. In this movement, the pastors hold the office of apostle, which Wagner viewed as someone who is commissioned by God with the duty of empowering and commissioning members of the church. The pastor-apostle is not necessarily a theologically trained, ordained member of the clergy, as the process of attending seminary and attaining formal ordination is long and burdensome, as well as inconsistent with how Wagner viewed the apostles of the first-century church. Rather, the pastor-apostle rises into the role through relationships with people in the church, thereby proving his or her character and calling to the apostolic ministry.

The New Apostolic Reformation is a movement that seeks to place apostles and empowered lay Christians in positions of authority, particularly within secular occupations outside the church, through which they are able to transform cities and nations for the Kingdom of God. Much of this transformation occurs by engaging in spiritual warfare against demonic beings that hold people, buildings, corporations, governments, and nations in spiritual bondage. Through spiritual warfare, the apostles and lay Christians are able to wrest power away from demons so that those once under bondage can experience prosperity as part of the Kingdom of God. Beliefs about demons and practicing spiritual warfare have long had a place in Christian thought and praxis; what sets the New Apostolic Reformation apart is that it looks at entire people groups as under demonic oppression and sees the exorcising of demons as eradicating all social evils, including systemic poverty, government corruption, and drug addiction. This view was communicated in the *Transformations* video series, which many churches, including Palin's, used as a model for understanding spiritual warfare.

In addition to apostles, the New Apostolic Reformation sees the office of the prophet as necessary for first-century models of the church. Prophets receive words from God, often about current events but also about decisions that people in the church should make, and pass those prophecies on. These extra-biblical prophecies do not carry the same weight as prophecies in the Bible, but the apostle and prophet can use them to make decisions about church governance. Not a few of these extra-biblical prophecies—such as the one that Palin's pastor made about Alaska, its oil, and the End Times (see Chapter 3)—are directly connected to how the apostles and prophets view government and world events. Along with apostles, prophets have the ability to hear directly from God and have a high level of authority in their communities; church members confer this authority to the prophet, like the pastor-apostle, as he (almost always he) comes into his position by earning their trust rather than acquiring formal theological training.

Wagner believed that the New Apostolic Era began in approximately the year 2001. Before that time, church government was too structured, in the form of denominations and church boards, to be effective in carrying out the church's mandate of exercising dominion (see Chapter 10 for dominion theology). He believed that with the move towards pastor-apostles as charismatic, trusted authority figures for church congregations and communities, church government shifted enough that Christians could begin to successfully carry out their apostolic roles. However, the vast majority of churches in the United States, even those that embrace Wagner's teachings on some level, continue to operate within denominations and/or have a leadership structure that includes church boards and administrative staff. In fact, the sector that embraces the teachings of Wagner more than any other Christian group, Pentecostals, still operate primarily through the Assembly of God denomination.

Many fundamentalists and evangelicals who are aware of what the New Apostolic Reformation is are very much opposed to it. Some denounce the idea of modern-day apostles and prophets as unbiblical, as those offices came to a close with the first generation of Christians. Many oppose Wagner's teachings on the prosperity gospel and claim that the call to take dominion contradicts Jesus' message of serving others and turning the other cheek. Yet many evangelicals opposed to the New Apostolic Reformation had the same goal as leaders in the movement, including getting an evangelical Christian in the White House and promoting a conservative agenda in public policy. George W. Bush, an evangelical Christian who was supported by leaders of the New Apostolic Reformation (particularly Lou Engle), carried 68% of the white evangelical vote in 2000 and 78% in 2004.[1]

There is a critical intersection between the fundamentalist-nationalist beliefs of Jerry Falwell and the Religious Right from the 1980s and the post-denominational views of the New Apostolic Reformation. Falwell and his followers believed that America is a Christian nation that will soon face the wrath of God unless the country instates biblical morality as a guiding principle. As such, the government needed to ban what Falwell viewed as immoral practices, particularly abortion and gay marriage, as well as bring voluntary prayer back to public schools and take a hard stance against the Soviet Union. The New Apostolic Reformation takes this idea of America as

---

1. Reported by Pew Research.

a Christian nation further by asserting that Christians need to be in positions of government authority. For many fundamentalist and evangelical voters in the year 2000—the year before when Wagner believed the New Apostolic Era would begin—that Christian was the current governor of Texas, George W. Bush.

NATIONAL: THE ELECTION OF GEORGE W. BUSH

> Christ, because He changed my heart.
> —George W. Bush, when asked who his favorite philosopher is

Prior to the 2000 election of George W. Bush, the United States had seen a national return to liberal values in the presidency of Bill Clinton (1993–2001). His Don't Ask, Don't Tell policy allowed for LGBTQ+ individuals to serve in the military, and he signed legislation that imposed environmental regulations on businesses, particularly regarding the use of pesticides and other chemicals in agriculture. He increased funding for public schools, pressed for laws aimed at gun control, and even made efforts at healthcare reform. Though Clinton was a moderate Democrat, for those who longed to see *Roe v Wade* overturned and voluntary prayer put back into public schools, he was a nightmare.

During the Clinton years, many fundamentalists and evangelicals were beset by fears of a New World Order and the Antichrist, due in no small part to Tim LaHaye's mega-bestselling *Left Behind* series. Some began wondering if Clinton, or perhaps his vice president and later Democratic presidential candidate, Al Gore, might actually be the Antichrist; for evidence, they pointed to both the liberal policies that Clinton promoted as well as the scandal that led to his impeachment. Leaders of the Religious Right, particularly Jerry Falwell and Tim LaHaye, deplored Clinton for undoing all of the progress that they had made during the Reagan and Bush years. They saw their challenge as re-invigorating the Religious Right to bring conservative values back to national life and restore America's moral sanity. Meanwhile, leaders of the growing New Apostolic Reformation wanted to find a like-minded Christian to take over the White House. George W. Bush, the evangelical governor of Texas, seemed to be the answer to their prayers.

Bush was far from the first evangelical to occupy the highest office in the land. His father, George H. W. Bush, was an evangelical, as was Jimmy Carter. What set Bush apart was that he was outspoken about his faith, particularly about how his faith shaped his view of politics and even his duties as president, in a way that nobody else had been. While George

Bush, Senior had been demure about his faith, George Bush, Junior was publicly open about how much Jesus had changed his life. In December 1999, while campaigning for the Republican presidential nomination, he attended a televised debate in Des Moines, Iowa. When the moderator asked the candidates who their favorite philosopher was, Bush responded, "Christ, because He changed my heart. When you accept Christ as Savior, it changes your heart. It changes your life." During his campaign, he publicly spoke about the importance of prayer, both in his personal life and in how he managed the affairs of the Texas government; to him, America was a nation of prayer, and the gift of prayer was the greatest thing the people could give him. Additionally, his political views on only recognizing heterosexual marriage, opposing abortion—as well as stem-cell research, on the grounds that an embryonic life was being destroyed—and providing federal funding to faith-based programs came directly from his personal faith. Though critics claimed he was using Jesus and evangelical Christianity for political gain, in the 2000 election, 40% of Bush's votes came from the Religious Right. Rather than being an evangelical Christian who happened to be president, Bush was the country's first evangelical president.

Prior to becoming president, when Bush was serving as governor of Texas, he implemented a series of faith-based initiatives, particularly regarding child-care services and drug-addiction centers. In "Bible-belt" areas like Texas, churches often run child-care services, as well as rehabilitation centers for drug and alcohol addicts. Like any other facility that deals in human services, these faith-based centers have long been subject to stringent state regulation and licensing requirements—which some saw as nothing more than bureaucratic red tape—in order to keep their doors open. Governor Bush passed legislation that would help them stay open without worrying about burdensome state regulation: faith-based child-care and rehabilitation centers could remain open without state licensure. Rehabilitation centers could apply for an exemption to licensure, while child-care centers could be accredited by the faith-based organizations that operated them.

Supporters lauded the opportunity for these centers to remain open, as they believed that the churches that ran them—rather than the state—would provide oversight and accountability. That they were run by faith-based organizations meant that they had an added spiritual component that state-run services could not provide. Critics derided what they saw as the opportunity for faith-based organizations to bypass basic health standards, such as requiring training for drug counselors, and potentially create abusive environments. One tragic situation in which the faith-based initiative did lead to abuse was through the Texas Association of Christian Child Care Agencies, which had been set up to accredit faith-based child-care centers in Texas.

Those that the association regulated received 50 times as many complaints of abuse and neglect as centers that the state licensed. The worst case may have been the Roloff Homes, which had been founded by the fundamentalist pastor Lester Roloff to reform troubled girls through biblical discipline. The girls would be beaten, forced to read the Bible instead of being allowed to sleep, and put into isolation, where they had to listen to sermons for hours, sometimes days on end. The violations were so severe that in 2001, the Texas legislature declined to renew the law allowing for alternative accreditation of faith-based child-care and rehabilitation centers.

Yet Bush saw the faith-based initiatives in Texas as having been a success, owing to the number of child-care and rehabilitation centers that had been able to remain open under the law. They had been able to provide services to people who might otherwise have not been able to procure the assistance that they needed. As president, he went on to establish the Office of Faith-Based and Community Initiatives to replicate, on a national level, the policies that he had instated in Texas. The office provided federal funding for faith-based organizations, particularly those in poor communities, that were poised to serve the needy. Many of these organizations only hired people of the same faith, with the vast majority only hiring Christians; many also engaged in evangelism as part of their services to try to get people to convert. That the office was using tax dollars to fund religious programs led to claims that Bush was violating the separation of church and state. However, for the conservative Christians who supported the president, the faith-based initiatives represented the best possible model for how the government should manage social services. Instead of giving welfare payments to the poor, the government could empower entire communities by helping to strengthen churches and the services that they provided.

Bush believed that he held the presidency not only because of the will of the sovereign people, but also because of the will of God. He also claimed that the only reason he had become president was because of how much Jesus had changed his life. Lou Engle, one of the leaders of the New Apostolic Reformation, believed that the prayers of faithful Christians had led to the Bush presidency, and Tim LaHaye saw Bush as hand-picked by God for the role. The fundamentalist megachurch pastor John Hagee said that any who oppose Bush are the incarnation of evil itself. Dr. James Dobson, the conservative evangelical leader who chaired Focus on the Family, saw Bush as God's own instrument to preserve the country.

A large number of evangelicals who lacked the public mouthpiece of individuals like Engle and Dobson supported Bush on more moderate grounds. They wanted to see an end to the national scourge of abortion, and Bush adamantly opposed abortion. Should he have the opportunity to appoint a justice to the Supreme Court, he would almost certainly pick one who would vote to overturn *Roe v Wade*. Some evangelicals feared that the government, if it continued the liberal policies of Clinton, would begin infringing on their rights as Christians by forcing conservative churches to hire LGBTQ+ ministers or requiring Christian schools to teach evolution to children. Having an evangelical in the White House would allay those fears and ensure that they could continue to freely practice their faith while promoting pro-life legislation.

GLOBAL: SEPTEMBER 11 AND THE WAR ON TERROR

> God has raised up America to be a tool in these last days,
> To get the Gospel to the uttermost parts of the earth.
> —Tim LaHaye, in a *60 Minutes* interview

Bush's life was deeply embedded in the oil that had fueled Texas' economy ever since Patillo Higgins had prophesied that Spindletop would flow with oil. In 1977, Bush started the oil and gas exploration firm Arbusto Energy, which merged with Spectrum 7 a few years later. Bush never proved to be a successful oilman—only about half of the wells that his company drilled struck oil—but during his oil years, his faith transformed into what he saw as true discipleship of Jesus Christ. When oil prices collapsed in the late 1980s, the event that threw Alaska into a severe recession, Bush nearly went bankrupt. His failing oil company was saved when the Harken Oil Company bought it, and he left the oil business completely shortly before the Persian Gulf War. Oil and faith would later prove to be the two defining features of the Bush presidency, particularly regarding the War on Terror.

The first few months of the Bush presidency dealt heavily with energy policies. His vice president, Dick Cheney, had been CEO of the oil giant Halliburton, and he encouraged energy policies that would grow US access to foreign reserves. Bush encouraged the production of fuel-efficient cars while also incentivizing drilling and exploration, particularly within the United States. The country continued to import much of its oil from the Middle East, particularly from Iraq, in what critics saw as subsidizing the oppressive Saddam regime. Rather than promote renewable energy and wean the United States off of oil, he proposed drilling in Alaska's ANWR region as an alternative to importing Iraqi oil. In 2002, instead of signing the Kyoto Treaty, which would have set targets for lowering greenhouse-gas emissions, he asked Americans to voluntarily reduce their carbon output; in January 2004, he claimed that energy production was more important than reducing CO_2 emissions. The faith-based presidency of the former oilman was not going to lead to a decreased dependence on oil.

On September 11, 2001, people's attention shifted—at least temporarily—from the president's faith-based policies and exploration and drilling incentives to the horrific scenes unfolding in downtown Manhattan, Washington DC, and a field in Pennsylvania. Osama bin Laden, another man made wealthy by oil, had financed an operation in which al-Qaeda terrorists hijacked commercial airliners and crashed them into high-profile targets—the World Trade Center, the Pentagon, and one aimed for the White House but diverted by passengers away from its intended target. The nation immediately went into mourning for the thousands of innocent lives lost in the worst attack on US soil since Pearl Harbor in 1941.

When images of hijacked commercial airplanes crashing into the World Trade Center hit televisions across the country on September 11, 2001, readers of Tim LaHaye's *Left Behind* series saw something so demonic that it had to have come straight out of the book of Revelation. The apocalyptic images seemed to parallel those of Saddam's 1990 invasion of Kuwait, which had sparked fears of Armageddon a decade earlier. Surely the End Times were at hand, and Christian America had a righteous duty to rid the world of the demonic terrorists who would commit such an atrocity. They looked to their Christian president for answers, and he directed them into a War on Terror that would penetrate the most oil-rich regions of the world.

A month after the September 11 attacks, on October 7, 2001, the United States invaded Afghanistan, where intelligence experts believed bin Laden was hiding. But attention soon turned to Iraq and Saddam Hussein amidst claims that he was making weapons of mass destruction (WMDs) intended to target the United States. In March 2003, Bush directed an American invasion of Iraq, in what he termed Operation Iraqi Freedom, to intercept any WMDs, dismantle the Saddam regime, and liberate the Iraqi people. Bush called the effort a crusade, alluding to the Medieval wars in which armies of European Christians traveled to the Middle East to take control of the Holy Lands from the Arab Muslims (along with a minority of Arab Christians and Jews) who lived there. Leaders of the Religious Right endorsed the war wholeheartedly.

Tim LaHaye claimed that God had given America a special task to accomplish in the Last Days, and he saw the war as fitting in with the End-Times prophecies of the Bible. Pat Robertson saw the war as consistent with biblical principles and believed there would be few to no civilian casualties. Jerry Falwell delivered a circular entitled "Is God Ever Pro-War?" dated January 29, 2004, in which he defended the war in Iraq on biblical grounds. He said,

President Bush declared war in Iraq to defend innocent people. This is a worthy pursuit. In fact, Proverbs 21:15 tells us, "It is joy to the just to do judgment, but destruction shall be to the workers of iniquity." One of the primary purposes of the church is to stop the spread of evil, even at the cost of human lives. If we do not stop the spread of evil, many innocent lives will be lost and the kingdom of God suffers.

C. Peter Wagner, the architect of the New Apostolic Reformation, saw anti-war protestors as emissaries of the devil, as he believed that the Christian life is about spiritual warfare. In a sermon that he delivered at the Freedom, Freedom, Freedom! conference in Everett, Washington on November 2–4, 2006, Wagner did not distinguish between spiritual warfare and armed combat that involves national troops. In an article that he wrote for the website Elijah List, he claimed that Saddam Hussein was a demonic leader and that the people of Iraq worshipped a demon who went by the name Allah ("Allah" is the Arabic word for "God" and is used by both Christians and Muslims). To him, America had been called by God to engage in a righteous war against the devil. For Wagner, the war in Iraq was the epitome of spiritual warfare.

Though many leaders in the Religious Right took a hard stance on the War on Terror and particularly the Iraq war as being a righteous cause, many evangelicals had a more moderate view. The vast majority supported the war, largely because they were concerned about national security, especially if Saddam was stockpiling WMDs. They saw Bush as the leader for the war, not because he was a righteous crusader, but because the Bible says that Christians are to honor those in authority. He may have seen himself as leading a righteous crusade, but for the majority of evangelicals, he was an American leader who was doing what he thought, based on national intelligence, was best for the country.

Critics of the war saw it as being waged not over a righteous cause or even to target terrorism (weapons of mass destruction were never found in Iraq, and the intelligence was found to be faulty) but rather to secure American access to Iraq's immense oil reserves. They derided the invasion of Iraq as a blood-for-oil campaign that cost thousands of American and Iraqi lives. Further, the War on Terror—which increased US influence throughout Central Asia, in countries such as oil-rich Azerbaijan as well as Afghanistan—was a cover to enable US-based oil companies to access the region's oil in a manner that bypassed the hostile countries of Iran and Russia. President Bush and his cabinet answered these critics by saying that oil revenues from Iraq would fund both the war and the country's reconstruction.

Ironically, some in the Religious Right who supported the war also saw it in terms of oil. Shortly after the invasion of Iraq, the late John Walvoord's former colleague, Charles Dyer, wrote a book entitled *What's Next? God, Israel and the Future of Iraq*. Dyer, a fundamentalist dispensationalist, had already written volumes on the role of oil in the fulfillment of End-Times prophecies, and he saw himself as an expert on the Middle East. In *What's Next?* he argued again for the significance of Iraq's oil reserves as underlying the economic power of Babylon in the Last Days.

Yet not everyone in the Religious Right supported the War on Terror. Richard Mouw, then the president of Fuller Seminary, worried that statements that people like Falwell, LaHaye, and Robertson were making—some of which pointed an unsympathetic finger at Muslims—would drive further antagonism against the United States and widen the gulf between Christians and Muslims. Some worried about the uncertain future of missionaries in Iraq and other Arab countries; those fears were well-founded, as Muslim extremists did kill several missionaries from the United States who were working in Arab countries. Others worried that the future of Christianity in the Middle East was at stake, fearing that if Arab Muslims began to associate Christianity with the American invasion of Iraq, they might begin persecuting Arab Christians. However, these voices were in the minority and could not stem the evangelical support of the War on Terror.

The overt evangelical support of the War on Terror and the underlying oil politics were not new to the United States. Bush Senior had forayed into the realm of faith-based oil politics in Operation Desert Storm a decade earlier in a war that had also cast Saddam Hussein in a demonic light and sparked fears of Armageddon. But Bush Junior solidified, at least in the American public consciousness, the relationship between the Christian faith, access to cheap oil, and the tangled web of Middle East politics. But in the country's northernmost state, that relationship had long been established.

LOCAL: ALASKANS ELECT GOVERNOR PALIN

In early 2003, as the possibility of an American-led invasion of Iraq became not only a possibility but also an inevitability, analysts began forecasting that decreased oil production in Iraq would cause prices to increase. The war did bring Iraqi oil to a virtual standstill, and the oversupply of oil, which had begun in the late 1980s, began to decrease, causing the price of oil to skyrocket. The Iraq war was one of a continuum of factors that caused the price of oil to begin an upward climb, moving from about $30 a barrel at the beginning of 2003 to nearly $150 a barrel by the middle of 2008. American consumers in some places were paying more than $4 a gallon to fill their cars with gasoline, more than double what they had paid before the war began. People who had experienced the energy crisis caused by the 1973 OPEC embargo could not help but notice, yet again, that events in the volatile, oil-rich Middle East had a direct impact on the lives and wallets of American citizens.

The state of Alaska, whose oil-based economy is directly tied to the oil fields of the Middle East, saw a different effect. While the price of gasoline rose for Alaskan consumers filling up their cars and ATVs, the increased price of a barrel of crude sent more money to the government and expanded the reserves in the Permanent Fund. The state went into a period of renewed, oil-based prosperity, and the people had a new, unlikely hero: the former mayor of Wasilla who, in 2004, had bucked the establishment of the Republican Party to expose the Randy Ruedrich scandal. When Sarah Palin was elected governor of Alaska in 2006, the war in Iraq was still reshaping life in the Last Frontier.

During this time, Alaska was experiencing a boom from the skyrocketing oil prices that were, at least in part, connected to the Iraq war. Through 2003, the cost of a barrel of North Slope crude oil remained under $30. That price began a steady upward trend in 2004 so that by 2006, the price had more than doubled, to more than $60. Yet an opaque oil-tax code, known as Economic Limit Factor, was so complicated that Alaskan residents—along with many legislators—could not understand how the government calculated oil taxes. In fact, despite the skyrocketing price of oil, PFD payments—which are based on the investment performance of the Permanent Fund and represent a percentage of oil revenue that the state receives—were actually lower in 2004 and 2005 than in 2003, before the price oil began to climb. Alaskans were not seeing the money that the higher price of oil should have been bringing in to the state.

The factors underlying Alaska's oil-based economy are certainly complex, but there was one reason in particular why oil money was missing from the government's coffers: bargains being made between VECO oil executives and some of the state's politicians. VECO is the same company that had been giving bribes to Ted Stevens, and an FBI raid in August 2006 revealed that his son, Ben Stevens—who was president of the Alaska state senate—had also been receiving bribes. In return for bribes, VECO executives were dictating how legislators voted on issues related to oil taxes; in some cases, the executives were calling legislators or passing notes to them while votes were taking place.

The FBI raid on Ben Stevens and other politicians suspected of taking oil bribes came just days after Sarah Palin won the Republican nomination in the gubernatorial race. Her opponent, Democrat Tony Knowles, was never charged in the investigation, but many believed he had also been receiving oil bribes. In 2004, Palin had sacrificed a high-paying, cushy job on the Alaska Oil And Gas Conservation Commission to expose the corrupt deals that Randy Ruedrich was involved in. Now, with the FBI investigating multiple scandals involving corrupt deals between oil executives and state politicians, the people of Alaska wanted to elect someone who could not be bought. Palin had proven that she was that person, and she won the governor's race by nearly 10 percentage points.

The first year that Palin was in office, she signed legislation that would end the opaque Economic Limit Factor tax code. The new tax code required that oil companies pay a percentage of their profits, minus some fees that they incurred and some tax credits. The improved transparency of the government under Governor Palin, coupled with a simplified tax code for oil companies, led to the state saving $17 billion over the next few years. The Permanent Fund grew substantially under Palin; in 2005, the year before she was elected, the earnings to the Fund were just over $532 million. In 2006, the earnings were nearly $689 million, and in 2007, when the new tax code went into effect, they were over one billion dollars. PFD payments more than doubled under Governor Palin's administration, peaking at $3000 for every eligible man, woman, and child in the state.

For some Alaskans, such as Jerry Prevo, the war in Iraq was a theological cause that was part of America's God-ordained mission to the world. For others, it was spiritual warfare that Christian America was waging against the demonic powers in the Middle East. But these voices were in the minority. For the vast majority of Alaskans, the war in Iraq, at least in its early years, was an opportunity to demonstrate their patriotism and support of the red, white, and blue. Meanwhile, the Iraq war helped increase the price of oil, and Palin made sure that increased revenue went back to the people, not to elite politicians taking bribes from oil executives.

GLOCAL: THE NEW APOSTOLIC REFORMATION IN ALASKA

When Sarah Palin ran for governor of Alaska, her Christian faith did not figure heavily in her campaign. Many voted for her because the way that she exposed the Randy Ruedrich scandal demonstrated that she would not be bought by oil bribes or cater to the whims of the establishment, even the establishment of the Republican Party. Much of her appeal came in her libertarian ethos, particularly regarding taxes, as many Alaskans want the government to manage the state's oil and leave them alone. Some did vote for her because they wanted to see a Christian running the state, but these voters were in the minority. Quite a few Alaskans who voted for her did not even know that she was a Christian until well into her term as governor.

The New Apostolic Reformation, which seeks to place "apostles" in positions of government authority, is far from mainstream in Alaska and was not on the minds of many Alaskans who voted for Palin. When she ran for governor in 2006, the New Apostolic Reformation in Alaska was very much a fringe movement, though it had been gaining strength, particularly in the Mat-Su Valley. It attracted a fair number of Alaskan Christians who consider themselves libertarians, as its followers asserted that societal transformation is not possible through human intervention; this belief aligned with those who believed that the human intervention of the government harms everything that it touches. Instead, the New Apostolic Reformation teaches that transformation comes only by the supernatural moves of God, by the hands of His apostles in working out spiritual warfare. The New Apostolic Reformation in Alaska grew steadily, with many churches in the Mat-Su valley subscribing to it. The church that Sarah Palin grew up in and attended for much of her adult life is part of the New Apostolic Reformation, and she was very much influenced by the movement.

The pioneer of the New Apostolic Reformation in Alaska is Mary Glazier, an Alaska Native who, since 1990, has been partnering with C. Peter Wagner and other NAR leaders and heading prayer ministries. Glazier herself grew up in a home filled with alcoholism and abuse, a too-common occurrence in Native villages, where social ills such as alcoholism, suicide, and abuse run rampant; many Native villages have abuse rates of 100%, meaning that every single child in the village has been abused. Glazier began a ministry called Intercessors of Alaska in 1990, with the mission of seeking "a battle strategy for the state," particularly regarding the plight of Alaska Natives. Intercessors of Alaska developed a network of prayer ministries throughout the state, those ministries being based on the teachings of the New Apostolic Reformation, particularly regarding spiritual warfare. Glazier became the leader of the Alaska branch of the New Apostolic Prayer Network, which activates Christians all over the world to pray for apostles as they engage in spiritual warfare and seek to have greater measures of influence.

The ministry that Glazier founded, Intercessors of Alaska, became Windwalkers International, a prayer movement that includes many of the apostles of the New Apostolic Reformation. The headquarters of Windwalkers International is in Anchorage, a mere 35 miles from Wasilla. In the early days of Intercessors of Alaska, a member of one of those prayer networks was a young city councilwoman in Wasilla who went on to become mayor and then governor. According to an announcement that Glazier made at a Seattle conference in the summer of 2008, Sarah Palin had joined the prayer network when she was 24 years old and just getting started in politics.[2]

Glazier had an ongoing relationship with Palin's long-time church, Wasilla Assembly of God, as did other leaders in the New Apostolic Reformation. One such leader is an apostle from Kenya named Thomas Muthee, who rose to prominence in the movement for his part in the *Transformations* video series. The series documents cities across the world that were hotspots of crime, endemic poverty, and—according to the series—demonic activity. *Transformations* presents an account in which Christian leaders prayed and engaged in spiritual warfare against the powers of darkness in the cities, driving out the devil and reclaiming the cities for Jesus Christ. In turn, each of the cities featured in the series experienced a transformation, including widespread revivals of people converting to Christianity and endemic poverty turning into endemic prosperity.

Transformations featured Muthee for his role in transforming the Kenyan city of Kiambu, near the capital of Nairobi. He blamed the extreme poverty and high levels of crime in Kiambu to a witch named Mama Jane, and he organized prayer networks to engage in spiritual warfare against her. Muthee claimed that the prayers of Christians expelled Mama Jane from the city, which saw a subsequent revival of people converting to Christianity and experiencing newfound prosperity. Yet rival claims said that Mama Jane never left Kiambu and was actually a pastor of a Christian church, just down the street from Muthee's church. Some went so far as to claim that Muthee had built a reputation for himself and gone on to become a leader of the New Apostolic Reformation by exploiting her.

Whatever the case may be, Muthee, like Glazier, developed a relationship with Wasilla Assembly of God and even visited on several occasions. In a highly publicized service from 2005, Muthee anointed Palin and prayed against any witchcraft that may be used against her. In the same sermon, he said that the engagement of faithful Christians was why George W. Bush held the office of president and that Christians, like Palin, should seek positions of government authority. Palin later credited his prayers as helping her become governor of Alaska.

One feature that the New Apostolic Reformation and dispensational theology have in common is a focus on prophecy. Dispensationalism looks

---

2. This information was provided by Glazier and has not been independently verified. In the same conference, Glazier claimed that at Governor Palin's inauguration, she dedicated the state of Alaska to Jesus Christ; however, this claim was false.

at prophecies in the Bible that have not yet literally been fulfilled within history and sees them as pointing to the End Times. Leaders in the New Apostolic Reformation make extra-biblical prophecies, which they see as normative as long as the prophecies do not contradict anything in the Bible. Leaders and adherents of the movement in Alaska—particularly those connected to Glazier—routinely make prophecies about the state of Alaska, many of them involving the End Times and/or the state's oil. They may prophesy about the people needing to stand strong together against greedy individuals and corporations that want to exploit the state's oil reserves, and some point directly to the state's oil as having a role to play in the End Times.

One such example is when, during the summer of 2008, Governor Palin spoke at Wasilla Assembly of God about the war in Iraq and construction of a new pipeline being God's will. Her pastor followed her talk by claiming that Alaska, with its immense energy reserves, will be a refuge state during the End Times. As shown in Chapter 3, he said,

> There are some things about the natural resources, about the state. There was some things that God wants to tap into to be a refuge for the Lower 48. And I believe Alaska is one of the refuge states. . .in the Last Days. And hundreds of thousands of people are going to come to the state to seek refuge. And the church has to be ready to minister to them. Amen.

This prophecy merged dispensational ideas about the End Times with the prophetic component of the New Apostolic Reformation to demonstrate the relationship between the state's oil and Christian beliefs (although those beliefs are not held by a majority of Christians).

To many of the Alaskans who voted for Sarah Palin in 2006, she represented libertarian values and a hard stance against the corruption that plagued the state's government. But for leaders of the New Apostolic Reformation—particularly for those who had a strong presence in the Mat-Su Valley, such as Mary Glazier and Thomas Muthee—her rise in politics meant much, much more. She was an apostle called by God to politics, and she would help lead the campaign of spiritual warfare, both in the state of Alaska, and later, in the rest of the country.

Chapter 9

McCain-Palin 2008

*Sarah Palin Becomes the New
Face of the Religious Right*

Conservative Christians helped re-elect Bush in 2004, but by 2006, his second-term election seemed like it might have been the last hurrah of the Religious Right. The war in Iraq—which Bush had claimed would be paid for with Iraq's oil money and that many believed would be short—was still raging and increasingly unpopular; thousands of soldiers had died, along with many more Iraqi civilians, and the cost of the war was putting the United States deeper into debt. Ending abortion had been the galvanizing issue of the Religious Right since its inception in the 1970s, but after nearly three decades of conservative activism, abortion was still legal on a national level. Some conservative Christian leaders began questioning whether the strategy of electing Republican politicians was an effective means of being a moral voice and effecting Godly change in the world.

Long-time leaders of the Religious Right, like Tim LaHaye and Pat Robertson, had less clout among 2006 voters than they had enjoyed in the 1970s and 1980s. Younger evangelical voters saw them as old-fashioned preachers with political ambitions, and concerns about the environment and the poor were more important to these new voters than ending abortion. Jerry Falwell, the man who had founded the Moral Majority in 1979, would die the next year, in 2007. After his death and especially going into the 2008 presidential campaign season, many believed that the Religious Right as an organized voting bloc had fallen apart.

Then Sarah Palin came onto the scene.

During his tenure as a US senator, the "straight-talking" John McCain had done little to accommodate the Religious Right. In fact, in a speech that he gave in 2000 when he was running against George W. Bush in the Republican primaries, he referred to its leaders—specifically Pat Robertson and Jerry Falwell—as "agents of intolerance." Understandably, when he ran for president in 2008, he did not carry much appeal with this bloc of voters. And when the fundamentalist leader John Hagee gave him an endorsement, he rejected it. James Dobson, of Focus on the Family, openly declared that he could not vote for John McCain.

Not that McCain was nonreligious; he claimed to be a devout Christian who had profound spiritual experiences while being tortured in a Vietnamese POW camp. But his vice presidential pick, Sarah Palin, was the one who re-invigorated the caucus of conservative Christians and won many of them over to the McCain campaign. The Alaska governor did more than say that she was pro-life. She had recently given birth to a child with Down's syndrome and, at the time of her nomination, was facing her teenage daughter's pregnancy. In both of these difficult circumstances, abortion was decidedly not an option for her. With Sarah Palin as the star of the campaign, James Dobson changed his stance and announced that he would absolutely vote for McCain.

In the end, Palin's pro-life stance was not enough to garner enough of the Religious Right's support and save the McCain campaign. Ironically, in 2008, Barack Obama poised himself as the "values" candidate, as he valued healthcare, the poor, and the environment. Many of the younger evangelical voters endorsed these values, rather than ending abortion, and threw their support behind the Democratic candidate. No longer staunch Republicans, evangelical voters were becoming more liberal.

By the time the election results were called on November 4, 2008, the obscure governor of the Last Frontier was in the national spotlight. And she was taking her place as the de facto successor to Jerry Falwell in remaking the Republican Party into something that would once again have appeal among conservative Christians. While Falwell's sons, Jerry Junior and Jonathan, would take over his leadership at Liberty University and Thomas Road Baptist Church, Palin would rebuild the Religious Right by bringing it back from the fringes of conservativism and make its ideals central to the Republican Party's platform.

IDEOLOGY: CHRISTIAN DOMINIONISM

A central component of the New Apostolic Reformation is something that C. Peter Wagner called "dominion theology," sometimes also referred to as Christian dominionism. Wagner saw the entire Bible through the lens of dominion, which he interpreted as the authority to exercise power and rule as kings, both over creation and over other people. In his view, God had commanded Christians to take dominion over the world and given them the authority to do so through the substitutionary death of Jesus and his resurrection. In exercising dominion, Christians can bring the Kingdom of God into areas that had been under the control of Satan and his demonic forces.

Matthew 28:18–19 records Jesus telling his disciples, shortly after his resurrection, "All authority in heaven and on earth has been given to me. Go therefore and make disciples of all nations, baptizing them in the Name of the Father and of the Son and of the Holy Spirit." (ESV) Christians, particularly those with conservative theology, have long viewed this passage as the Great Commission because in it, Jesus instructs them on what their task is as his disciples. They are to tell people of all different nations who he is, baptize new Christians upon conversion, and disciple converts to become life-long followers of Jesus. Yet Wagner interpreted this passage as Jesus mandating that his disciples turn not just individual people but entire nations into disciples. Christians had to exercise dominion by rising into positions of authority—such as being manager of a company or even president of the United States—and then casting out the demons that prevented the populations under their rule from converting to Christianity. In this manner, Wagner believed, populations that had suffered under systemic oppression would quickly become prosperous as evidence that the Kingdom of God had come to them.

Wagner frequently spoke about what he called the "seven mountains of dominion." The seven mountains are education, religion, family, business, government and military, arts and entertainment, and the media. Christians have focused most of their energy on the mountain of religion by building up churches, yet they have neglected the other mountains. Wagner and his followers believe that Christians need to take over all seven mountains by coming into positions of authority in those areas. For example, they need to take over the mountain of education by becoming superintendents and school board members, the area of business by becoming CEOs, the mountain of government and military by becoming executive-level politicians and high-ranking military officers. From their places of authority in these mountains, Christians should exercise dominion and spiritual warfare by casting out demons so that they can claim the mountain for the Kingdom of God.

Wagner was aware of what would be necessary for Christians to come into these positions of authority and exercise dominion: massive amounts of what he called "kingdom wealth." He said that the first sign of gospel transformation is that the good news ("gospel" means "good news") is preached to the poor; good news for the poor is the absence of poverty, in other words, wealth. The true gospel message brings people wealth because, according to Wagner, Jesus does not want Christians to be poor. When confronted with accusations that he was preaching the prosperity gospel, Wagner's response was that yes, he was. He believed that Christians having large amounts of wealth was not only biblical but necessary in order for the Kingdom of God to expand on earth.

Another way that leaders in the New Apostolic Reformation have described the mandate for Christians to take authority over the seven mountains is that they should "infiltrate" the different spheres of national life. They don't go to Hollywood studios or publishing houses declaring that they are going to take over arts and entertainment for the Kingdom of God; rather, they go into the seven mountains as "marketplace apostles" who perform their jobs to the best of their abilities. While doing their jobs and presumably rising up the employment ladder, they cast out the demons that hold that mountain in bondage. None of the secular employees may even be aware of what the marketplace apostles are doing until the Kingdom of God falls upon the entire mountain. The Kingdom presence is measured in terms of the prosperity that comes alongside it.

Critics of the New Apostolic Reformation and dominion theology are particularly concerned about the idea of Christians taking over the mountain of government. In fact, some leaders in the New Apostolic Reformation use the term "overthrow" to refer to how they intend to take over government. Critics believe that this idea represents theocracy, a system in which a country is governed by religious laws and led by religious leaders. The way that George Bush, Junior used his presidency to advance Christian causes, even drawing the country into a war that he described with religious terms, further heightened concerns that the United States could very well be headed towards a theocratic form of government.

Yet Wagner denied that dominion theology promoted theocracy and believed that Christians could take over the government by purely democratic means. Even though Bush had used the office of the president to promote Christianity, he had been democratically elected—not once, but twice. As such, he was supported by the sovereign will of the American people and the hand of God, both of which had worked together to promote him to the highest office in the land. Leaders of the New Apostolic Reformation wanted to continue putting Christian leaders in high positions of authority, from which they could exercise spiritual power and cast out demons, so that they can fulfill the Great Commission of discipling entire nations.

The use of national political office to promote Christianity is nothing new in American history. Civil religion in the United States has a long history, and there has long been a conflation between civil religion and Christianity (particularly Protestant Christianity) among fundamentalists and evangelicals. The New Apostolic Reformation is unique in that its scope is much broader than anything that William Jennings Bryan or Billy Graham could have imagined. Through overseas engagements, such as the War on Terror, leaders of the New Apostolic Reformation saw the opportunity to achieve their goal of evangelizing the world by discipling entire nations. In other words, they could use the pulpit of the United States to fulfill their interpretation of the Great Commission. When Sarah Palin stepped onto the national scene in 2008, the Religious Right was ready for her.

NATIONAL: SARAH PALIN BECAME JOHN MCCAIN'S 2008 RUNNING MATE

John McCain was a United States senator from Arizona who had a reputation for being a straight talker; he would sit with reporters until he had answered every question to their satisfaction. As a moderate Republican, he promoted environmental protections; improvement of the country's public schools, particularly those with failing standards; and development of renewable energy, in addition to off-shore drilling, to create energy independence. He also strove for bipartisan engagement and compromise, rather than ideological entrenchment, on divisive issues. Some compared him to Nelson Rockefeller, the liberal Republican who inherited part of the Rockefeller fortune. Like Rockie, McCain set his sights on the presidency; he lost the Republican nomination to George W. Bush in 2000 but won it in 2008.

When the straight-talking McCain selected the obscure governor of Alaska to be his running mate in 2008, he thought Sarah Palin was a straight-talking moderate like himself, someone who could talk to journalists and satisfy their most probing questions. She had proven herself by standing up to oil interests while serving on the AOGCC and again as governor of Alaska, even though doing so made her an outsider to the Republican establishment. Like McCain, she was willing to go against the grain of her own party to maintain her sense of personal integrity and do what she believed was best for the people. Yet when Palin entered the 2008 race as McCain's vice-presidential nominee, she showed herself to be not a straight-talking moderate but rather a populist who appealed to the far-right voters that felt neglected by the establishment.

When Sarah Palin's name was announced as McCain's vice-presidential candidate at the 2008 Republican National Convention in Dayton, Ohio, journalists and analysts scrambled to find out just who this unknown governor of the isolated state of Alaska was. Overnight, the national media descended on the small town of Wasilla and neighboring Anchorage to uncover the story of the populist politician whose rhetoric had fired up every person in attendance at the RNC. When they arrived, they found people who fondly remembered Sarah as the girl who took the basketball team to the state championship in 1982; they also found people who recalled her divisive small-town politics as mayor and plenty who celebrated her pro-life stance. In her acceptance speech at the RNC, she had presented herself as a down-to-earth hockey mom whose son was in the military and would soon deploy to Iraq. She believed that America is still the land of opportunity, and she knew by name the Wasillians who had first voted for her onto the city council, then into the mayor's office, and finally the governor's mansion. Governor Palin, McCain's vice-presidential nominee, was still Sarah of Wasilla.

Not that Palin was the only populist in the 2008 election. McCain had been characterized as a populist by the Republican Party, having broken ranks with its establishment in the past and won votes from people who felt that the party had lost touch with them. Democratic presidential hopeful Barack Obama's campaign motto was "We Can Change," and he positioned himself as the candidate who could feel the pain of voters. What set Palin apart was that while Obama and McCain resonated with the anger of voters who felt ignored by Washington, Palin seemed to feed into their anger. When President Obama was trying to push through healthcare reform in 2009, Palin coined the term "death panels" and insisted that his socialized medicine would lead to the most vulnerable Americans being euthanized. The charge of death panels was entirely false, but there was another "death panel" that had long concerned the Religious Right: a Supreme Court that had legalized abortion and allowed for the state-sanctioned murder of tens of millions of unborn babies. Palin stoked fears of state-sponsored euthanasia by a government that was willing to slaughter innocent babies.

To leaders of the Religious Right, Palin's presence showed that the country, which had strayed from its founding principles of life, liberty, and the pursuit of happiness, could return to God and find renewed prosperity. One leader in particular who was drawn to Palin's rhetoric was Lou Engle, one of the apostles of the New Apostolic Reformation. *Vanity Fair* obtained an email that he wrote to her just before the vice-presidential debate, in which she would face off with Joe Biden in front of the country. The email read,

> Dear Sarah,
>
> Many thousands are fasting and praying for you. I know you've heard it, but I believe this is an Esther moment in your life. Esther hid her identity until Mordecai challenged her to risk everything for such a time as this. Your identity is "Sarah Barracuda." Esther removed corruption from the Persian government and Haman fell. She didn't have experience, she had grace and favor. Sarah, don't hide your identity tonight. There will be questions given to you that you don't know, and I have been weeping over you. I believe the Lord would have you be real. If they ask you a question that you don't know, don't be ashamed to say: "I don't have the experience of 30 years of politics like Senator Biden, but what I have is character, truth, and integrity, and I haven't been seduced by 30 years of political and moral compromise like these men in DC. I believe America is not looking for more knowledge, they are looking for more character and more truth, and that is who I am. I refuse the politics of neutrality. I will stand for the family, I will stand on foundations of truth and this nation will be better for it.
>
> Sarah I'm sure you're doing this, but take a moment to still yourself before the Lord. The Lord is a shield about you. To those who have no strength, the Lord will show Himself powerful.
>
> Sarah, I could be wrong, but I've been praying for five years for an Esther, with dreams of being a Mordecai to that Esther. I believe you're the one and I think you're even wearing a life band. Tonight don't be ashamed to plead for the life of the unborn and all the wounded woman who have gone through this holocaust. You can throw this email away, but I have 50 young people fasting and praying day and night who are shouting tonight: "Grace, grace to you!"
>
> We love you,
> Lou Engle[1]

In referring to Palin as "Esther," Engle characterized her as the biblical heroine who hid her Jewish identity and entered the Persian king's harem. Esther became queen, and when she learned of a plot by the king's trusted advisor to kill all of the Jews in the empire, she prevented a complete genocide. Her uncle, Mordecai, told her that she had been brought into

---

[1] Michael Joseph Gross, "Is Palin's Rise Part of God's Plan?" in *Vanity Fair*, September 17, 2010.

the palace "for such a time as this," to prevent a disastrous slaughter of the Jewish people. Leaders of the New Apostolic Reformation—not only Engle, but many others as well—saw Palin as an Esther figure who God had also raised up "for such a time as this." For Engle, the slaughter that Palin would end was abortion. As her "Mordecai," he saw himself as her beloved uncle who would advise her in the difficult days ahead. Palin was their "apostle" to take dominion over the mountain of government and thereby bring the Kingdom of God back to the United States of America.

McCain and Palin would lose the election, but she would become the de facto leader of a populist organization known as the Tea Party, which also had strong connections to the New Apostolic Reformation and the broader Religious Right. Her down-home appeal as a common-sense, pro-life hockey mom, combined with her persona of incorruptibility because of her dealings with oil companies, would make her the new spokesperson of the Religious Right.

GLOBAL: OIL POLITICS AND SARAH PALIN'S RISE

When Obama took office in January 2009, he inherited a crumbling economy that had become completely derailed by the financial crisis of 2008. The rising price of oil, which translated into higher gas prices at the pump, had left middle-class Americans reeling. Many working-class Americans could no longer afford to fill their cars up with gas to go to work, and, with an unfolding banking crisis, unemployment and foreclosure rates soared. Furthermore, the unending War on Terror had put the government trillions of dollars deeper into debt and eroded people's faith in what they could expect from their elected officials. President Bush had committed the nation to liberating Iraq on the premise that Saddam had weapons of mass destruction; those weapons were not there, but more than five years later, the United States was still mired in a foreign war.

Despite the lack of WMDs in Iraq, Palin had claimed the summer before the election, when speaking at her church in Wasilla, that the war in Iraq was a task from God. More than half of evangelicals still supported the war, but by 2008, the voting bloc was divided on whether or not the time had come to withdraw US troops from Iraq. With the country in an economic freefall, many evangelicals wanted to see the government focus more on domestic issues, including increased unemployment and homelessness among Americans, the banking crisis that had precipitated the economic recession, and immigration reform. Furthermore, there was still the issue of abortion, and Obama had promised to expand abortion access, not just in the United States but all across the world. Palin's populist ethos resonated particularly strongly among disaffected Republicans, especially those in the Religious Right.

Whereas Palin promoted civil religion during the 2008 presidential campaign, following the victory of Obama, she spoke passionately about the role of the Christian faith in American life. She frequently quoted Bible verses while also speaking about the Founding Fathers and the Christian principles inscribed in the country's founding documents. In 2015, she published a devotional entitled *Sweet Freedom*; in it, she did exactly what Jerry Falwell did with the naming of Liberty University: she referred to the Christian and American notions of "liberty" as if they are the exact same thing. For Palin, like Falwell and other leaders of the Religious Right, protecting American liberty requires the promotion of Christian values, as the Christian religion and American nation both reinforce each other.

In addition to Palin's belief that America is a Christian nation, her foreign policy resonated with the Religious Right. Her foremost policy concern on the campaign trail was energy, particularly as it related to national security. She wanted to increase production in the United States—particularly in Alaska—to put more Americans to work and meet the country's energy and security needs, as had been the goal with the construction of the Alaska pipeline in the 1970s. Further increasing domestic energy production would mean drilling in ANWR, a move that she (and many other Alaskan politicians) supported, as opening up the Arctic to more drilling would create more jobs. Yet increasing domestic oil production was not Palin's only objective in foreign policy. She wanted an increase in American troops in Iraq to bring about victory over there because, as previously shown, she believed that the war was God's will. To her, the war was not being fought over oil, as critics claimed, but rather over the security needs of Christian America and the freedom of the Iraqi people. In other words, Palin's foreign policy was defined by Alaskan oil politics and the belief that Christian America had a God-given mission to the world.

Yet for leaders in the Religious Right, including the dominionists of the New Apostolic Reformation, Christian America could not fulfill its God-given destiny in places like Iraq while the country's courts failed to protect the lives of unborn babies. And Palin was something that Falwell and other leaders of the Religious Right could never be: she was a woman who had refused to abort her Down's syndrome baby and supported her teenage daughter through pregnancy. Whereas the vast majority of leaders in the Religious Right had been white males, Palin came onto the national scene as the embodiment of the pro-life movement. She talked about her love for her son with Down's syndrome at her speech at the RNC and even shared personal details of her pregnancy experience in her autobiography, *Going Rogue*. Her presence alone inspired both male and female conservative Christians to not abandon hope on the pro-life cause and to keep it at the center of both faith and politics.

By 2008, a number of evangelicals, particularly those under 30, had added the environment to their list of concerns. They were becoming increasingly uneasy about fossil fuel emissions contributing to global warming, which was beginning to take a toll on the world's poorest people. Rising sea levels were eroding islands in places like the South Pacific and forcing villages to evacuate, and melting Arctic ice was harming fragile ecosystems. Palin had an answer for these evangelicals, as well: Climate change is real, but it is not manmade. The burning of fossil fuels is not harming the environment, and wildlife can thrive alongside oil wells as long as proper standards are followed. She claimed that oil wells in the United States are less destructive than those in other countries, which do not have the same environmental protections and are more prone to catastrophic spills. Further, God had put the oil into the ground for the people to use wisely and attain the prosperity that was so evident in Alaska and across the country. While developing renewable energy was necessary for American energy independence, there was no reason to stop drilling for oil.

Palin combined the Christian nationalism of the Religious Right with a pioneer ethos that, while still somewhat true of Alaska, does not connect with the reality that most Americans in the Lower 48 live with. She would tell people that Alaskans eat plenty of organic food, after they go out into the woods and shoot it, yet most Americans live in urban centers and do not hunt. The America that she spoke of is a simpler place, unburdened by heavy taxes that prevent entrepreneurship and a force for good in its apprehension of terrorists. People in this America can thrive without a white-collar job or a college degree because they have everything that they need on the rural homestead. This "Middle America" of small-town values looks a lot like Alaska's Mat-Su Valley, at least before oil dollars brought in Targets and Wal-Marts and eroded the pioneering values of its early residents.

But Alaska is no longer the pioneering state that it once was; it has been transformed by the oil pipeline that bisects it. While there are still some homesteads from the state's pioneering days, most of them have been sold and turned into subdivisions. Plenty of Alaskans hunt and fish, thereby getting the "organic protein" that Palin often referred to, but plenty also buy their food at the grocery store and/or farmers markets. Alaskans do not pay a state income tax because oil money funds the state's coffers; instead of paying a state income tax, they get an annual PFD check. Palin's Christian

America was an idealized Alaska, where oil money, not taxes, pays for the government.

Sarah Palin was not an expert on foreign policy, nor was she a theologian who understood the complex relationship between the Christian religion and the United States government. She was an Alaskan politician who knew state-level oil politics, the names of many of her constituents, and how to run a government that derived its income from oil rather than taxes. Yet for many in the Religious Right, which was becoming decidedly more populist in the wake of the election of President Obama, her lack of experience was a bonus. As Lou Engle said in his letter to her, "Don't be ashamed to say: 'I don't have the experience of 30 years of politics. . . I haven't been seduced by 30 years of political and moral compromise." To people like Engle, she was an ideologue who represented the purity of the Christian American nation.

LOCAL: GOVERNOR PALIN RESIGNED

Not that all American evangelicals supported Palin; that she garnered 80% of the evangelical vote in 2008 left 20% on the other side of the fence. Reasons for not supporting her included her insistence that climate change is not manmade and her absence of meaningful policy—other than more drilling for oil to create more jobs—on addressing poverty and unemployment in the United States. Because Obama addressed environmental concerns and promised universal access to healthcare regardless of income, he was able to attract some of the evangelical vote. Of the evangelicals who did support her, most were unaware of the New Apostolic Reformation, and many who knew of the movement did not endorse it. It was on the fringes of evangelicalism and had been decidedly rejected by the majority of evangelicals who had read C. Peter Wagner's version of the prosperity gospel.

Meanwhile, Alaskans watched their governor's foray into national politics with shock and some confusion. Plenty were proud to see Sarah of Wasilla, the "Saracudda" who had led her high school sports teams, represent the Last Frontier on a national stage. She spoke for their home-grown, libertarian values of freedom and hard work against the encroachment of Big Government and socialized medicine. Yet others reeled when the figure making appearances on Fox News and other major media outlets looked like their Sarah but acted completely differently. Governor Palin had worked across the aisle in Juneau to get the job of running the state done, but the vice-presidential nominee was unwilling to compromise with those that did not agree with her. After losing the election, Palin returned to a state that no longer recognized her and that she could no longer govern.

While the rest of the United States was reeling in the 2007–2009 economic recession that included record-high prices at the pump, the state of Alaska was in another oil boom. In addition to high oil prices bringing more money into the state, Governor Palin had passed legislation to build a second pipeline, this one for the natural gas in the North Slope. The natural-gas pipeline was never built, but it would have brought more drilling to the edge of the Arctic Ocean and even greater revenue to the state and its Permanent Fund. Governor Palin anticipated that it would also bring more jobs and provide for the country's energy independence, thereby improving national security. That the pipeline would be built by private companies—Exxon and TransCanada—was a boost to the Falwell-type libertarian mindset that promotes free-market capitalism without government interference.

Following Obama's inauguration, he passed an economic stimulus package to help bring the country out of the recession. The stimulus package strengthened welfare programs while also striving to create new jobs by providing federal investment in infrastructure and energy programs, including renewable energy. Governor Palin saw government spending in energy programs as taking away from the private sector as well as an encroachment on states' rights, as the federal spending would come with new regulations that states would have to follow. She was the only governor in the country who rejected the stimulus package; even when Alaskan residents and politicians pleaded with her to accept the money to help develop renewable energy and provide for rural communities, she refused to be beholden to the Obama administration and his economic policies. She vetoed the federal dollars, but the Alaskan legislature overrode her veto. "The people" of Alaska wanted the federal dollars that Palin had rejected.

Governor Palin's rejection of the federal stimulus package was not the only divisive issue in Alaska. Alaskan residents brought a series of ethics charges against her, beginning when McCain first tapped her to be his running mate and continuing well after they lost the election. Many of the charges were frivolous and included Palin wearing a jacket with the logo of the company that sponsored her husband in a snow machine race. Yet the state had an obligation to investigate all of the charges, and though every single one was dismissed, investigations took thousands of hours and cost millions of dollars. Palin herself incurred $500,000 in legal fees defending herself against the charges. Mired in investigating the frivolous ethics charges, parts of the state government, including the governor's office, came to a standstill.

In the summer of 2009, Governor Palin announced that she was going to resign her post as governor. The divisive issues that the state was facing had taken a front seat to further developing the oil and gas industry, and she wanted to focus on the national issue of restoring the country's Christian freedoms that, in her view, were being eroded under Obama. Her resignation speech, given in Wasilla, spoke of the need to continue promoting private industry while resisting the growth of the federal government. She said,

> People who know me know that besides faith and family, nothing's more important to me than our beloved Alaska. Alaska's mission—to contribute to America. We're strategic in the world as the air crossroads of the world, as a gatekeeper of the continent. Bold visionaries knew this—Alaska would be part of America's great destiny. Our destiny to be reached by responsibly developing our natural resources. This land, blessed with clean air, water, wildlife, minerals, and oil and gas. It's energy! God gave us energy...
> We created a petroleum integrity office to oversee safe development. We held the line for Alaskans on Point Thomson—and finally for the first time in decades—they're drilling for oil and gas. We have AGIA, the gasline project—a massive bi-partisan victory (the vote was 58 to 1!)—also succeeding as intended—protecting Alaskans as our clean natural gas will flow to energize us, and America, through a competitive, pro-private sector project. This is the largest private sector energy project, ever. THIS is energy independence...
> I wish you'd hear more from the media of your state's progress and how we tackle outside interests—daily—special interests that would stymie our state. Even those debt-ridden stimulus dollars that would force the heavy hand of federal government into our communities with an "all-knowing attitude." I have taken the slings and arrows with that unpopular move to veto because I know being right is better than being popular. Some of those dollars would harm Alaska and harm America. I resisted those dollars because of the obscene national debt we're forcing our children to pay, because of today's Big Government spending; it's immoral and doesn't even make economic sense![2]

In stepping down from state-level politics as the governor of Alaska, Palin would continue the position that she had inherited as John McCain's running mate, that of the de facto leader of the Religious Right. With the support of the New Apostolic Reformation, which still lay on the fringes of

---

2. From Governor Sarah Palin's Resignation Speech, July 3, 2009.

evangelicalism, she would soon emerge as the spokesperson of a movement that was, in some ways, a re-invigorated Religious Right: the Tea Party.

GLOCAL: CLIMATE CHANGE IN ALASKA

Though the popular image of Alaska is a frontier of fresh air, roaming wildlife, and clean water, Alaska's interior city of Fairbanks—the state's boom-and-bust hub on the pipeline—has the worst air pollution in the entire country. Sources of renewable energy, which could provide equitable access to cheap, clean heat during the winter, are almost nonexistent in Alaska's interior. Much of the air pollution in Fairbanks is due to people burning wood to heat their homes, as in the isolated interior of Alaska, gas prices can be double or even triple the national average. When gas is unaffordable and winter temperatures plunge to minus 50 Fahrenheit, people burn whatever they can to heat their homes; the result is toxic levels of air pollution that blanket the city every winter. That people in a state whose economy is fueled by oil, in a city that has long been a hub on the pipeline, cannot afford gas presents a compelling picture of how uneven the benefits of oil are.

Despite Palin's insistence that burning fossil fuels does not harm the environment, the situation for Natives in rural parts of Alaska is even more precarious than for residents of Fairbanks. Many Native villages are not only unable to afford fuel; they are also experiencing the worst effects of climate change. Whereas the Arctic Ocean was once full of ice, that ice has now melted; the melted ice is now causing coastal villages to experience a catastrophic level of erosion. Melting glaciers have caused inland flooding in which hundreds of feet of embankment collapse into rivers, and invasive species that thrive in Alaska's warming climate are decimating local ecosystems. Furthermore, toxic fumes from the oil industry on the North Slope have poisoned the air and water and caused high rates of cancer, both among people and Alaska's wildlife. However, like Palin and other Alaskan politicians, leaders of the New Apostolic Reformation and other movements in the Religious Right deny that human activity is causing climate change and continue to promote faith-based oil politics.

Conservative Christians in the United States have long been skeptical about science, particularly since the creation versus evolution debate of the nineteenth century that helped fuel the fundamentalist movement. As with the rise of Darwinism then, the question for conservative Christians—evangelicals, fundamentalists, and many others—today is whether the source of truth is the Bible or modern science. Fundamentalist leaders in particular, including leaders of the New Apostolic Reformation, see the

Bible and modern science as incompatible. Instead of Darwinian evolution, they promote creation science to show that geological and biological markers indicate that the earth was created less than 10,000 years ago.

Because fundamentalists believe that the earth was created relatively recently, they do not see oil as having been formed by geological processes over the lapse of millions of years. Rather, they see oil as having been created by God very early in the earth's history; many believe that God put oil in the ground for people to use. This view was reinforced in Palin's resignation speech, when she said, "Our destiny to be reached by responsibly developing our natural resources. This land, blessed with clean air, water, wildlife, minerals, and oil and gas. It's energy! God gave us energy."

This general distrust of mainstream science and the view of oil that emerges out of creation science are two reasons why so many leaders in the Religious Right today deny that climate change is man-made or that it is even happening at all. Lance Wallnau, Lou Engle, and other leaders in the New Apostolic Reformation see claims about climate change as pseudo-science that contradict the truth of the Bible. Rick Joyner, the apostle who bought Jim and Tammy Faye Bakker's Heritage USA, was himself a climate-change denier; he changed his mind after he went on a documentary with his daughter, an environmental activist who teaches environmental stewardship as a component of Christian faith and praxis, and talked with environmentalist evangelicals about climate change. Yet the vast majority of leaders in the Religious Right today deny climate change or that it is caused by burning oil and other fossil fuels.

Palin is not the only Alaskan politician whose views about climate change are consistent with those of the New Apostolic Reformation. Don Young, the Alaskan congressman who has been serving in the House of Representatives in Washington DC since the 1970s, said on his website,

> Alaska is the focal point in the global warming debate. I do not challenge that climate change is occurring, but the central question awaiting an answer is to what extent man-made emissions are responsible for this change. Contrary to popular opinion, that question remains unanswered. Those who claim otherwise perpetrate a tremendous disservice to science and society, and I am shocked by the continued marginalization of any dissenters.
>
> Our state is witnessing the effects of climate change more so than any other state in the Nation. This has caused some in Congress to use Alaska as an example for the need to curb these effects. However, these proposals seek to legislate a solution to a problem we do not fully understand, and if enacted,

could result in drastic consequences for our State's and Nation's energy, economy, and national security.[3]

In addition to doubting the science that climate change is happening and that it is man-made, some of these leaders see claims about climate change as part of a liberal agenda to impede on capitalist and libertarian values. Environmental controls and federal involvement in the development of renewable energy represent further encroachments of the government, as well as impede on individual freedoms and free-market capitalism. When Governor Palin vetoed the federal stimulus package that would promote renewable energy in Alaska, she was aligning herself with this aspect of the Religious Right: federal dollars going into the energy sector would erode the freedoms of private business to practice free-market capitalism. The nemesis of free-market capitalism and private business is the archenemy that both Billy Graham and Jerry Falwell spoke out against during the early years of the Religious Right: a state-controlled economy, leading to communism.

The oil industry remains an undercurrent of the New Apostolic Reformation's goal of taking dominion over the seven mountains of culture. For many of the leaders of the Religious Right today, acknowledging that burning fossil fuels has caused harm to the environment means acknowledging that libertarian capitalism is not always compatible with the Bible and their interpretations of Christian thought. It means changing how they think about creation, creation science, and the truths of the Bible. It also means changing how they view the American nation, the notion of Christian freedom, and what the nation's mission to the world really is.

In other words, changing the way that conservative Christians think about oil means changing the way that they think about the Bible and what being a Christian in the world really means.

---

3. Don Young, "Global Warming," on Don Young, Congressman For All Alaska. https://donyoung.house.gov/issues/issue/?IssueID=5006 Accessed February 9, 2020.

Chapter 10

The Birther Movement and the Tea Party

In the Obama years, the Religious Right had a new leader, one who was every bit as charismatic as Jerry Falwell and able to attract crowds to events that, in some ways, mimicked Falwell's "I Love America" rallies from the 1970s and 1980s. These rallies were known as Tea Parties, named after the far-right movement that Sarah Palin was activating in the wake of the Obama election. Like the Religious Right that Falwell galvanized in the 1980s, Tea Partiers believed that the government was infringing on their personal freedoms and liberties. They relied heavily on a theological movement that also emerged in the 1980s but did not gain the same traction as Falwell's Moral Majority: Christian Reconstruction and theonomy.

At Tea Party rallies, Tea Partiers often wore costumes that represented either their view of how America currently stood or the ideals to which it should return. The most popular costume was colonial garb, which included knee breeches and a three-corner hat for men and a long dress with a bonnet for women. Some Tea Partiers draped themselves with either the American flag or the "Don't Tread On Me" Gadsden flag, which has a picture of a coiled snake ready to strike. The prevailing idea behind the regalia was that America needed to return to the Christian principles that the Founding Fathers had in mind when they wrote the United States Constitution.

Speaking to the costume-infused rallies of the Tea Party was a politician whose experience was largely confined to Alaska's oil politics and a government that collected very low taxes from the people, as it derived its income from oil. For Sarah Palin, that oil was part of the Christian-American tradition and proved that the national economy could be rebuilt with lower taxes, more private businesses, and less welfare and social spending. Her faith-based oil politics, coupled with Alaska's libertarian ethos, reflected the political and economic views of theonomy and Christian Reconstruction.

IDEOLOGY: THEONOMY

> Government will occur at the state and local level,
> and society will center on families.
> —Rodney Clapp, in a 1987 expose on theonomy

Possibly the greatest dividing line among American Christians today is the question of how they should understand the Bible's relationship to modernity and to national life. Should Christians apply modernist critiques to the Bible and acknowledge that society and culture today, particularly in the United States, are vastly different than in biblical times? Or should they continue to uphold the Bible as normative and authoritative for all aspects of modern life, including approaches to science? Perhaps there are other ways, as well, with which Christians can apply the Bible to modern society.

In 1973, as Jerry Falwell's fundamentalist-nationalist movement was beginning to take root, a theologian named Rousas John Rushdoony promoted the idea of Christian Reconstruction and theonomy. Rushdoony's parents immigrated to the United States from Armenia to escape the genocide of 1915–1916, in which 1.5 million Armenians were slaughtered by the Ottoman Turks. Christianity had become the state religion of Armenia in the fourth century, and most Armenians remained Christian when the predominantly Muslim Ottoman Empire conquered the country 12 centuries later, in 1555. The genocide from which Rushdoony's family fled began with systematic massacres of Armenian Christians, and his parents nearly became casualties. This background of Christianity as the state religion of a country that became subject of a genocide undoubtedly influenced Rushdoony's thought on Christian nationalism in the United States. Christian Reconstruction is a system of belief that asserts that Christians must reconstruct society so that it conforms to biblical law. Theonomy, in the view of Rushdoony and the Reconstructionists, is the belief that biblical law must be normative for how governments and societies function; otherwise, they are doomed to fail.

Rushdoony grew up in California and attended the University of California at Berkeley during the Great Depression years of the 1930s. In this milieu, his professors taught communism as a progressive ideology while the federal government was implementing the socialist policies of President Roosevelt's New Deal. During those same years, the Soviet government was heavily persecuting Christians, including Armenians who had fled to Russia during the genocide. Rushdoony's work was, in some ways, a reaction against the times in which he lived. He taught that because society had rejected the Creator God and instead substituted paltry theories of Darwinian evolution, people had lost their sense of meaning in life and society had lost its sense of order. People had replaced the sovereignty of God with statism, in which power became concentrated in a central government; people trusted in that government, rather than the timeless truths of God as revealed in the Bible, to solve their problems and create a better society. Rushdoony believed that modern society had become so sick, due to its reliance on the state and its socialist policies, that its only hope for survival was to be "reconstructed" according to the laws of God as laid out in the Bible.

That reconstruction would not come from a theocratic takeover of the federal government but rather a severe restriction of its scope and a return to small-town values. Rushdoony saw the Bible as promoting a limited government, which had to be centered on small, local institutions, particularly individual churches, small businesses, and families. Leaders of these institutions would promote biblical law within their communities; government institutions, such as welfare programs, public schools, and homeless shelters, would be abolished in favor of churches functioning as the center of society. He was a champion of the homeschool movement and believed that in order for a Christian society to thrive, parents should educate their children at home instead of sending them to a government-run public school. Rushdoony taught that, in homeschooling children, parents were raising up a generation of children who would take dominion for the Kingdom of God.

In the 1950s and 1960s, Rushdoony received money from the Volker Fund, a libertarian charity that promotes free-market economics, so that he could develop his ideas, particularly his approach to education. He went on to found the Chalcedon Institute in 1965 to promote his views on theonomy and Christian Reconstruction. The Chalcedon Institute continues to advocate free-market capitalism as the economic system endorsed by biblical law and libertarianism, albeit with the biblical consequences for sins such as homosexuality, as the basis for government. In promoting a biblical government via a reconstructed society, Rushdoony taught that Christians were bringing the Kingdom of God to earth. Followers of Rushdoony's thought see their economic and political principles as a Bible-based libertarianism that is supported by the United States Constitution.

Rushdoony's writings on theonomy, particularly a 1973 compendium on the 10 commandments entitled *Institutes of Biblical Law*, had a significant influence on some of the leaders of the Religious Right in the 1970s and 1980s. In 1974, Billy Graham's magazine, *Christianity Today*, declared *Institutes of Biblical Law* as the most important theological work of 1973. Some of the country's leading fundamentalist universities, including Liberty University and Oral Roberts University, began using Rushdoony's writings on theonomy—the rule of God as the normative means by which societies function—in their law schools; additionally, Rushdoony made appearances on shows run by televangelists, including Pat Robertson's *The 700 Club*. However, though leaders in the Religious Right embraced theonomy, during the years of the Moral Majority in the 1980s, it remained on the fringes of evangelical theology. Many evangelicals rejected theonomy, along with Christian dominionism.

In 1987, an article in *Christianity Today*, entitled "Democracy as Heresy" by Rodney Clapp, analyzed the movement of theonomy and Christian Reconstruction and said,

> In the Reconstructed society, there will be no federal government. Nor will there be a democracy, which Reconstructionists regard as "heresy.".. [G]overnment will be republican, with the Bible as the charter and constitutional document. Government will occur at the state and local level, and society will center on families. The family will be ordered in a patriarchal fashion. . . Parents will be responsible for the education of their children. Public, or "government," education is thought to rob the family of the right to shape its children by biblical beliefs.[1]

In the 1950s, as Rushdoony was beginning to develop the ideas of Christian Reconstruction and theonomy, a journal called *The Christian Economist* caught the attention of Gary North, who had recently graduated from high school. The journal was financed by an ultra-wealthy oil businessman, J. Howard Pew, and promoted what is known as the Austrian school of economics. The Austrian school of economics rejects socialism and government intervention in the economic realm, as it sees government activities as harming markets and preventing them from correcting themselves. Austrian-school economists believe that private property and private businesses, which must be deregulated and allowed to function

---

1. Rodney Clap, "Democracy as Heresy," in *Christianity Today*. February 20, 1987.

solely according to the needs of the market, lead to the greatest freedoms of individual people and the best economic outcomes for society. *The Christian Economist* influenced North, who promoted theonomy and Christian Reconstruction in the sphere of economics.

North married Rushdoony's daughter, Sharon, and he and his father-in-law became an influential force in the promotion of free-market capitalism as a biblical economic system. He described his calling as working to understand the relationship between free-market economics, namely the Austrian school, and Christianity. The Volker Fund, which financed much of Rushdoony's early work, also provided funding for some of North's work, as he advocates libertarianism as the basis for sound economic policy. The Austrian economics that North promoted, along with other libertarian aspects of Rushdoony's theonomy and Christian Reconstruction, became embedded in the Tea Party movement that emerged following the 2008 election of President Obama.

GLOBAL: THE GREAT RECESSION

The Religious Right years of the 1980s, when the Moral Majority and other Christian-based, neoconservative groups were gaining cultural and social capital, saw the slow but steady rise of Christian Reconstruction and theonomy. Though theonomy remained on the fringes of the Religious Right, during the latter Bush years, particularly when the housing crisis began in 2007, it saw a resurgence among conservative Christians who were dissatisfied with the country's economic policies. Gary North in particular had been advocating free-market capitalism, deregulation, and the government no longer getting involved in the economy.

Alan Greenspan, who had served as the Chairman of the Federal Reserve from 1987 until 2006—spanning the presidencies of Ronald Reagan, George Bush Sr., Bill Clinton, and George Bush Jr.—had also advocated for free-market capitalism, deregulation, and the government no longer getting involved in the economy. With minimal government oversight, in the late 1990s and early 2000s, banks began offering highly risky mortgages to people who did not have the means towards home ownership; in some parts of the country, such as California, banks would offer a mortgage to anyone, regardless of income and credit. The terms of the mortgages were often so complex that the people who bought homes with them did not understand how the interest rates would fluctuate or that their monthly payments would double, triple, or even quadruple. Millions of the country's poor took out these subprime mortgages, and to keep up with the demand on the mortgage market, the real-estate market entered a boom. Real-estate companies were selling houses as quickly as banks could produce the subprime mortgages, and government regulators were nowhere to be found to put an end to the unethical and risky financial practices. When mortgage payments skyrocketed and hundreds of thousands of people went into foreclosure, the real-estate and mortgage markets—which had flooded investment portfolios with toxic assets—collapsed. The result was the global recession of 2008–2010.

The recession, which began with the toxic mortgage and housing assets that had been freely written to the American poor, jumped across the United States' borders and entered countries from Great Britain to Iceland to Dubai to China. Banks in places like London and Paris held the toxic assets—billions of dollars' worth—in their own portfolios; furthermore, the British prime minister promoted "light-touch" economics, in which the government would only minimally regulate the financial practices of the country's banks. Banks all across the world began trading on speculations of credit—essentially buying IOUs from each other—and hemorrhaging money when those assets, which were essentially subprime mortgages from the United States, were found to be insolvent.

When the first US bank failed due to the toxic assets of the subprime lending market—Bear Stearns in early 2008—the US government, under the advice of President Bush's Secretary of the Treasury, Henry Paulson, bailed the bank out to keep the American people from losing money that they had invested in Bear Stearns. Yet the bank failed anyways, and thousands of Americans lost all of their savings. When Lehman Brothers failed shortly thereafter, the government decided not to bail the bank out. It collapsed and nearly took the global financial sector down with it.

The collapse of the banks in the United States reverberated all across the world. In London, the failure of Lehman Brothers meant that the London branch had no money to pay its employees, who suddenly lost their jobs. In France, workers who were being laid off without getting paid organized kidnappings of their bosses; the American-based companies that they worked for were becoming defunct as a result of the financial collapse, and thousands of French workers were becoming unemployed. In Spain, unemployment skyrocketed so high that the government offered to pay immigrants to return to their home countries. In Dubai, the glamorous capital of the oil-rich United Arab Emirates, the government forcibly rounded up immigrant workers who were out of work but waiting for paychecks that would not come. And in the United States, foreclosures forced so many families into homelessness that sidewalks turned into tent cities.

More banks began to go under—Goldman Sachs, Merrill Lynch, Morgan Stanley, and the insurance group AIG. The response to the financial meltdown, and the very real possibility of a global depression, was the greatest level of government intervention in the American economy since the Great Depression. Paulson authorized billions of dollars' of emergency relief funds to bail out the troubled financial institutions, the very same institutions that had caused the crisis by engaging in unethical lending practices. Yet critics saw Paulson—himself the former CEO of Goldman Sachs, in which position he had also engaged in unethical and risky financial practices—as heavily responsible for the crisis. To add insult to injury, after he authorized the unpopular move of funding the troubled banks, their CEOs used a large portion of the taxpayer money that they had received to award themselves bonuses.

When President Obama took office in January 2009, he inherited the failing economy. His administration continued the program of bailouts to the troubled banks, as allowing those banks to fail would cause Americans to lose billions of investment and retirement dollars and deal a catastrophic blow to the country. Yet once again, the CEOs of banks who received the Obama bailout money used those taxpayer dollars to award themselves multi-million-dollar bonuses. American investments and jobs were safe—at least, for some—but the American public became incensed that while they were experiencing foreclosures and layoffs, their tax dollars were funding corporate bonuses.

President Obama went on to pass the Homeowners Affordability and Stability Plan to help homeowners who had taken on subprime mortgages and were in danger of losing their homes. The plan put the mortgages under government jurisdiction—funded by taxpayer money—rather than the private jurisdiction of the banks that had written the mortgages. Critics of Obama's economic policies saw him as using their tax dollars to reward people who had taken out irresponsible mortgages. Furthermore, they decried that the government was regulating the private financial sector and putting troubled banks under government jurisdiction.

Austrian-school economists, such as Gary North, saw no benefit to the deprivatization of the banks. North saw free-market capitalism and the ownership of private property as not only in keeping with biblical principles but as the basis for a healthy society. Meanwhile, private oil companies in the United States—which remained subject to little government regulation—thrived. Investors saw oil shares as safe investments, because even in an economic downturn, people still had to buy gas for their cars. While oil-based economies, such as in the Middle East and Alaska, certainly felt the shock of the financial crisis, they fared much better than other parts of the world. For theonomists and other Austrian-school economists, the reason was simple: a privately owned business that the government does not regulate will, by its very nature, fare better economically and, in the process, promote the public good.

NATIONAL: THE RISE OF THE TEA PARTY AND THE BIRTHER MOVEMENT

The financial collapse of 2008 began only two weeks after John McCain introduced Sarah Palin as his running mate in the election; the announcement came on August 30, and Lehman Brothers filed for bankruptcy on September 15. While Palin may not have been a theonomist herself, at least not as Rushdoony promoted theonomy, her faith-based oil politics and small-town, populist appeal made her a favorite of the theonomist movement and Austrian-school economists. She promoted private businesses without government interference and burdensome regulations, and she saw her small hometown of Wasilla as emblematic of what the rest of the country could be. While she did not talk about its high rate of homeschoolers—which both Rushdoony and North heavily promoted—or its lack of diversity, the message was clear: she stood for the old-fashioned, small-town values of Middle America, the Christian communities that had been run over by Wall Street and the government's response.

Gary North was intrigued by Palin. Shortly after her nomination by McCain, he wrote of her, "In one week, she has changed the face of American politics... In short, she can re-make the office of Vice President—re-make it by returning it to the Constitution. She can define it. She can become the lady with the gavel."[2] When she and McCain lost the election, she only temporarily returned to her post as governor of Alaska. A few months later, she emerged as the de facto leader of a resistance movement against not the banks behind the collapse but the American government itself: the Tea Party.

The Tea Party took its name from an event that helped spark the American Revolution, the Boston Tea Party of 1773. The British crown had instated a series of taxes on the American colonists to help pay for the French and Indian War; all of the taxes provoked outrage from the Americans who were subject to British law but had no representation in British parliament or recourse in British courts. Colonists decried "taxation without representation" and, in the middle of the night on December 16, 1773,

---

2. Gary North, "Sarah Palin: The First Good Old Girl in America's National Politics." September 9, 2008.

a group dressed like Mohawk Indians boarded a ship loaded with imported tea. They proceeded to dump all of the tea into Boston Harbor as a means of protesting the tax and demanding fair representation in the political process.

For adherents of the Tea Party movement, the "tea" was an acronym for "taxed enough already." They decried taxes that took away from private property and private businesses to support socialist welfare programs and, even more enraging, the bank bailouts and corporate bonuses. While there was no single leader of the Tea Party, its most prominent patron was Sarah Palin. Her speeches, which railed against the Obama administration's deficit spending and what she saw as backroom deals, aroused anger among people who were being hit hardest by the housing crisis and ensuing recession.

More than deficit spending and bailouts to the Wall Street giants who had caused the 2008 recession, the issue that angered Tea Partiers the most was that the election of Obama was, in itself, a violation of the United States Constitution. The constitution stipulates that the president must be a native-born citizen of the United States, but a so-called "birther" movement, which began during Obama's campaign, called into question whether he was, in fact, born a citizen. The conspiracy actually began when supporters of Hillary Clinton, against whom Obama was running in the Democratic primaries, circulated information online claiming that he had not been born in the United States. At first, the Obama campaign did not take the rumor seriously. However, it grew perniciously enough that in June 2008, the candidate released the short form of his birth certificate, which proved that he had been born in Hawaii.

After Obama clinched the Democratic nomination, Republicans took up the accusation that he was not a natural-born citizen. Claims suggested that he had actually been born in Kenya or that he had dual British-American citizenship. Long after even conservative Fox News host Bill O'Reilly affirmed that Obama was a native-born US citizen, the birther movement continued to incite anger that the Obama presidency was altogether a violation of the constitution.

The person inciting the anger that continued to fuel the birther conspiracy was not Sarah Palin but rather the person that she would endorse as the Republican candidate for president in January 2016: Donald Trump. By that point, the Tea Party had moved from the fringes of the Republican Party to being its central platform. People who held to the Tea Party ideology would embrace him wholeheartedly and earn a new moniker: the Alt Right, for the far-right views that have not historically been part of the Republican Party.

In 2011, the Pew Research Center issued a report on the Tea Party and the Religious Right. Researchers had found that white evangelicals—the demographic most represented in the Moral Majority of the 1980s—were disproportionately represented in the Tea Party. Indeed, the Tea Party's platform, which opposed same-sex marriage and promoted a strong national defense while lowering taxes, especially for the rich, and severely curbing welfare, strongly resembled the tenets of the Moral Majority. More than the Moral Majority, though, it is also a revamping of the Christian Reconstruction and theonomy movement from the 1980s.

Not that the Tea Party was synonymous with the Religious Right. In fact, it was bigger than the Religious Right and had a wider base of support. Yet the Tea Party, which established the "Freedom Caucus" (a name reminiscent of Falwell's Liberty University), re-invigorated conservative Christian voters in a way that the McCain campaign had been unable to in 2008. The Tea Party took one of the most primeval symbols of the American nation, the Boston Tea Party, and imbued it with Christian meaning by appealing to a biblical form of government and economics based on the theonomic system of Rushdoony, North, and their followers.

LOCAL: GOVERNOR WALKER AND ALASKA'S PERMANENT FUND

When Sarah Palin served as governor of Alaska, she initiated tax reforms that changed how oil companies operating in Prudhoe Bay paid income to the state. The effect on the state's budget was pronounced: In fiscal year 2006, tax revenue from oil stood at just under $2 billion, but in fiscal year 2007, when her reforms went into effect, that amount was nearly $3 billion; by fiscal year 2008, oil taxes stood at nearly $8 billion. The increase in oil revenue under Palin's new tax laws meant that the state government could fund new roads and better schools while also balancing the budget. With the increase in oil revenue, Alaska was in a period of prosperity while the rest of the world was suffering from the effects of the financial crisis and ensuing recession.

By 2009, though, oil prices had crashed from $140 a barrel to $30 a barrel, and Alaska's revenue was reduced by half. Furthermore, the financial crisis of 2008 had hurt the Permanent Fund, which had investments in banks and stocks that had crashed. The recession did hit Alaska—the state's unemployment increased by just over 1% in 2009, and PFD payments decreased as there was less money in the Permanent Fund—but not nearly as hard as other parts of the country. Soon, with a lower budget and a first-time budget deficit, the oil-financed Permanent Fund would become the center of Alaskan politics.

To compound the financial woes that the state was now becoming mired in, in 2013, Palin's successor, Governor Parnell, changed the tax reforms that she had implemented. Her ACES tax code had provided more transparency to the state's petrodollars and how oil companies paid taxes; the result was a budget surplus, and the state saved $17 billion over the six years that ACES was in effect. Yet productivity on the North Slope was down, and some politicians blamed the ACES tax formula for de-incentivizing oil companies to drill in Alaska. In 2013, Parnell replaced ACES with SB 21, also known as the More Alaska Production Act (MAPA) to try to increase oil production by cutting oil taxes. Under ACES, oil companies paid roughly 30% of their revenue in taxes, but under MAPA, that amount bottomed out to as little as 1.5%. With a combination of low oil prices and reduced oil taxes, the state began to spend down the $17 billion that Palin had saved in order to finance its deficits. When that money disappeared, some Alaskan politicians looked to the Permanent Fund to meet the state's budgetary needs.

When Governor Jay Hammond created the Permanent Fund in 1976, there was no legislation that stipulated exactly how the money in it should be used. Some thought that the money should be re-invested into the state's economy by developing new industries outside of oil; that way, when the oil stopped flowing or oil prices tumbled, the entire economy would not go down. Others saw the Permanent Fund as an endowment for the state, whose sole purpose was to generate interest that would be paid back to the people every year in their annual PFD payments. Still others saw the Permanent Fund as a back-up supply of money in case of a budget deficit. When Alaskans elected Bill Walker as governor in 2014, nearly four decades after the establishment of the Permanent Fund, the debate as to its purpose had still not been settled.

In addition to debates over how to use the Permanent Fund, the state was now in a massive budget shortfall due to MAPA's decreased oil taxes. While the libertarianism behind the decreased oil taxes appealed to many Alaskans, the fact remained that the state's budget was almost entirely dependent on oil money. To help fund the state's growing budget crisis, Governor Walker attempted to tap into the Permanent Fund. He intended to use the money to fund programs such as education, but doing so would reduce the amount of interest that the Permanent Fund earns. As such, tapping the Fund would reduce the PFD payments that Alaskans would receive for years to come.

The response was overwhelmingly negative, especially from people who saw the purpose of the Permanent Fund as generating revenue for their annual PFD checks. Alaskans do not own the mineral rights on their property, so they are not allowed to turn a profit on any natural resources on their land without a special permit from the state. Instead, all of the state's natural resources are held in a collective trust, which prevents one private business—such as the Standard Oil juggernaut at the turn of the twentieth century—from building monopolies and halting capitalist competition. Under this system, the oil under Alaska's ground actually belongs to the people, and they have the legal right to receive a share of the oil money in return for the fact that they do not have mineral rights on their own private property. Hence, many Alaskans see the PFD as a pre-tax tax that the oil companies, via the state, pay to them for the natural resources that they own. If the governor attempted to tap into the Permanent Fund to finance the state's budget, he would be taking the money that they are rightfully entitled to.

Additionally, many libertarians in Alaska, particularly Christian nationalists who subscribe to ideologies such as those of the Moral Majority and Christian Reconstruction, do not think that the government should be funding so many programs in the first place. They want to privatize education, Medicare and Medicaid, and other public programs that the state pays for so that the only thing that the government does is protect their individual rights.

Resistance against Governor Walker's attempt to tap into the Permanent Fund was so fierce that he lost his re-election campaign in 2018 to a Republican, Mike Dunleavy, whose campaign promise was to restore the PFD. Meanwhile, the state's budget woes have compounded, as the state remains tied to the oil industry, the ups and downs of oil prices, and incentives to make sure that companies continue to produce on the North Slope, all while attempting to receive a fair share of taxes to redistribute to citizens via the PFD. Following Dunleavy's election, he would attempt to instate a budget that would closely resemble the libertarian platform of the Tea Party (see Chapter 11).

The biggest problem associated with Governor Walker's attempt to use the Permanent Fund to make up the state's budget deficit was not that it would reduce people's PFD payments. The biggest problem was that the state was still addicted to oil and financed almost entirely with oil money. Any change in oil prices or production on the North Slope might mean that the state is unable to pay public school teachers or pave roads; furthermore, the petrodollars fueling the government mean that the state's politicians remain easy targets for oil magnates who need people in power to advance their agendas.

GLOCAL: THE KOCH BROTHERS IN ALASKA

Closely associated with the Tea Party, and providing much of its funding, is the organization Americans for Prosperity. Americans for Prosperity, centered in Arlington, Virginia and headed by Tim Phillips, actively campaigns for deregulation of energy, especially the fossil fuels that scientists say are contributing to climate change. This deregulation includes significantly reducing, or eliminating altogether, corporate taxes (especially on energy companies) and revitalizing America's coal industry; it also supports increased drilling, especially in places like ANWR and Native lands throughout the United States. Like Palin, Americans for Prosperity calls for privatization of the energy sector and denies that climate change is happening and/or that it is caused by the burning of fossil fuels and other human activities. Americans for Prosperity also wants to limit the powers of the Environmental Protection Agency, if not abolish it altogether.

Behind Americans for Prosperity is not a grassroots organizing effort of concerned citizens but rather two of the richest oilmen in history: Charles and David Koch (David died in 2019). The Koch brothers are longtime libertarians who have used their immense fortunes to promote legislation that favors their private corporation, Koch Industries. Koch Industries includes many chemical, petroleum, and paper companies, amongst others, as well as 4000 miles of oil pipeline. All of these oil- and chemical-based companies contribute to Koch Industries being—according to a 2010 study—one of the 10 biggest polluters in the entire country. In addition to wanting to curtail the EPA, the Koch brothers have long funded programs that deny climate change; there is even a hall at the Smithsonian Institute named the David A. Koch Hall of Human Origins, which shows that climate change is normal and necessary for the development of human civilization. By promoting deregulation of private industry and gutting the EPA, the Koch brothers have been able to protect their business assets and build a fortune worth tens of billions of dollars.

Koch Industries, under the subsidiary Flint Hills Resources, from 2004 until 2014 operated the largest oil refinery in Alaska, near the pipeline's hub city of Fairbanks. The North Pole refinery contracted with the United States government to provide jet fuel to the nearby Eielson Air Force Base until a massive chemical leak in 2014 contaminated much of the soil and water in and around Fairbanks. The spill polluted hundreds of residential water wells and also further damaged ecosystems that are already collapsing due to the exacerbated effects of climate change in the Arctic. Though the Koch brothers only operated the refinery for 10 years, that timeframe was long enough for them to develop a vested interest in the state's pipeline, as well as its libertarian ethos.

Determining which politicians have received money from the Koch brothers is a challenge, as one of their lobbying groups, Citizens United, won a Supreme Court case that said that private companies and individuals do not need to publicly report their campaign donations. But in 2013, when Alaska's legislature, under the urging of Governor Parnell, repealed Palin's ACES tax system, which had generated a $17 billion surplus for the state, and replaced it with lower taxes under MAPA, the state's government played into the libertarian agenda of the Koch brothers. The man elected governor in 2018, Mike Dunleavy, was heavily funded by Koch money; Americans for Prosperity supported his controversial budget vetoes that slashed the states' social services, healthcare, and educational sector (see Chapter 11). One Alaskan politician who may not have fallen into the entanglements of Koch money is Sarah Palin, who ironically went on to lead a national movement—the Tea Party—that was heavily funded and trained by the Koch-backed Americans for Prosperity.

Americans for Prosperity, FreedomWorks, the Institute for Free Speech, and other Koch-funded groups present themselves as if they are grassroots organizing efforts that are led by concerned citizens. Yet what they represent is something called astro-turfing, in which corporate and/or political sponsors push their agenda in such a way that it appears to be the concern of everyday citizens. The way that the oil industry in Alaska has become the personal interest of the state's residents, though they no longer see a fair share of revenue from it and are experiencing severe effects of climate change, is a prime example of astro-turfing. That many Alaskans vote for politicians based on their promises about the PFD demonstrates just how intimately linked oil money and the state's politics are. Oil industries, such as those of the Koch brothers, present their corporate interests for lower taxes and government deregulation, particularly of environmental policies, as if they are in the best interests of "the people" (assuming that "the people" are a coherent whole). But the people that those policies benefit are oil magnates who have been using their money to expedite the political process.

Today, the massive industry run by the Kochs looks strikingly similar to the global monopoly that JD Rockefeller held in Standard Oil at the turn of the twentieth century. Like Rockefeller, the Koch brothers have given exorbitant amounts of money to philanthropy, including funding for healthcare, the arts, and research grants. Also like Rockefeller, they have used their money to exert power over the Republican Party so that it supports their own business interests. Like Rockefeller, they make those interests look like the will of the people, whom they are benefiting by providing oil. And like

Rockefeller, they have helped make sure that the world remains addicted to oil, in their case, by promoting deregulation of oil, stripping legislation that imposes environmental restraints, and denying that fossil fuels are driving any kind of climate change.

The Tea Party, which relied heavily on the economic libertarianism of the Religious Right—including the Moral Majority, but more importantly, Christian Reconstruction and theonomy—was indebted to the oil money that funded it. That money came from the Koch brothers, who paid for the new leader of the Religious Right, Sarah Palin, to travel to and speak at many of the Tea Party's events. The Religious Right in the United States today is every bit as bound up to petrodollars as the fundamentalist movement was at the turn of the twentieth century.

Chapter 11

Make America Great Again

The Religious Right's Support of Trump

In November 2016, the editors of *Oxford Dictionary* announced that the word of the year was "post-truth." Post-truth refers to "circumstances in which objective facts are less influential in shaping public opinion than appeals to emotion and personal belief."[3] Other words that made the shortlist for word of the year were "Brexiteer," "adulting," and "alt-right." But with the divisive vote on Brexit in the United Kingdom and the election of Donald Trump in the United States, the editors of *Oxford Dictionary* decided that "post-truth" best encapsulates the spirit of the age in which we now live.

In our post-truth world, people no longer trust "the establishment" or the-so-called "facts" that it panders. Hence the rise of another term in 2017: alternative facts. The term was coined during a debate about the size of the crowd at President Trump's inaugural ceremony; Sean Spicer, then the press secretary for the new president, claimed that "this was the largest audience to ever witness an inauguration, period." In a CNN interview in which she defended Spicer's statement, Trump's then senior advisor, Kellyanne Conway, claimed, "Our press secretary gave alternative facts." Later in the interview, she said, "Think about what you just said to your viewers.

---

3. "Word of the Year 2016." (Oxford University Press, 2016).

That's why we feel compelled to go out and clear the air and put alternative facts out there."[4]

Post-truth politics and alternative facts are only symptoms of a greater malaise, the origins of which are much deeper than Trump's election and inaugural ceremony. Much of that malaise can be traced to the oil politics and religious fervor of the 1970s, which seemed to be a foreshadowing of the 2010s.

From a global perspective, Donald Trump's administration represents only one in a slew of populist governments that came to power in the 2010s. These governments embrace "illiberal democracy," to use a phrase coined by Hungary's populist autocrat, Viktor Orbán. These illiberal democracies are characterized by polarizing rhetoric, division, othering, nativism, and alternative facts. Sarah Palin's endorsement of Trump in January 2016 was part of a broader, global movement that saw the rise of populist governments with nationalist views of religion and that systematically exclude those who are not of "the people."

IDEOLOGY: TRUMPISM

Some of the more technical theological points of the New Apostolic Reformation and Christian Reconstruction are incompatible with the dispensationalism of Falwell's Moral Majority. However, Christian Reconstruction and theonomy, along with their close relative, Christian dominionism, have the same goal as Falwell, of remaking the United States into the Christian nation that, in their view, the Founding Fathers intended. They sought to restore Christian and American values, particularly liberty, by bringing biblical principles to bear on the national government; more than converting individuals to Christianity, they aimed to revert the nation to Christianity. Falwell sought to restore what he saw as the Christian element in the Constitution and other founding documents, while Rushdoony and the theonomists sought to make the Bible the constitution of the land.

In 2016, journalists from all over were perplexed as to why so many conservative Christians in America's Religious Right supported the candidacy of Donald Trump. Yet the evangelical support of Trump did not emerge in a vacuum; rather, it is the product of Moral Majority-style American nationalism and Christian patriotism, the prosperity gospel, the New Apostolic Reformation's Christian dominionism, and Christian Reconstructionism's

---

4. Eric Bradner, "Conway: Trump White House offered 'alternative facts' on crowd size." CNN. January 23, 2017.

theonomy, all brought to the forefront of the re-invigorated Religious Right through the faith-based oil politics of Sarah Palin.

The evangelical support of Trump came as a shock to many who had not been party to Christian Reconstruction and/or the Tea Party. Trump had been divorced twice and was then married to a woman who is 24 years younger than him and had posed nude for magazines. During his campaign, he made inflammatory statements aimed against racial minorities, immigrants, and people with disabilities, as well as misogynistic statements towards women. He was known to engage in affairs with women and make sexual advances without the woman's consent; on one recording, he bragged about grabbing women's genitals. Few people expected that the Religious Right would back such a figure, and then continue backing him as one scandal after another unfolded.

Yet Trump also represented all of the political goals endorsed by the Religious Right since Jerry Falwell and his colleagues organized it in the 1970s. Despite statements made before his 2016 campaign, he appealed to the Religious Right by saying that he wants to overturn *Roe v Wade* and outlaw abortion. For Christian dominionists in the New Apostolic Reformation, Trump was God's voice on the mountain of government; that he is not a Christian is irrelevant to how God has used him to restore the American nation. His efforts to deregulate businesses by loosening government restrictions and lowering corporate taxes promote the libertarian capitalism that Falwell believed was the country's best defense against communism in the 1980s. Coal is one of the most heavily polluting forms of energy and releases high levels of greenhouse gases into the air; Trump's support of America's coal industry, which had been weakened under Obama, told creationists that he is on their side in denying climate change and the need for developing renewable energy sources. He also loosened regulations on oil drilling, automobile gasoline, and other sources of fossil fuel emissions, while opening up the ANWR region of Alaska to drilling. His libertarian approach to deregulating private business, including the oil industry, appeals to Christian Reconstructionists, who blame government intervention for the country's economic woes.

The central feature of Trump's 2016 campaign was to build a border wall between the United States and its southern neighbor of Mexico to try to prevent would-be illegal immigrants from crossing the border. The border wall is the ultimate expression of Christian nationalism in the United States: True Americans are Christians, and they have a God-given duty to protect their nation's sovereignty against any who might seek to undermine it. For those who support Trump, the people who are most undermining the American nation are illegal immigrants from Central America and

Mexico that are attempting to sneak across the border so that they can collect welfare payments and benefit from the country's advanced healthcare system. Robert Jeffress, the pastor of First Baptist Church of Dallas and full-fledged Trump supporter, appeared on Fox News on September 29, 2019 and said, "The Bible says even Heaven itself is gonna have a wall around it. Not everybody is going to be allowed in. So if walls are immoral, then God is immoral."[5]

Jerry Falwell's son, Jerry Junior, has been one of the most outspoken Trump supporters, using his position as chancellor of Liberty University to promote the president's populist and divisive politics. Jerry Junior has regularly appeared alongside President Trump, who has made multiple visits to Liberty University and garnered the endorsement of the Falwell family. Yet not all evangelicals feel the same way about Trump as the chancellor of Liberty University; in 2016, dozens of graduates of Liberty University returned their diplomas to the school, and 2000 students and faculty of the school signed a statement that admonished both Trump and Jerry Junior for the former's statements about women.

While many leaders in the Religious Right—Franklin Graham (son of the late Billy Graham), Jerry Junior, James Dobson, Lou Engle, John Hagee, Rick Joyner, and a number of others—are outspoken about their unconditional support of President Trump, other conservative Christians are equally outspoken about recovering the Christian faith from Trumpism and the Christian nationalism of the Religious Right. Beth Moore, an influential Bible study leader, said in a Tweet in 2018,

> For many of us about whom people say, "I liked them better before they got political," we liked us better, too. Who wanted to be where a mountain of manure was hitting the fan? This manure came to us in the church. We didn't go to it. For a lot of us it's a fight for the faith.[6]

The evangelical support of Donald Trump is about far more than his controversial statements on racial minorities, women, people with disabilities, and politicians who disagree with him. It is about the fact that he embodies the political aspirations of movements within the Religious Right from the 1970s onwards, particularly the Moral Majority, the New Apostolic Reformation, and Christian Reconstruction. He also represents the prosperity gospel, not only because he is a billionaire but because he promises to bring prosperity back to the American nation.

5. Carol Kuruvilla, "Evangelical Pastor Defends Trump's Border Plan: 'Heaven Itself Is Gonna Have A Wall,'" in *Huffington Post* October 1, 2019.
6. Beth Moore as BethMooreLPM on Twitter, March 12, 2018.

NATIONAL: SARAH PALIN'S ENDORSEMENT OF TRUMP

Yet fully 80% of white evangelicals voted for Donald Trump in the 2016 election, and they have been his most solid support base throughout his presidency. Jerry Junior has insisted that nothing—no corruption scandal, no allegation of sexual misconduct—could make him waver in his support of Trump. When the United States Senate impeached him for obstruction of congress and abuse of power, the Religious Right and its leaders staunchly stood by their president, some even comparing him to Jesus Christ for how they felt he was being persecuted by the establishment.

Populism is the illiberal response to the central challenge of democracy: determining who "the people" are. In a populist movement, "the people" are those that the populist leader represents, in the case of Donald Trump, the Tea Partiers, members of Jerry Falwell's "Christian American nation," and Christian libertarians who supported Rushdoony's and North's Christian Reconstruction and theonomy. These Christians began to throw their weight behind Trump long before he won the Republican nomination for president in the summer of 2016. In January 2016 at the Iowa caucus—the first of the presidential primaries—Sarah Palin spearheaded the evangelical support of him when she endorsed him as the man suited to represent the people as the president of the United States of America.

In her endorsement speech at the Iowa caucus, which kickstarts the presidential primaries, Palin addressed her talk to the essence of Middle America,

> . . .you hard-working Iowa families. You farm families, and teachers, and teamsters, and cops, and cooks. You rockin' rollers. And holy rollers! All of you who work so hard. You full-time moms. You with the hands that rock the cradle. You all make the world go round, and now our cause is one.[7]

Her appeal was specifically to blue-collar, working-class men and women who, due at least in part to the inflammatory rhetoric of the Tea Party, felt left out by the Obama administration. Minority groups—African Americans facing increased racial tensions, immigrants on a path to citizenship, the queer community, et. al.—are not included in her address. Her endorsement of Trump was a tribute to the Middle America that looks a lot like her hometown of Wasilla and nothing like the big, diverse cities where most of the country's population lives.

After an attack on Obama, she went on to say of Trump,

---

7. Sarah Palin, "Endorsement Speech for Donald Trump," January 19, 2016.

Only one candidate's record of success proves he is the master of the art of the deal. He is beholden to no one, but we the people, how refreshing. He is perfectly positioned to let you make America great again. Are you ready for that, Iowa? No more pussy footin' around! Our troops deserve the best. You deserve the best!

In saying that Trump is only beholden to "we the people," having just a few minutes earlier defined who "the people" are, she appealed to the populist notion that Trump would only represent Middle America and not minority or urban communities.

Palin's political experience is limited to a state that derives its revenue from the oil industry, which is run by private businesses. She championed this notion of private business when she went on to say of Trump, "He is from the private sector, not a politician. Can I get a 'Hallelujah!'" With Trump's experience in the private sector, she knew that he would deregulate industries that are subject to environmental laws and taxes that cost them money every year. She believed that Trump, by deregulating the private sector, would do what he believed is best for "the people." "The people" were the hard-working families who ran farms and worked in the small towns of Middle America, and who have been losing their homes and jobs under Obama's policies. The solution for "the people" was to bring back private industry without government regulation.

Palin went on to describe "the people"—those who have been ignored not only by Obama but also by the Republican Party, labeling them as "the rest of us"—as "right-wingin', bitter-clingin', proud clingers of our guns, our God, and our religion, and our constitution." Of the wars in the Middle East which the United States has been engaged in since Bush launched his War on Terror in 2001, she said, "Where they're fighting each other and yelling 'Allah Akbar' calling jihad on each other's heads for ever and ever, like I've said before, let them duke it out and let Allah[8] sort it out." She concluded her speech by saying, "Iowa, you say a lot, being here tonight, supporting the right man who will allow you to make America great again. God bless you! God bless the United States of America and our next president of the United States, Donald J. Trump!"

Palin's endorsement of Trump came 10 days before Jerry Junior endorsed him. One after another, leaders of the Religious Right—and soon the voting bloc itself—came to see the populist leader as God's man to restore the nation. Yet not all Republicans, including those who have enjoyed the favor of the Religious Right, supported Trump. John McCain, the man who

---

8. "Allah" is the Arabic word for "God" and is used by both Christians and Muslims in Arabic-speaking countries.

brought Palin onto the national scene in 2008, was one of Trump's most vocal critics. When Trump launched his campaign by promising to build a border wall with Mexico, McCain accused him of firing up the radical, far-right "crazies" of the Republican Party. He later voted against Trump's healthcare bill, which would have repealed much of Obamacare. Before he died of brain cancer in 2018, he requested that neither Trump nor Palin attend his funeral.

McCain represented the last of the Rockefeller Republicans, those who promoted financial conservativism while also believing that the government could have a positive role in people's lives. He did not pander to the Religious Right and, at times, even rejected endorsements given by its leaders. Trump's populist, nationalist Republican Party, which promoted the supposedly homegrown, Christian values of Middle America, looked more like the one that JD Rockefeller and other oilmen funded at the turn of the twentieth century than the one that Rockefeller's grandson, Rockie, helped lead during the Cold War.

GLOBAL: THE RISE OF POPULISM IN THE 2010s

Populist governments, especially right-wing ones that appeal to nationalism and appeals of one religious group—such as conservative Christians and Jerry Falwell's idea of the American nation—rely heavily on identifying an enemy and targeting it. For Trump and his supporters, that enemy is immigrants from Mexico and Central America; hence, the promise of a border wall between the United States and Mexico was the only policy goal that he presented during his presidential campaign in 2016. Once in office, that common enemy of the American nation expanded to include Muslims; many Trump supporters have long feared that Muslims in the United States want to replace the country's Christian founding documents—the Declaration of Independence and the constitution—with Islamic law, known as Sharia. Trump responded to those fears by implementing a travel ban on people from several Muslim-majority countries, including Libya, Yemen, Syria, Somalia, and Iran.

Other groups in the United States also found themselves the target of heightened tensions and "othering" that excludes them from the American nation. In Charlottesville, Virginia on August 12, 2017, a group of far-right Trump supporters held a "Unite the Right" rally, which was attended by neo-Nazis, Ku Klux Klan members, and other white supremacists who carried swastikas and Confederate flags; in reaction to a counter-protest, one white supremacist from Unite the Right drove a car into a peaceful gathering, killing one and injuring 19. For the LGBTQ+ community, 2017, the year that Trump took office, was the deadliest year in history. While Trump was not directly responsible for any of the hate crimes committed against minority groups, his nationalist, populist rhetoric empowered hate groups and made them believe that they had an ally in the White House. Trump's border wall and Muslim travel ban had made their "others"—immigrants and Muslims—the enemy of "the people." The United States is not alone in this surge of right-wing nationalism, populism, and othering, The election of Donald Trump was only one in a global surge of populist movements that appeal to a mythologized ideal of a nation and strive to recreate an imagined golden age.

One of the first and most longstanding of the global populist governments is in Hungary. In 2010, while the economies of Europe were still recovering from the financial crisis that began in 2008, Hungarian nationalists elected Viktor Orban as prime minister. Hungarians who voted for him were wary of the European Union[9] imposing on their freedoms and the sovereignty of Hungary; they saw the EU's liberal policies as hostile to Hungary's Christian heritage and Christian identity. In the time since, Orban's cronies have bought out media outlets—newspapers and television stations—throughout the country so that the news people see is favorable to him. He has pressured liberal universities to close down or leave the country and blacklisted charity groups that assist refugees and other immigrants; additionally, he appointed those who are loyal to him to preside over the country's courts. Orban himself coined the term "illiberal democracy" to describe his government and vision for returning Hungary to its glorious past of a pure Hungarian, Christian nation.

Shortly after European markets recovered from the 2008 financial crisis, in 2015, waves of refugees fleeing violence in countries such as Syria, Libya, and Nigeria crossed the Mediterranean Sea in boats and arrived in Europe, looking for safe asylum. Questions of how to manage the tens of thousands of migrants that poured in month after month began to dominate governments in Europe: Which countries should open their borders to receive the refugees? And how might this mass immigration change the face of Europe? Nationalist groups in Europe are nothing new, but the mass migration of 2015—with many of the refugees being practicing Muslims and arriving from Muslim-majority countries—prompted a surge of right-wing populism and nationalism among citizens who feared for their own safety and the future of their Christian nations.

9. The European Union is the central governing body of Europe and supports liberal values, such as secular democracy and support of minority groups, throughout the continent.

Right-wing populist movements need an enemy, and in Orban's Hungary, that enemy is the Hungarian-born billionaire, George Soros. Soros has donated money to causes that promote liberal democracy—such as Hungary's Central European University, which Orban has been trying to close—and is a common bogeyman of other populist movements. Right-wing populists in the United States blame him for the asylum seekers that continue to arrive from Mexico and Latin America, making him the primary cause of their nation's woes. In the United Kingdom following the mass immigration of 2015, the populists' bogeyman was the European Union itself, and in the 2016 "Brexit" referendum, "the people" of the United Kingdom chose to leave the EU altogether. In Italy, Matteo Salvini's populist party gained momentum by appealing to the immigration crisis and targeting refugees as the enemy of "the people" of Italy. Similar movements have flourished in France, Germany, Austria, the Netherlands, and many other European countries.

The right-wing, nationalist-populist movements of the 2010s were not limited to the so-called "Christian" nations of the West that wanted to preserve their Christian heritage against Muslim immigration. In India, Hindu nationalists helped secure the election of Narendra Modi as prime minister in 2014. Modi went on to strip the citizenship or deny a path to citizenship for millions of Muslims living in India and promoted one religious group—Hindus—as being the pure substance of the nation. Like Trump, he also weakened laws that protect the environment, and the two have made several appearances together. In the Philippines, an archipelago in South Asia, populists elected Rodrigo Duterte, who was known for a tough stance on crime that frequently involved him engaging in illegal activities himself, including extrajudicial killings. His straight-talking, anti-elitist, illiberal style appealed to populists who wanted to rid the Philippines of crime, especially drug crime; when elected, he launched a War on Drugs that allowed police officers and local militias to kill suspected drug offenders with impunity. For Duterte and his populist base, the "others" that undermine "the people" are drug criminals, and the only solution is to rid the country of them.

In Brazil, populists elected Jair Bolsonaro as president in 2018, and he took office on January 1, 2019. He had been part of the military dictatorship that ruled Brazil until 1985 and, during his campaign for president, publicly spoke about how Brazil might be better off if it returned to military rule. Bolsonaro, though a long-time politician with inflammatory rhetoric, positioned himself as one of "the people" and promised to end the corruption that plagued Brazil's government. But "the people" that Bolsonaro represented did not include the Amerindian tribes that live in the Amazon rainforest, half of which lies in Brazil. During the summer of 2019, while much of the world was smothering in climate-change-related heatwaves that were causing massive forest fires, the biggest fires were in the Amazon rainforest. Bolsonaro, like so many other populist leaders, had cut environmental laws and dismantled organizations dedicated to protecting the environment, including the rainforest. That summer, deforestation of the Amazon nearly doubled, with many setting fires to it so that they could use the cleared land for farming and industrial development. Smoke from the fires covered half of the country and could even be seen by satellites orbiting the earth. The fires threatened every aspect of life for the Amazon tribes, who were facing not only the elimination of their hunting grounds and food sources but the burning of their very homes and villages.

Yet the burning of the Amazon has ramifications far beyond the Amazon tribes. The Amazon rainforest absorbs as much as 25% of the world's carbon dioxide, which is emitted by fossil fuels and is a driver of climate change. Most populist leaders, however, deny that climate change is even happening or that it is caused by burning fossil fuels, as scientists say. Like the libertarian leaders of oil companies that astro-turf their corporate interests, populist leaders around the world promote an ongoing dependence on oil and other fossil fuels, as well as gutting of environmental laws that hamper economic growth, as being good for "the people."

LOCAL: ELECTION OF GOVERNOR DUNLEAVY AND THE 2019 BUDGET VETOES

The state of Alaska has one of the largest savings accounts in the country—the Permanent Fund—and pays out a portion of the interest that it earns every year to its residents in the PFD payments. Yet despite this large savings account and the PFD payments, Alaska has some of the highest markers of poverty in the country. For the year 2008, when Sarah Palin's government paid record-high PFDs of $3000 to every eligible man, woman, and child in the state, the Annie E. Casey Foundation found the state of Alaska to rank #31 in the entire country for child well-being. By 2018, with reduced oil revenue under MAPA forcing the state to withdraw funding for many social services, that ranking had slipped to #45. The libertarian values promoted by Gary North and the Koch brothers, along with other oil executives whose companies work on Alaska's North Slope, have not eliminated poverty or improved the well-being of children and families.

Following the institution of MAPA in 2013, lower oil prices coupled with reduced tax burdens for oil companies led to a budget crisis in which the state could no longer meet its budgetary needs. Furthermore, the libertarian ethos of the state's residents, many of whom believe that the only function of the government is to protect their individual rights and ensure that they get their fair sure of oil revenue in the form of PFD payments, convinced many Alaskans that the state does not even have an obligation to fund social services. That libertarian belief regarding the state's role in social services is shared by the Koch brothers, who financially supported the campaign of Mike Dunleavy, who became governor of Alaska in 2018.

In 2015, the year that Governor Bill Walker attempted to tap the state's Permanent Fund in order to make up its budget deficit, he also signed an order for Medicaid expansion in Alaska. The Medicaid expansion program was an Obama initiative that provided federal dollars to ensure that those who could not afford health insurance had access to healthcare; the program had been vetoed by Governor Palin and by her successor, Governor Parnell, on the grounds that they did not want Alaska to become indebted to the federal government, especially to a socialist healthcare program. When Governor Walker signed Medicaid expansion in 2015, he met fierce resistance by Alaskans who saw the taking of federal dollars to fund healthcare as a violation of their libertarian values. That he had also tried to tap the state's Permanent Fund that same year made many believe that Medicaid expansion was further inflating an overstretched budget and would force the state into bankruptcy.

Americans for Prosperity, the Koch-funded libertarian group, had recently been established in Alaska and swiftly organized against Medicaid expansion there. People who had worked with Governor Walker to push forward Medicaid expansion were harassed by people from Americans for Prosperity, including its Alaska director, Jeremy Price. Members of Americans for Prosperity organized residents to give testimonies at public hearings about how Medicaid expansion would harm Alaska and was not in the best interest of the people. Americans for Prosperity and other Koch-funded organizations threw their support behind Mike Dunleavy who, during his 2018 bid for governor promised to balance the state's budget and restore the PFD so that the people would get their fair share of oil revenues. Following Dunleavy's election in 2018, serving as his chief of staff was Jeremy Price, the director of Americans for Prosperity Alaska.

In the summer of 2019, just a few months after taking office, Governor Dunleavy made good on his promise to balance Alaska's budget by slashing funding to the state's social services. He did so in the same way that his predecessor, Governor Palin, had also cut social services during her tenure as governor: by using a line-item veto, in which he selectively eliminated terms of a budget bill that had already passed the Alaska legislature. One of the hardest-hit programs was Medicaid; the legislature reduced funding for

Medicaid by $70 million, and the governor used the line-item veto to reduce that amount by an additional $50 million; the budget vetoes also eliminated Medicaid dental coverage for adults and the state's senior benefits program. He cut over $130 million of funding to the University of Alaska—over 40% of what the government gives it each year, effectively gutting the state's higher education—but later restored $110 million. Americans for Prosperity in particular applauded Governor Dunleavy's move to get the government out of people's lives. Other Alaskan libertarians, such as former legislator Ray Metcalfe, believed that the state needed to bring back Palin's ACES tax code to force oil companies to pay their dues to the state for taking its resources out of the ground. Metcalfe and like-minded libertarians see the role of the government as protecting the rights of individuals, which, in their case, means securing fair compensation for the mineral resources that oil companies extract for a profit; that fair compensation requires a tax system that will support Alaska's budgetary needs.

The people who were hit hardest by the budget vetoes—University of Alaska students who would lose their scholarships and professors who would lose their jobs, working-class families who would lose their healthcare, and senior citizens who would have to choose between buying food and buying medicine—organized against them by urging their legislators to vote against the budget vetoes. Governor Dunleavy held legislative sessions in Wasilla—the town that both he and Palin call home—instead of the capital city of Juneau. Public testimony in the legislative sessions raged between people who would experience hardship because of the vetoes and libertarians who supported the notion that the government should not be involved in providing social services. In the end, the legislature did not override the governor's budget vetoes.

Many of those who supported the budget vetoes endorsed the libertarian economics of Gary North and his father-in-law, RJ Rushdoony, who believed that the church rather than the state should be at the center of the American Christian nation. Others took an even stronger approach, including white supremacists groups that, at the legislative sessions in Wasilla, made white power fists to people coming and going. For many, the consensus was that those who relied on the government to fund social services were not of "the people" and did not belong in Alaska.

In a state that has a long history of military support, strong nationalist values, and many veterans, one of the groups hit hardest by the budget vetoes were seniors who live at the state's Pioneer and Veterans Homes. The Pioneer Homes provide residential nursing care to veterans and other seniors who helped settle the state; many of the residents came to Alaska when it was still a territory, and not a few worked on the construction of the oil pipeline during the 1970s. When the 2019 budget vetoes went into effect, the cost of the Pioneer Homes became prohibitively expensive; without Medicaid and other senior benefits, some of the residents had to leave. When the budget debate was settled, seniors who had spent their lives contributing to the state were not seen as "the people," and the state's politicians did not represent them or find room for their care in the budget.

GLOCAL: OILMEN IN PRESIDENT TRUMP'S CABINET

During the 1973 OPEC oil embargo, ensuing energy crisis, and economic recession, the United States government decided not to invest in renewable energy. Instead, President Nixon urged congress to approve construction of the Alaska pipeline and continue the country's addiction to oil. In the time since, Alaska's economy has become so dependent on the pipeline and oil revenue that any fluctuation in oil prices—as with the Saudi oil glut of the 1980s—or decrease in oil taxes—as with Governor Parnell's MAPA tax plan—can send the state into a tailspin. Though Alaska is no longer a libertarian haven or wilderness for pioneers to settle, Alaskans continue to see themselves as independent and not in need of government intervention in their lives. For many of Alaska's libertarian voters, the only role of the government is to make sure that they continue receiving PFD checks—paid for by private oil companies rather than public funds—every year.

Meanwhile, the Permanent Fund, PFD payments, and astro-turfing by oil companies have helped ensure that the state does not diversify its economy and remains entirely dependent on oil. In turn, the United States has remained dependent on oil, while politicians continue to astro-turf the libertarian interests of private oil companies to the country's citizens. The astro-turfing of politicians and oil companies can be seen in President Trump's cabinet, which included many oilmen with connections to the Alaska pipeline.

Rex Tillerson, who served as Trump's Secretary of State, previously served as the CEO of Exxon-Mobil, which has a significant presence in Alaska's oil fields and was behind the *Exxon-Valdez* oil spill. In 2008, when Palin was serving as governor of Alaska and Tillerson was serving as CEO of Exxon, the oil spill had still not been cleaned up, and Exxon had not paid the court-ordered punitive damages for the loss of livelihood to fishing villages on Prince William Sound. Under Tillerson's leadership, Exxon took the case regarding the company's punitive damages—which a court declared to be $2.5 billion—to the Supreme Court. In a ruling that favored the oil company, the Supreme Court ruled in *Exxon v Baker* that Exxon only had to pay $500 million in damages, as it had already paid $3.4 billion towards recovery efforts in Prince William Sound. To this day, oil still covers beaches in Prince William Sound, and Exxon remains one of the biggest oil producers in Alaska.

Tillerson played a mostly peripheral role in the White House and often butted heads with the president until being fired in March 2018, just over a year after taking office. Yet other oilmen, many in less prominent positions, have exerted a greater level of influence over the Trump administration and influenced policies that benefit the corporate interests of oil companies. Trump selected congressman Ryan Zinke to serve as Secretary of the Interior, placing him over the country's mining, drilling, and management of the country's public lands and wilderness areas. As Secretary of the Interior, Zinke used language that Christians in the Religious Right would recognize; instead of speaking of "energy security," he spoke of "energy covenant renewal." Protestants in particular see covenants as agreements that God made with people in the Bible and that Christians make with each other in the name of faith. Zinke's energy covenant included immediately reversing the environmental protections that Obama had instated and opening new areas of United States wilderness to drilling by private oil companies. By overturning environmental protections and promoting further drilling, Zinke effectively declared that as Trump's Secretary of the Interior, he did not support the development of renewable energy. Further, his "energy covenant renewal" speech had been given at an event hosted by the Heritage Foundation, an organization that is financially supported by the Koch brothers.

Turning over public lands for private development is one of the tenets of the Alaska Republican Party's platform, a tenet that directly benefits the oil companies that finance the state's budget. Zinke had been supported by oil companies during his campaigns to become a congressman; as Secretary of the Interior, he pushed forward opening more areas of Alaska—including ANWR—to drilling. Many Alaskans celebrated that more drilling would create more jobs and more revenue for the state, but that increased revenue would further indebt the state to oil companies. Shortly after Zinke's speech on "energy covenant renewal," Joe Balash, an Alaskan with deep ties to the state's oil industry, became Assistant Secretary of the Interior in December 2017. All three of Alaska's congressional representatives—Senator Lisa Murkowski, Senator Dan Sullivan, and Representative Don Young—celebrated that one of their own would now help oversee energy policy for the entire country.

Zinke resigned his position in January 2019 and was replaced by David Bernhardt, a former oil lobbyist who had built a career in promoting corporate oil interests in Washington, DC. Bernhardt had worked for the Department of the Interior under President Bush from 2001 until 2009, where he produced reports for congress that had been funded by oil companies and tried to open up more public wilderness areas in Alaska for drilling. Following the election of Obama, Bernhardt returned to lobbying for oil companies; as Trump's new Secretary of the Interior, he further scaled back environmental protections and regulations on the oil industry.

Rick Perry, the former governor of oil-rich Texas who has long been supported by the New Apostolic Reformation, also received a high position in Trump's cabinet when he became Secretary of Energy. As governor of Texas, Perry signed legislation that would boost the state's reliance on renewable energy, particularly wind. Yet he, like Palin and other politicians who have worked with the oil industry, denies climate change and other harmful effects of fossil-fuel emissions; further, Perry himself received hundreds of thousands of dollars from oil companies to finance his election campaigns. Prior to becoming Secretary of Energy, Perry served on the board of the oil companies Energy Transfer Partners and Sunoco, both of which have pushed for building the Keystone XL pipeline through Native lands in the Dakotas. While he and Palin both served as governors of oil-producing states at the same time—from 2006 until 2009—the two frequently worked together on promoting private business by deregulating the oil industry. Indeed, Trump cited Perry's experience in promoting the oil industry when tapping him for the position.

Trump's choice for the director of the Environmental Protection Agency, Scott Pruitt, was not directly connected to the Alaska pipeline and its oil industry. Yet when he served as attorney general for the state of Oklahoma, Pruitt led his state's charge against Obama's Clean Power Plan and other Obama-era environmental and energy policies. Like the oil companies that have donated hundreds of thousands of dollars to Pruitt's campaigns, he denies climate change; after building his political career by undermining environmental policies, when Pruitt became the director of the EPA, he gutted the organization and made it unable to enforce environmental regulations. Like many of his colleagues in the Trump administration, Pruitt opened up more wilderness areas in Alaska to oil drilling and mining, further embedding the evangelical support of the Trump presidency into the corporate interests of oil companies.

The Trump presidency represents the culmination of faith-based oil politics, not only of Sarah Palin but of the larger Religious Right. Those faith-based oil politics have been present among conservative Christians since the rise of fundamentalism coincided with the rise of oil, when oilmen used their wealth to finance the fundamentalist movement. The connection between the Religious Right and oil became cemented during the Cold War, when Billy Graham and Jerry Falwell promoted American capitalism as a Christian value and the nation's oil-based prosperity as evidence of God's blessing.

During the Cold War, the Yom Kippur War pitted a Soviet alliance with the Arab states against an American alliance with Israel. The result was an embargo on oil from OPEC countries and an oil crisis in the United States, along with a theological rationale in dispensationalism that asserts that oil is a divine resource that God is using as part of the End Times drama. The embargo led to the approval of the Alaska pipeline, which came to dominate Alaskan politics and provide all of the money for the state's budget. It also fueled the faith-based oil politics of Sarah Palin, who went on to lead the Religious Right after the death of Jerry Falwell.

Meanwhile, the growing field of creation science came up with an explanation for the presence of oil that contradicted mainstream science: Oil was put in the ground directly by God for the purpose of people furthering His Kingdom on earth. Just as in the fundamentalist movement, oil money should be used to enhance the prosperity of Christians and strengthen their political power; this view of oil-based wealth was endorsed by the prosperity gospel and later New Apostolic Reformation. Because oil was put in the ground by God, burning it cannot be harmful for the environment, and oil spills that devastate wildlife do not indicate that oil and wildlife cannot co-exist. Rather, the production and use of oil are Christian enterprises that underpin a biblical economic system.

That economic system endorses private industry, particularly the oil industry, in a campaign of astro-turfing that gives the appearance that the corporate interests of oil companies are the same as the everyday interests of common people. For Palin, governing a state that is funded by the private oil industry, "the people" that oil supports represent the Christian American nation that Billy Graham and Falwell promoted during the Cold War. Alaska's Permanent Fund and its PFD payments, which provide Alaskans a check every year instead of them having to pay an income tax, helped ensure that the interests of the oil companies became the interests of Alaskan voters. In Alaska, where 80% to 90% of the budget comes from oil money and people get a check every year, no matter who gets elected, oil companies always win.

Events in the news today are a long time in the making. They are the product of not just far-right agendas that support white supremacism against racial diversity and Christian nationalism against religious pluralism; they are the product of a longstanding relationship between conservative

Christianity and oil. The renewable energy sources—which would provide clean, carbon-free energy to people—that have been present for decades have not been developed, in lieu of supporting government policies that continue America's addiction to oil and oil's place in the theology of the Religious Right.

Conclusion

Blessed are the poor in spirit,
For theirs is the kingdom of heaven.

—Jesus of Nazareth

American evangelicals have a long history of being at the forefront of reform movements. To help end religious persecution in the newly formed country, they advocated for separation of church and state to be a central pillar of the United States. They pushed for the abolition of slavery, and many opened their homes—at severe personal risk—to slaves fleeing to freedom on the Underground Railroad. They ran hospitals, schools, and orphanages at a time when the government was being run by corporate interests and had no ambition to promote social order or public welfare. They promoted laws that would restrict child labor and make work safer for men and women in industrial factories. Even before *Roe v Wade* and the call for ending abortion became a national crusade,, they ran crisis centers to help women who were facing a difficult pregnancy.

But along the way, evangelicals in the Religious Right confused the United States Constitution with the Word of God and the oil industry with the Kingdom of God. Now, instead of leading reform movements, the majority of evangelicals are not only helping to drive climate change but also making sure that the world remains addicted to the oil that is causing it. Climate change is already harming the poorest people in the world and, if not stopped immediately, will soon create a new mass migration of people fleeing areas that are now uninhabitable. Yet the world continues to drill for more oil.

What would evangelicalism look like if it no longer found itself mired within the matrix of oil politics? I ask this question first to myself, as I am an evangelical in search of an authentic faith that represents the message preached by prophets in the Old Testament and embodied in Jesus of Nazareth. I ask this question second to my fellow evangelicals, who may not have realized how much the faith that they love bears a stain so deep that it cannot be easily washed away. And I ask this question third to those who do not hold to an evangelical faith yet want to see a world that is no longer divided over oil.

I did much of the research for this book in and around Wasilla, Alaska between the summer of 2019—when Governor Dunleavy vetoed funds for the state's social services—and New Years of 2020. On Christmas Eve, I attended church with a friend who lives near Wasilla and is on the same quest as me. We sang the hymn "What Child Is This," the second verse of which has a line which asks a ponderous question:

> Why lies he in such mean estate
> Where ox and ass are feeding?

The infant Jesus lay in such mean estate because the Incarnation was a scandalous event that disrupts everything we think we know about how to please God. Jesus came to earth in dire poverty, yet we rush to meet him with our offerings of oil. We have constructed elaborate theologies centered around the Millennial Reign, when he will return to earth in all the splendor and majesty that befit the King of Kings. But those theologies say more about the relationship that American evangelicalism has with oil politics, American nationalism, and the prosperity gospel than they say about the King who was born in a stable.

He is not impressed with the money that we can make by extracting oil out of the earth, how we can use that money to fund missionaries, or with the theologies we design that support oil politics. Nor is he impressed with our "prophetic" ideas that some nations are uniquely righteous and blessed by God, while others have been wicked since time immemorial. Saluting the American flag is not the same as worshipping God, and being a patriotic American is not the same thing as being a Christian. I do not think Jesus even cares if we win theological debates about whether the Bible should be taken literally or insist that creationism be taught in public schools, especially when in the process, we turn our love of God into a political agenda and force others to abide by it.

In searching for an authentic, biblical faith, what I have found is that Jesus is impressed when we go to the poor, not only to help them, but to find the image of God in them. When we stop looking at the poor as people that we need to convert to our faith and instead look at them as bearers of the Imago Dei who have a message that we ourselves need to hear. Loving the poor changes us and forces us to ask questions that are harder than those posed by creation-versus-evolution debates: Are my political views actually creating oppression for other people? Is my unilateral support of Israel causing Arab Christians to suffer persecution? Is the way that my faith has co-opted Jewish traditions and beliefs about Israel depriving the Jewish people of the dignity of being able to speak for themselves? Is my support of oil politics causing people in areas hit hardest by climate change to suffer from droughts, wildfires, or flooding? These are the questions that we do not want to have to ask, but an authentic, biblical faith, one that is not mired in theologies of oil, requires us to ask them.

We cannot profess to love God while damning entire nations in the name of theology. Nor can we profess to love God while destroying the earth that He created because we have convinced ourselves that oil is a divine resource to further our Christian society. We love God by loving the poor. We love God by giving them the ability to speak for themselves so that they can have a voice in our fractured and polarized world. We love God by no longer claiming to speak for everybody, or even worse, claiming to speak for God, when all that we have is a Republican agenda that cannot be separated from corporate oil interests.

In my opinion, the greatest witness that American evangelicals can have in the world today is to confess how badly wrong we were about oil. Constructing theologies of oil and celebrating it as God's blessing on America have not furthered the Kingdom of God on earth. But our theologies of oil and belief that America is truly exceptional have led to wars, oppression of some of the world's most vulnerable people, and an environmental catastrophe. As evangelical Christians, we have failed to represent Christ to the world.

In terms of creation science, we need to emphasize care for God's creation through environmental stewardship. We need to invest in renewable energy that will not only benefit us but also benefit the global poor. We need to support diversified economies that do not depend on oil dollars to support the state. And we need to seriously consider what we can do to reverse climate change.

For the foreseeable future, evangelicals and the broader cohort of "conservative Christians" will remain one of the largest voting blocs in the United States. In terms of American public life, the evangelical voice will continue to be heard, and the direction that evangelicals take regarding oil politics will have a significant impact on American public policy. I want to see my fellow evangelicals champion the environment—the world that God created and called humans to be stewards of—and the poor over any short-term victories that they may see in oil.

Bibliography

1958. ""Text of Rockefeller's Resignation as US Adviser and Eisenhower's Reply." *New York Times.*
Alaska Oil and Gas Association. n.d. "History—1980's." *Alaska Oil and Gas Association.* Accessed January 1, 2020. https://www.aoga.org/industry/history-1980s.
Alaska Republicans. n.d. *Alaska Republican Party Platform 2018.*
All-Alaska Weekly. 1980. "A Moral Majority? Church Group Takes Over Alaska GOP." March 14.
Ammerman, Nancy. 1991. *North American Protestant Fundamentalism.* Vol. 1, in *Fundamentalisms Observed,* by Martin Marty and R Scott Appleby. Chicago: The University of Chicago Press.
Ammerman, Nancy. 1991. *The Dynamics of Christian Fundamentalism: An Introduction.* Vol. 4, in *Accounting for Fundamentalisms,* by Marty Martin and R Scott Appleby. Chicago: The University of Chicago Press.
Anderson, Benedict. n.d. *Imagined Communities: Reflections on the Origin and Spread of Nationalism.* London: Verso.
Annie E. Casey Foundation. 2018. "Kids Count Data Book."
Annie E. Casey Foundation. 2008. "Kids Count Data Book."
April 26, 2018. *Viktor Orban's "Illiberal Democracy."* Produced by BBC Newsnight. Performed by BBC.
Bellah, Robert. 1967. "Civil Religion in America." *Daedalus* (MIT Press) 96: 1–21.
Biola University. n.d. "Biola University's Theological Positions." *Biola Uiversity.* www.biola.edu.
Boraas, Alan. 2012. "'Prosperity theology' embraces wealth." *Anchorage Daily News.*
Bowler, Kate. 2013. *Blessed: A History of the American Prosperity Gospel.* New York: Oxford University Press.
Bradner, Eric. 2017. "Conway: Trump White House offered 'alternative facts' on crowd size." (CNN).
Bradner, Mike, and Tim Bradner. 2017. "How the PFD came to be." *Mat-Su Valley Frontiersman,* October 15.
Braun, Stephen. 2016. "Perry brings oil industry ties as Trump's pick for Energy Dept." *Alaska Journal of Commerce* 40 (51).

Brooks, James. 2019. "Dunleavy vetoes $444 million from operating budget—The University of Alaska is the biggest target of the governor's line-item veto pen, losing $130 million in state support." *Anchorage Daily News*.

Brown, Garrett, Iain McLean, and Alistair McMillan. 2018. "Social Darwinism." In *A Concise Oxford Dictionary of Politics and International Relations*. Oxford: Oxford University Press.

Carnegie, Andrew. 1889. "The Gospel of Wealth." *North American Review* (North American Review).

Christianity Today. 1991. "Leaders Wrestle with Faith and War." February 11.

Clapp, Rodney. 1987. "Democracy as Heresy." *Christianity Today*, February 20.

Coates, Peter. 1991. *The Trans-Alaska Pipeline Controversy*. London and Toronto: Associated University Presses.

Coghlan, Skip. 2016. *Wasilla: A Great Place Among The Lakes*. Big Bend, WI: Among The Lakes Publishing Co.

Cohen, Michael. 2016. *American Maelstrom: The 1968 Election and the Politics of Division*. Oxford: Oxford University Press.

Cole, Dermot. 2008. *North to the Future*. Kenmore, WA: Epicenter Press.

2017. "Congressional Delegation Congratulates Alaskan Joe Balash on Confirmation as Assistant Secretary of the Interior." *State News Service*.

Coyne, Amanda. 2008. "A Visit to Palin's Church." *Newsweek Magazine*, September 1.

Dewar, Helen. 1980. "Republicans Capture Seats of Senate Liberals McGovern and Bayh." *The Washington Post*, November 5.

Dochuk, Darren. 2019. *Anointed With Oil: How Christianity and Crude Made Modern America*. New York: Basic Books.

Dochuk, Darren. 2012. "Blessed by Oil, Cursed with Crude: God and Black Gold in the American Southwest." *The Journal of American History* 51–61.

Dochuk, Darren. 2017. "Extracted Truths: The Politcs of God and Black Gold on a Global Stage." In *Outside In: The Transnational Circuitry of US History*, by Andrew Preston and Doug Rossinow, 153–176. Oxford: Oxford University Press.

———. 2011. *From Bible Belt to Sun Belt: Plain-Folk Religion, Grassroots Politics, and the Rise of Evangelical Conservativism*. New York: WW Norton and Company.

Dochuk, Darren. 2012. "Tea Party America and the Born-Again Politics of the Populist Right." *New Labor Forum* 15–21.

n.d. "Dr. Jerry Prevo." *Anchorage Baptist Temple*. Accessed October 24, 2018.

Duffy, Michael. 2002. "Marching Alone." *Time*, September 11.

Dyer, Charles. 1999. "Chapter 5—Babylon: Iraq and the Coming Middle East Crisis." In *The Road to Armageddon: A Biblical Understanding of Prophecy and End Time Events*, 105–144. Nashville: Word Publishing.

Edsall, Thomas. 1985. "Onward GOP Christians, Marching to '88." *The Washington Post*, June 30.

Edwards, Bob. February 26, 2003. *Profile: Silent Evangelical Support of Bush's Proposed War Against Iraq*.

Encyclopedia Britannica. n.d. "Yom Kippur War." *Encyclopedia Britannica*. Accessed December 1 2019.

Fairbanks Daily News Miner. 1980. "Moral Majority likely to prevail, GOP district sessions on again." March 11.

Fairbanks Daily News Miner. 1980. "Murkowski to seek Gravel seat." March 20.

Falwell, Jerry. 1979. "1980 Update on Prophecy, Part 1." *Dr. Jerry Falwell Teaches Bible Prophecy.* Lynchburg: Old-Time Gospel Hour.
———. 2004. "Is God Pro-War?" *Falwell Family Papers.* January 29.
———. 1980. *Listen, America!* New York City: Doubleday.
———. 1976. "Our Citizenship As Americans." Lynchburg: The Old-Time Gospel Hour, March 7.
———. 1983. "Press Release to Pastors, "The Day After" Article." Moral Majority.
———. 1980. *The Fundamentalist Phenomenon: The Resurgence of Conservative Christianity.* New York: Doubleday Galilee.
Fitzgerald, Frances. 1981. "A Disciplined, Charging Army." *The New York Times*, May 18.
Freeman, Louise. 2011. "Military money in Alaska: colossal contributor to the economy." *Alaska Business Monthly*, November 1.
Gibbs, Nancy, and Michael Duffy. 2007. *The Preacher and the Presidents: Billy Graham in the White House.* New York: Center Street.
July 31, 2001. *Governor George W. Bush's faith-based initiative in Texas.* Produced by National Public Radio.
Graham, Billy. 2011. *Just As I Am: The Autobiography of Billy Graham.* Harper Collins.
Gross, Michael Joseph. 2010. "Is Palin's Rise Part of God's Plan?" *Vanity Fair*, September 17.
Gutjahr, Paul, and Randall Stephens. 2017. "The Bible and Fundamentalism." In *The Oxford Handbook of the Bible in America.* Oxford: Oxford University Press.
Harder, Amy, and Michael Bender. 2016. "Donald Trump Picks Former Texas Gov. Rick Perry as Energy Secretary." *Wall Street Journal.*
Harding, Susan. 1991. *Imagining the Last Days: The Politics of Apocalyptic Language.* Vol. 4, in *Accounting for Fundamentalisms*, by Martin Marty and R Scott Appleby. Chicago: The University of Chicago Press.
Heath, Sr., Chuck, and Chuck Heath, Jr. 2012. *Our Sarah: Made In Alaska.* New York: Center Street.
Hesse, Josiah. 2017. "Donald Trump is no saint, but I know why evangelicals love him." *The Guardian.*
Hummel, Laurel. 2005. "The US Military as Georgaphical Agent: The Case of Cold War Alaska." *Geographical Review*, January: 47–72.
Hyman, Anthony. 2002. "Nationalism in Afghanistan." *International Journal of Middle East Studies* 34 (2): 299–315.
Ingersoll, Julie. 2011. "Christian Reconstructionism." In *Encyclopedia of Global Religion*, by Mark Juergensmeyer and Wade Clark Roof. Sage Publishing.
Johnson, Kirk, and Kim Severson. 2008. "In Palin's Life and Politics, Goal to Follow God's Will." *The New York Times*, September 5.
Joyner, Rick. 2004. "2004 Special Bulleting #5." *MorningStar TV.* Accessed January 25, 2020. https://prod.morningstarministries.org/publications/morningstar-purchases-former-heritage-usa.
Kelly, Devin. 2015. "Anchorage, Alaska Passes Gay Rights Law." *Anchorage Daily News*, September 30.
Kleveman, Lutz. 2004. "Oil and the New "Great Game."" *The Nation*, February 16.
Komarnitsky, S. J. 1996. "Republicans Draw Fire For Backing Candidates In Mat-Su's Elections." *Anchorage Daily News*, September 28.
Komarnitsky, S.J. 1996. "New Mayor, Sharp Knife—Wasilla Winner Says She'll Halve Taxes, Take Pay Cut." *Anchorage Daily News*, October 3.

———. 1996. "New Wasilla Mayor Asks City's Managers To Resign In Loyalty Test." *Anchorage Daily News*, October 26.
———. 1996. "Palin Wins Wasilla Mayor's Job." *Anchorage Daily News*, October 2.
Kuruvilla, Carol. 2019. "Evangelical Pator Defends Trump's Border Plan: 'Heaven Itself Is Gonna Have A Wall'." *The Huffington Post*.
LaHaye, Tim. 1972. *The Beginning of the end*. Wheaton: Tyndale House.
Langfitt, Frank. 2008. "Supreme Court Cuts Damages in Exxon Valdez Spill." *NPR*. June 25.
Lardner, George, and Lois Romano. 1999. "Bush Name Helps Fuel Oil Dealings." *Washington Post*.
Leary, Alex, and Timothy Puko. 2019. "Trump to Nominate David Bernhardt as Interior Secretary; The former oil-and-gas industry lobbyist has been serving as acting head of the department since January." *Wall Street Journal*.
Lee, Lydia. 2017. "Gog and Magog." In *End of Days: An Encyclopedia of the Apocalypse in World Religions*, by Wendell Johnson. Santa Barbara, CA: ABC CLIO.
Leung, Rebecca. 2004. "Rise of the Righteous Army: Evangelical Movement Shapes Culture With 'Left Behind' Series." *CBS News, 60 Minutes*. February 5. Accessed January 20, 2020. https://www.cbsnews.com/news/rise-of-the-righteous-army/.
Marty, Martin. 2011. "Fundamentalism." In *The International Encyclopedia of Political Science*, by Bertrand Badie, Dirk Berg-Schlosser and Leonardo Morlino. Sage Publications.
Marty, Martin, and R Scott Appleby. 1992. *The Glory and the Power: The Fundamentalist Challenge to the Modern World*. Boston: Beacon Press.
Mayer, Jane. 2010. "Covert Ops: The Billionaire Brothers Who Are Waging A War Against Obama." *The New Yorker*.
McVicar, Michael. 2013. ""Let them have dominion": "dominion theology" and the construction of religious extremism in the US media." *Journal of Religion and Popular Culture* (University of Toronto Press) 25 (1).
Miller, Lisa. 2010. "How Sarah Palin Is Reshaping the Religious Right." *Newsweek*, June 11.
Moore, Beth. n.d. "Tweet from March 12, 2018." Twitter.
Mudde, Cas, and Cristobal Rovira Kaltwasser. 2017. *Populism: A Very Short Introduction*. Oxford: Oxford University Press.
Murkowski, Frank. 1994. "Senator speaks out on mining law reform." *Engineering & Mining Journal*, February 1.
2005. *Why Sarah Palin?* Performed by Thomas Muthee. Wasilla Assembly of God, Wasilla. October 16.
New York City Anti-Violence Project. 2018. "Crisis of Hate." New York City.
Newsweek Magazine. 1983. "Where God is the Teacher." February 28.
Noell, Edd. 2014. "Theonomy and Economic Institutions." In *The Oxford Handbook of Christianity and Economics*, by Paul Oslington. Oxford: Oxford University Press.
Noll, Mark. 1992. *A History of Christianity in the United States and Canada*. Grand Rapids: William B. Eerdman's Publishing Company.
North, Gary. 2012. *Economics: Job vs Calling*.
———. 2008. "Sarah Palin: The First Good Old Girl in America's National Politics." garynorth.com. September 9. Accessed February 13, 2020. https://www.garynorth.com/public/3979.cfm.

O'Donoghue, Brian. 1993. "Mat-Su Residents Renew Abortion Fight As Board Elections Near, Groups On Both Sides Focus On Valley Hospital." *Anchorage Daily News*, April 2.

———. 1992. "Vote Count Is Delayed In Mat-Su." *Anchorage Daily News*, October 7.

———. 1992. "Wasilla OKs Taxes To Pay For Police." *Anchorage Daily News*, October 8.

1865. "Oil in the Pulpit." *American Phrenological Journal* 109.

OPEC. n.d. *OPEC*. Accessed December 1, 2019. www.opec.org.

Ostling, Richard, Laurence Barrett, and Joseph Kane. 1987. "A Jerry-Built Coalition Regroups: Falwell's exit changes the landscape of the Religious Right." *Time Magazine*, November 16.

Oxford Dictionaries. n.d. "Word of the Year 2016 is. . ." (Oxford University Press).

Palin, Sarah. 2010. *America By Heart: Reflections on Family, Faith, and Flag*. New York: Harper Collins.

———. 2007. "Bible Week." *Alaska Governor's Office Press Release*. Juneau, October 17.

———. 2007. "Christian Heritage." *Alaska Governor's Office Proclamation*. Juneau, September 14.

Palin, Sarah. 2016. *Endorsement Speech for Donald Trump*. Iowa, January 19.

———. 2009. *Going Rogue: An American Life*. New York: Harper Collins.

Palin, Sarah. 2009. *Governor Sarah Palin's Resignation Speech*.

———. 2008. "Transcript: Gov. Sarah Palin At The RNC." *NPR*. September 3. Accessed February 7, 2020. https://www.npr.org/templates/story/story.php?storyId=94258995&t=1581102154908.

Palin, Sarah, and Ed Kalnins. 2008. *Master's Commission Service at Wasilla Assembly of God, June 8, 2008*.

Parr, Susan Sherwood. 2008. *Sarah Palin: Faith, Family, Country*. Alachua, FL: Bridge-Logos.

Pew Research Center. 2008. *Religion and Politics '08: Sarah Palin*. Pew Research Center.

———. 2004. "Religion and the Presidential Vote: Bush's Gains Broad-Based." December 6. Accessed January 18, 2020. https://www.people-press.org/2004/12/06/religion-and-the-presidential-vote/.

Phillips-Fein, Kim. 2009. *Invisible Hands: The Making of the Conservative Movement from the New Deal to Reagan*. New York: WW Norton and Co.

Politics Magazine. 2010. "Alaska Influencers." February: 48.

Powell, Michael. 2008. "Obama, The Populist." *The New York Times*, April 1.

Riesebrodt, Martin. 1998. *Pious Passion: The Emergence of Modern Fundamentalism in the United States and Iran*. Berkeley: University of California Press.

Roderick, Jack. 1997. *Crude Dreams: A Personal History of Oil & Politics in Alaska*. Kenmore, WA: Epicenter Press.

Ruthven, Malise. 2004. *Fundamentalism: A Very Short Introduction*. Oxford: Oxford University Press .

Ryrie, Charles. 1965. *Dispensationalism Today*. Chicago: Moody Press.

Sandlin, Andrew. 1996. *A Comprehensive Faith: An International Festschrift for Rousas John Rushdoony*. San Jose, CA: Friends of Chalcedon.

Schmidt, Samantha, and Amy Wang. 2017. "Jerry Falwell Jr. keeps defending Trump as Liberty University grads return diplomas." *The Washington Post*.

Schor, Elana. 2008. "Alaska Senator Stevens found guilty of accepting gifts from oil executive." *The Guardian*, October 27.

n.d. "Scopes Trial Transcripts, 1925." Hanover University archives.

2017. "Secretary Zinke Signs Order to Jump-Start Alaskan Energy." *Pipeline and Gas Journal* 244 (7).

Settje, David. Winter 2000. "'Sinister' Communists and Vietnam Quarrels: The Christian Century and Christianity Today Respond to the Cold and Vietnam Wars." *Fides et Historia* 32 (1): 81–97.

Smith, Anthony. 2000. *Myth and Memories of the Nation*. Oxford: Oxford University Press.

Smith, Gary Scott. 2006. *Faith and the Presidency*. Oxford: Oxford University Press.

Southern Baptist Convention. 2018. "Annual Meeting Resolutions." *SBC Annual Meeting*. sbcannualmeeting.net.

———. n.d. "GuideStone Financial Resources." www.sbc.net.

State of Alaska Department of Revenue. 2009. "Permanent Fund Dividend, 2008 Annual Report."

State of Alaska Tax Division. 2008. *2008 Annual Report*. Juneau: State of Alaska.

Steinfels, Peter. 1991. "Gulf War Proving Bountiful For Some Prophets Of Doom." *The New York Times*, February 2.

Stockemer, Daniel, ed. 2019. *Populism Around the World: A Comparative Perspective*. Springer International Publishing.

Stoddard, Ed. 2008. "Divided evangelicals key to election." *Reueters*, February 8.

———. 2007. "U.S. evangelical support for Iraq war slipping." *Reuters*, January 19.

Strober, Gerald, and Ruth Tomczak. 1979. *Jerry Falwell: Aflame for God*. Thomas Nelson.

Sullivan, Colleen. 2011. "Persian Gulf War." In *The SAGE Encyclopedia of Terrorism*, by Gus Martin. SAGE Publications.

Tabachnick, Rachel, interview by Terry Gross. 2011. "The Evangelicals Engaged in Spiritual Warfare." *Fresh Air*. (August 19).

TC. 1903. "J.D. Rockfeller's Religion." *Life* 42: 403.

The Economist. 1991. "The Perils Of Hyphenation." January 26.

The Editors of Encyclopedia Britannica. n.d. *John D. Rockefeller*.

The New York Times. 1988. "Robertson is Victor in Alaska." March 3.

1985. *Moral Majority Report*. Performed by Cal Thomas. April 9.

Thornburgh, Nathan. 2008. "Mayor Palin: A Rough Record." *Time Magazine*, September 2.

Trump, Donald. n.d. "Executive Order 13769, Protecting the Nation from Foreign Terrorist Entry into the United States."

Turner, Wallace. 1980. "Group of Evangelic Protestants Takes Over The G.O.P. in Alaska." *The New York Times*, June 9.

United States Republican Party. 2016. *Republican Platform 2016*.

University of Chicago Faculty. n.d. *Office of the President: William Rainey Harper*. Accessed November 26, 2019.

University of Massachusetts at Amherst Political Economy Research Institute. 2010. "Toxic 100 Names the Top US Climate, Air, and Water Polluters."

Wadhams, Nick. 2008. "False claims exposed of Kenyan pastor who protected Sarah Palin from witches." *The Telegraph* , October 15.

Wagner, C Peter. 2006. *Freedom, Freedom, Freedom!*

Wagner, C. Peter, interview by Terry Gross. 2011. "A Leading Figure in the New Apostolic Reformation." *Fresh Air*. (October 3).

Wagner, C. Peter. 2000. "The New Apostolic Reformation." *Renewal Journal #15: Wineskins*.

Walters, Philip. 1986. "The Russian Orthodox Church and the Soviet State." *The Annals of the American Academy of Political and Social Science* (Sage Publications) 483: 135–145.

Walvoord, John. 1990. *Armageddon, Oil, and the Middle East Crisis: What the Bible Says About the Future of the Middle East and the End of Western Civilization.* Grand Rapids: Zondervan.

———. 1962. *Israel in Prophecy.* Grand Rapids: Zondervan Publishing House.

———. 1993. *The Final Drama: 14 Keys to Understanding the Prophetic Scriptures.* Grand Rapids: Kregel Publications.

———. 1967. *The Nations in Prophecy.* Grand Rapids: Zondervan.

———. 1957. *The Rapture Quesiton: A Comprehensive Biblical Study of the Translation of the Church.* Grand Rapids: Dunham Publishing Company.

Werner-Muller, Jan. 2016. *What Is Populism?* Philadelphia: University of Pennsylvania Press.

Winters, Michael Sean. 2012. *God's Right Hand: How Jerry Falwell Made God A Republican And Baptized The American Right.* New York: Harper One.

Worland, Justin. 2016. "What You Need to Know About Scott Pruitt, Trump's Pick for EPA." *Time Magazine.*

Yardley, William. 2009. "Anchorage Gay Rights Measure Is Set Back by Mayor's Veto." *New York Times*, August 18.

YCharts. n.d. "Alaska North Slope Crude Oil First Purchase Price."

Young, Don. n.d. "Global Warming." *Don Young, Congressman For All Alaska.* Accessed February 9, 2020. https://donyoung.house.gov/issues/issue/?IssueID=5006.

Zinke, Ryan. 2017. "A Vision for American Energy Dominance." September 29.

Zurlo, Gina. 2015. "The Social Gospel, Ecumenical Movement, and Christian Sociology: The Institute of Social and Religious Research." *The American Sociologist* (Springer) 46 (2): 177–193.

www.ingramcontent.com/pod-product-compliance
Lightning Source LLC
Chambersburg PA
CBHW062037220426
43662CB00010B/1536